M000158965

A PIECE OF THE ACTION

A PIECE
OF THE
ACTION

RACE AND LABOR IN
POST-CIVIL RIGHTS HOLLYWOOD

EITHNE QUINN

Columbia University Press   New York

Columbia University Press
Publishers Since 1893
New York   Chichester, West Sussex
cup.columbia.edu
Copyright © 2020 Columbia University Press
All rights reserved

Library of Congress Cataloging-in-Publication Data
Names: Quinn, Eithne, 1971– author.
Title: A piece of the action : race and labor in post–civil rights Hollywood / Eithne
    Quinn.
Description: New York : Columbia University Press, 2019. | Includes bibliographical
    references and index.
Identifiers: LCCN 2019023881 (print) | LCCN 2019023882 (ebook) | ISBN 9780231164368
    (cloth) | ISBN 9780231164375 (paperback) | ISBN 9780231551014 (ebook)
Subjects: LCSH: African Americans in motion pictures. | Race in motion pictures. | Race
    relations in motion pictures. | African Americans in the motion picture industry. |
    Motion pictures—United States—History—20th century.
Classification: LCC PN1995.9.N4 Q54 2019 (print) | LCC PN1995.9.N4 (ebook) |
    DDC 791.43/652996073—dc23
LC record available at https://lccn.loc.gov/2019023881
LC ebook record available at https://lccn.loc.gov/2019023882

Columbia University Press books are printed on permanent
    and durable acid-free paper.

Printed in the United States of America

Cover image: Director Melvin Van Peebles on the set of
    Watermelon Man (1970). Courtesy of Columbia Pictures/Photofest.
Cover design: Lisa Hamm

CONTENTS

ACKNOWLEDGMENTS

Many people have helped me write this book, and I am so grateful for their support. Scholars, editors, and teachers have taken time to meet and correspond with me and to contribute rich ideas, make subtle refinements, suggest source materials, and invite me to present work, which generated further productive conversations. They include Bridget Byrne, Steve Chibnall, Gary Cross, Tom Doherty, Melvin Donalson, Jeffrey Geiger, Paul Grainge, Herman Gray, Lee Grieveson, Martin Halliwell, Heather Hendershot, Dave Hesmondhalgh, Jan-Christopher Horak, Darnell Hunt, Mark Jancovich, Robin Kelley, Stephanie Lewthwaite, Ed Linenthal, Peter Ling, Karen Lury, Dan Matlin, Sharon Monteith, Jonathan Munby, Steve Neale, Simon Newman, Anamik Saha, Bevan Sewell, Judith Smith, Cara Rodway, Will Turner, William Van Deburg, Craig Watkins, James West, John Williams, Howard Winant, and Janet Wolff.

I am deeply grateful to Philip Leventhal at Columbia University Press for his early interest in the project and expert help in guiding it to completion. Thanks also to Monique Briones in editorial, Zachary Friedman in marketing, Michael Haskell in production, and faculty board members. I am indebted to Annie Barva, whose copy editing of the manuscript was superbly deft and clarifying. For assisting me in accessing images used in the book, thanks to Minerva Diaz at the Dwyer Cultural Center, Espen Bale at the British Film Institute, and superefficient Kristine Krueger at the Margaret Herrick Library. Special thanks are owed to the anonymous reviewers of the book proposal and manuscript: I am grateful for their thoughtful suggestions and belief in the project.

Part of chapter 2 was published in earlier form as "Sincere Fictions: The Production Cultures of Whiteness in Late 1960s Hollywood," *Velvet Light Trap* 67 (Spring 2011): 3–13, copyright © 2011 by the University of Texas Press; all rights reserved. Parts of chapters 3 and 5 were published in earlier form as "Closing Doors: Hollywood, Affirmative Action, and the Revitalization of Conservative Racial Politics," *Journal of American History* 99, no. 2 (September 2012): 466–91; reprinted with permission of Oxford University Press. Part of chapter 4 was published in earlier form as " 'Tryin' to Get Over': Super Fly, Black Politics, and Post–Civil Rights Film Enterprise," *Cinema Journal* 49, no. 2 (Winter 2010): 86–105, copyright © 2010 by the University of Texas Press; all rights reserved. I am grateful to the journal editors and to the presses for permission to include revised versions here. I benefited enormously from a research fellowship from the Leverhulme Trust, which allowed me extended time and resources to conduct interviews and archival work. Heartfelt thanks to all the great interviewees, including Dick Anthony Williams, Michael Campus, Joel Freeman, Cliff Frazier, Jack Hill, Larry Cohen, Richard Heffner, and Sam Goldwyn Jr., and to the many archivists at U.S. research libraries who helped me find materials for the project.

Many lovely colleagues in English and American studies at the University of Manchester have helped make working life good and contributed to aspects of this project, including David Alderson, Naomi Baker, Anke Bernau, Dave Brown, Dani Caselli, Michelle Coghlan, Laura Doan, Andrew Fearnley, Douglas Field, Molly Geidel, Hal Gladfelder, Ben Harker, Maria Hyland, David Matthews, Monica Pearl, Ian Scott, Jackie Stacey, Anastasia Valassopoulos, and Natalie Zacek. Special thanks to my supportive department head and longtime friend Peter Knight.

The most sustained intellectual support has come from Peter Krämer, who has read drafts of the whole book, pushed me to develop arguments, and offered great conversation along the way. I am fortunate to have a mentor and friend like Peter. Other close readers have helped develop the project. Brian Ward was a very astute reader of several early draft chapters, and gave me great reading suggestions; my colleague Molly Geidel has provided superb, full, provocative feedback at various stages; and Judy Smith emerged as a late, generous, incisive reader. Many thanks also to the meticulous film studies scholars Joshua Gulam and Pete Jones for research suggestions and proofing chapters.

My friends have been a constant source of fun and warmth, including Anastasia Valassopoulos, Molly Geidel, Sue Attwood, Sam Hills, Sarah MacLachlan, Rachel Rich, David Yelland, and Bridget Byrne, whom I count on for laughs and advice. Special thanks to Jill Solomon, who has been a source of friendship and inspiration my whole adult life (as well as someone to stay with during numerous research visits to Los Angeles). Thanks to my lovely family, especially my mum, Noirin, and brothers, Eugene and Jeremiah Quinn, as well as to Trisha, Roisin, and Rory Quinn and to Kath Jones, Mary Curtis, and Monika Kalcsics. Thanks, in memory, to my wonderful dad, Victor Quinn. Special thanks to my partner, Steve Jones, who has cast an astute eye over the whole manuscript while remaining calm, funny, and loving, and to our beloved children, Sean and Des Jones.

INTRODUCTION

Movie stars played an important role in the historic March on Washington in August 1963. Organized by civil rights groups and unionists to protest state-sanctioned discrimination and build an antiracist movement, the 250,000-strong marchers included many black and brown entertainers. The singer and actor Harry Belafonte, who was deeply involved in the freedom struggle of the 1960s, coordinated these celebrity participants, including Lena Horne, Ruby Dee, Ossie Davis, Dick Gregory, Diahann Carroll, Rita Moreno, Nat Cole, Eartha Kitt, Sammy Davis Jr., and Sidney Poitier. The march was a showcase of Hollywood integration, with many of the white film elite also in attendance. Marlon Brando, Burt Lancaster, and Charlton Heston—members of the civil-rights-supporting Arts Group founded in June 1963 during Martin Luther King Jr.'s Rally for Freedom visit to Los Angeles—were accompanied by other white celebrities such as James Garner, Shelley Winters, Judy Garland, Billy Wilder, Paul Newman, Tony Curtis, and Joseph Mankiewicz. Brando had initiated planning meetings for the march by the Arts Group, forming the Hollywood March Committee, which Heston, who had been a high-profile presence at a civil rights protest in Oklahoma City in 1961, agreed to chair.[1] At a press conference at Heston's home in July 1963, the committee announced its intention "to express our support for the Civil Rights legislation now before the Congress and to urge its passage." The press statement that came out of the meeting at "Brando's bungalow" went further, pressing "to improve the legislation . . . now pending before Congress."[2] Voicing ambivalence and guarded optimism about the march's show of integrated support, the actor and singer Eartha Kitt remarked: "The white people do not really understand the problems of the Negro. How could they? They have been brainwashed all their lives. But I believe in the sincerity of white marchers."[3]

On the day of the march, the celebrities both entertained the marchers and garnered publicity for the demonstration. The playwright, actor, and activist Ossie Davis—who in 1970 would become only the second African American director of a Hollywood film with *Cotton Comes to Harlem*—was in charge of entertainment. During the near mile-long walk up the National Mall, which included lengthy periods of waiting, he used music to galvanize and amuse the protestors and served as an emcee at the postmarch rally in front of the Lincoln Memorial. Numerous celebrity speakers came to the podium before King gave his historic "I Have a Dream" speech. They included the singer Josephine Baker (marking an exhilarating return from her European exile, she declared, "This is the happiest day of my entire life"[4]); Brando (enthralling the crowd with a cattle prod, a totem of oppressive policing from a civil rights demonstration he had recently attended in Gadsden, Alabama); and Heston (delivering an Arts Group statement written by the celebrated writer and attendee James Baldwin). The march was widely seen as a success, and, indeed, it steered the nation closer to its historic watershed in strengthening and then passing the Civil Rights Act the following year. With the film stars' participation extensively (and often negatively) reported in the mainstream media, Hollywood's association with racial liberalism was consolidated.[5] As Belafonte later recalled, "To see Marlon and Charlton Heston, and Sidney Poitier, Paul Newman, Mahalia Jackson . . . one after another after another, in a posse, shaking hands as we all went by, talking, offering uplifting words: The effect was electrifying."[6]

However, this electrifying image of racial solidarity stood in stark contrast with the reality of exclusion in Hollywood workplaces in 1963. The full title of the demonstration was the March on Washington for Jobs and Freedom, but film jobs, as advocacy groups such as the National Association for the Advancement of Colored People (NAACP) were at pains to point out, were next to nonexistent for minorities offscreen and severely restricted for actors onscreen.[7] Some technical- and craft-union locals in film, from grips to soundpersons, included no minority members at all. The March on Washington was spearheaded by the Negro American Labor Council led by A. Philip Randolph, who helped win support from some major unions for the march. But the American Federation of Labor–Congress of Industrial Organizations (AFL-CIO), the national umbrella organization for U.S. unions, declined to endorse the demonstration. Moreover, the AFL-CIO's constituent organization representing cinema's many technical workers, the International Alliance of Theatrical Stage Employees (IATSE), also failed to support it. Hollywood's management and ownership class, which included some movement fund-raisers and donors, was even whiter than film's technical-craft workforce, with no people of color on any of the major studios' executive boards.[8]

Indeed, despite the growing political pressure since the 1940s to combat job exclusion in Hollywood's creative, executive, and technical spheres, it was only in the wake of the landmark Civil Rights Act of 1964, amid mounting political activism and unrest, that minority workers were charged with the means of legally challenging America's motion-picture industry. The Civil Rights Act ended formal job discrimination on the basis of race (as well as gender, religion, and national origin), and Title VII of the act created the Equal Employment Opportunity Commission (EEOC) to enforce the new law. It equipped those locked out of jobs and promotions, including in the film industry, with sufficient political and legal resources to demand action. When the EEOC came to investigate the film business in the late 1960s, it found Hollywood's "gross underutilization" of minority workers to be more severe than in other Southern Californian industries—including other media industries such as radio and television.[9] Thus, it was only when the Title VII challenge got under way, powered by broad politicization, that the industry's image of racial liberalism, exemplified by those whom Kitt referred to as "sincere white marchers," was put to the test. Many, as she feared, did "not really understand the problem." Nor, as a consequence, had they thought through the solutions. The ramifications of the legislation and activism would mean turning the spotlight around to the ignominious labor practices in cinema's own workplaces. For Hollywood's overwhelmingly white workforce, it would mean being asked to give up some of its unwarranted yet largely unexamined racial advantages in an industry full of highly prized, well-paying jobs on many employment levels.

This book explores what happened next. In these post–Civil Rights Act years, black film workers came to test, to an unprecedented degree, cinema's white-dominated work zones, film content, and revenue streams. Along with activists, advocacy groups, political organizations, and the federal government, African American filmmakers tried ambitiously to operationalize civil rights laws and to bring microlevel and mesolevel (institutional) change to cinema. I trace many of the political and commercial forces that enabled black filmmakers to finally push into the mainstream industry and tell some of their stories. By attending to the distinct experiences of African American actors, directors, writers, technicians, producers, and activists, I offer a layered account of black film practice. African American political identities, racial critiques, cultural repertoires, and vernacular modes came to be credibly staged in popular film in unprecedented ways during this period, from the Bill Gunn–scripted dark satire about Brooklyn gentrification *The Landlord* (Hal Ashby, 1970) and the intergenerational family comedy *Five on the Black Hand Side* (Oscar Williams, 1973) to the hip, black-nationalist-informed action picture *The Mack* (Michael Campus, 1973) and a coming-of-age drama set in the 1950s, *Cooley High* (Michael Schultz, 1975). In this book, I show that this black-oriented film wave—often reductively dubbed the "blaxploitation era"—was in many ways complex, extensive, and politically vital. It would set blueprints for cross-platform black cultural-industries practices for decades to come.

The problem is that these developments stirred powerful and complex counterforces. The new black film culture and employment interventionism came up against shifting forces of conservatism in Hollywood. The film business in the late 1960s and 1970s started to catalyze new, post–civil rights models for incorporating and stalling racial progress. To ward off and capitalize on racial activism, the industry mounted "color-blind" expressions of tolerance in its corporate and (some of its) onscreen communication, but these outward expressions were combined paradoxically with continuing widespread practices of racial exclusion in its division of labor and wealth distribution.[10] The racist typologies that also continued to be fielded in the industry's storytelling repertoires came to be accompanied by liberal-pluralist rhetoric and imagery that had putatively taken aboard the import of the Civil Rights Movement. I show that the Motion Picture Association of America (MPAA) and Hollywood films developed and deployed racially meritocratic language at strategic moments to mask the industry's still starkly racialized political economy. Notwithstanding the existence of individual white progressives, the new limits-of-tolerance discourses, I suggest, shielded the industry from both racial self-knowledge and lasting constructive change to its exclusionary job practices, financial arrangements, and persisting racist imagery. Indeed, I argue that cinema was singularly placed to help guide the nation's post–civil rights retreat from racial justice—negotiating some of the discursive and material terms of what the sociologists Lawrence Bobo and Ryan Smith have called the shift from "Jim Crow racism" to post–civil rights "laissez-faire racism."[11] This book shows that the film industry helped germinate and channel corporate- and labor-driven race reaction at the dawning moment of conservative rehabilitation and neoliberalization.

Indeed, after the wave of black-oriented filmmaking and serious attempts to integrate the industry chronicled in this book, the fight for racial justice in cinema rapidly fizzled. By the late 1970s, the film industry had incorporated few, if any lasting movement demands. It had faced down the challenge mounted by creative workers, activists, and the federal government, and the rate of black-directed film releases dropped precipitously. In 1976, when the California Advisory Committee of the U.S. Civil Rights Commission came to investigate racial-inclusion rates in Hollywood's studios and craft unions, it found an industry shirking its affirmative-action responsibilities. There had been very little improvement since the passage of the Civil Rights Act, and the committee could not see any industry appetite or government requirement to intervene going forward.[12] By this time, the studios had shifted from being mainly producer-distributors of films to being (nonproducing) financier-distributors, making it increasingly difficult for cultural-industry workers, including black workers, to organize against exclusion and to mount a politics of redress.[13]

In the year that the Civil Rights Commission found that whiteness remained the Hollywood workplace norm, *Rocky* (John Avildsen, 1976) emerged as the industry's runaway hit. It was a preeminent text of "white ethnic revival":[14] the story of the Italian American underdog boxer taking on the flashy, underhanded black heavyweight champion. *Rocky*'s revivalism sprang not just from the film narrative but also from the celebrated publicity image of self-made newcomer Sylvester Stallone, who played Rocky, conceived the story, and wrote the script. Stallone stands for the honest, plucky film-industry mobility of white, working-class men cast in antithesis to the pampered might of new black celebrity entertainers like the boxing champ. This narrative of arrogant black privilege, against which the white man is the all-American bootstrap striver, was, of course, belied by continuing film-industry racial job marginalization. But the film's symbolic salience, channeling white resentment, helped deepen racial inertia in cinema's behind-the-scenes workplaces. By 1980, the year of Ronald Reagan's first election victory, next to no black-focused films were released, a lack attended by little if any handwringing among industry whites. As film scholar Ed Guerrero explains in his classic book *Framing Blackness*, the African American actors who had emerged in the early 1970s "found themselves in bit parts and increasingly shuttled into oblivion by the film industry."[15]

Race and Labor in Post-Civil Rights Hollywood

This book adopts an interdisciplinary approach to race, representation, and cultural production, drawing on labor history, film studies, African American studies, race sociology, cultural studies, political science, and critical race theory. This eclectic method allows me to explore the interplay among economic, political, and cultural trends in understanding how film shaped and was shaped by the politics of race. My approach, drawing on the Marxist-informed cultural-industries approaches of David Hesmondhalgh and Anamik Saha, foregrounds unequal power relations in commercial cultural production without being overly deterministic. The model reveals the profit-driven, risky business of cinema to be racist and exclusionary while also being "complex, ambivalent, and contested," to use Hesmondhalgh's keywords.[16] My interdisciplinary approach gives rise to four linked contentions about racial continuity and change in Hollywood: first, that cinema played a powerful, underexplored role in America's early post–civil rights racial politics; second, more specifically, that national ideological battles about employment and economic justice were dramatically contested in and through cinema; third, that neglected white identity politics are crucial to understanding the film industry's role in processes of racial formation; and, finally, that cinema's ideological power derives in large part from what I call *reflexivity* between industry politics and narrative themes.

This book suggests that cinema played a leading role in what critical race theory scholars identify as the crucial "transitional decade" that spanned from the ending of the old Jim Crow era in the mid-1960s to the start of the modern racial era in the late 1970s, heralded by Reagan's first presidential campaign and then victory.[17] Following the "racial break" with the old regime of state-sanctioned white supremacy ushered in by the historic if limited civil rights victories, this transitional period saw particularly intense contestation about the meaning of race and the terms of racial equality.[18] The immediate post–civil rights period was marked by continuing and evolving activism as the black movement shifted away from an inclusion-centered, rights-based challenge to U.S. institutions and toward a more expansive vision of racial justice connected to other mobilizations (anticolonial, labor, feminist, antiwar, etc.). The transitional period is crucial in part because, at least in its first half, so much seemed possible.

Hollywood faced two major racial-justice challenges during these transitional years, both backed by movement protest: the federal activism of the EEOC and Justice Department that set out to integrate the industry in 1969–1970 and the mobilization of black advocacy groups in 1972–1974, including the NAACP, Operation PUSH, and the Coalition Against Blaxploitation, which strove for more decision-making power and better representation on screen. When the industry faced these periods of heightened pressure, some real, if belated advances were made. But what is striking in the story told here is the film industry's structural intransigence to racial justice despite individual whites actively supporting constructive change. I show that the MPAA, reacting to movement demands, played a crucial role in the forging of "neoconservative" racial discourses around the turn of the 1970s that found new and far-reaching ways to rehabilitate laissez-faire policies.[19] If new forms of racial reaction were mobilized by management, they were also adopted by many labor unions and white filmmakers and percolated in countless film narratives. Management and labor institutions learned to incorporate movement themes and some moderate movement demands while remaining deeply racially unequal. Ultimately, the film business not only served to disseminate backlash ideas in the transitional period but also was an important site where these ideas were incubated and their policy implications were tested and made normative. I argue that Hollywood was a fertile ground for incubating these ideas because the conditions of relative stability in many other industries across the 1960s had not been shared by the ailing motion-picture business, which was, as a result, at the leading edge of crisis-driven corporate reorganizing (and what would become neoliberalizing) trends of the 1970s.

At the heart of the racial struggle in these years were arguments about fair access to jobs and resources. As labor historians such as Nancy MacLean have explored, the struggle for job equity was particularly acute in the immediate post–Civil Rights Act period as marginalized groups with mounting employment and political expectations faced continuing widespread workplace rejection.[20] In its report on the urban rebellions of the mid-1960s, the National Advisory Commission on Civil Disorders (Kerner Commission) found in 1968 that "pervasive unemployment and underemployment are the most persistent and serious grievances in minority areas. They are inextricably linked to the problem of civil disorder."[21] U.S. policy makers and publics debated how to respond to the pervasive unemployment and inequality in the post–Civil Rights Act moment. Should labor markets be left to their own devices now that formal discrimination had been outlawed, as advocated by an increasingly vocal contingent of whites who argued that employment practices had become basically racially meritocratic? Or, in the face of what others understood as vestigially and persistently exclusionary employers, should interventionist affirmative-action measures—including minority-training programs, diversity quotas in hiring, and grants and subsidies for minority businesses—be deployed to redistribute some jobs and wealth? Or did America's workplaces and wealth holdings require more radical transformation, proposed by those who believed race-reform efforts within U.S. capitalism, including its motion-picture industry, to be inadequate and even harmful?

Given the heated ideological battles over race, employment, and redistribution in the transitional period, the way they played out in the flagship cultural industry of cinema is important. The film business was a highly desirable (if also often insecure and exhausting) job sector: from the "below the line" blue-collar craft workers to the "above the line" writers, actors, producers, and directors, and from the studio executives, talent agents, and lawyers who put together the movie deals to the marketers, the distributors, and the exhibitors who managed and owned the film theaters. Despite mounting national civil rights activism, in the mid-1960s almost all of these jobs were monopolized by white men, and the industry had never really engaged with its own white opportunity hoarding. In the pivotal years that followed, many white film workers and executives maintained the racial status quo by interpreting as unfair and antimeritocratic those initiatives aimed at minority hires while deeming unproblematic the continuing de facto system of white racial preference in the industry. These new anti-affirmative-action perceptions among whites came to be reproduced and contested in the period's films, as black workers and the EEOC mounted robust challenges. Indeed, as I show, many of the most influential race-themed film narratives of the early post–civil rights years in very different ways staged and renegotiated battles over workplace integration, wealth and property inequity, institutionalized racism, and economic precarity, from *In the Heat of the Night* (Norman Jewison, 1967), *The Angel Levine* (Jan Kadar, 1970), *Buck and the Preacher* (Sidney Poitier, 1972), and *Super Fly* (Gordon Parks Jr., 1972) to *Coffy* (Jack Hill, 1973), *The Spook Who Sat by the Door* (Ivan Dixon, 1973), and *Blue Collar* (Paul Schrader, 1978).

The role of white people and white-led institutions in these racial battles over creative labor and cultural representation in cinema was crucial. As the dominant racial group in U.S. society and its cultural industries, whites have been central to reinforcing or disrupting film's racialized employment relations, its revenue streams, and, in turn, its regimes of representation. To fully understand the racial politics of the transitional years, we need to borrow frameworks and mobilize insights from race theorists and labor historians who have exposed the significance of white practices and discourses in institutional and employment contexts and how they work to reproduce (as well as sometimes dismantle) majority-white workforces.[22] These theorists and historians insist on the importance of analyzing white racial self-perceptions: what the race sociologists Joe Feagin, Hernan Vera, and Pinar Batur term "sincere fictions," which are "sentiments about the white self, elicited by encounters with 'others.'"[23] Conducting extensive public-opinion surveys of white people in the 1990s, they identified attitudes that allowed whites to see themselves as racially benign even as they acted in discriminatory ways. This book argues that early formulation and fomentation of such discourses, which would fully crystalize in the later post–civil rights period, happened in the film industry and film storytelling of the early post–Civil Rights Act breach.

An examination of whiteness in the film industry during the transitional years requires us to scrutinize the notion of the "white liberal," which in common parlance (and in scholarship) tends to be used to mean quite different things. This book draws a clear distinction between the many "liberals" in the industry who in response to concrete movement demands turned to laissez-faire, implicitly pro-white racial politics and those progressive white liberals who became self-conscious about their own racial privilege and actively supported, to lesser and greater degrees, antiracist practices. For the sake of clarity, I call these two groups *retreatist liberals* and *interventionist liberals* (or progressives) and argue that this distinction is vital to understanding continuity and change in U.S. racial formation as it was negotiated in film.[24] As both a workplace and representational medium, the cinema of the transitional years started to illuminate what the sociologist Steven Steinberg calls "the liberal retreat from race."[25] To be sure, not all the retreatist liberals were white—some were among the new, precarious black elite, whose emergence was propelled in part by their function as ratifiers of an only slightly altered racial status quo. But most were white. The industry's new retreatists joined many of its racial conservatives in the realization that, following the racial break, the best way to maintain the racial order was to profess tolerance in principle in order not to have to bring about change in practice. As the historian Thomas Sugrue insists, racial separatism among whites following the watershed moment of the mid-1960s was still widely practiced but increasingly "dared not speak its name." Popular understanding of white racism during this period and since then has too often been consigned to overt white supremacists or working-class "hard-hat" whites.[26] This consignment obscures the more widespread and influential practices of informal white separatism among retreatist liberals and new conservatives, groups that in the period discussed here had many powerful advocates in Hollywood.

The underplaying of insidious white separatism in the center ground has too often traveled into film-historiographical accounts of these years. One scholarly tendency is to suggest that well-meaning white filmmakers were forced away from racial-justice concerns by a radicalizing and white-repudiating black freedom movement. In my research for this book, I repeatedly found, by contrast, a rejection of racial equity by white executives and institutions, from top management to grassroots labor organizations such as the Group for Union Equality. The racial recalcitrance of many white people (rather than of black people) in cinema during these years was the central impediment to constructive change. The sincere-fiction underestimation of white resistance to racial equality, evident in some of the film historiographies, fits within a larger and long-standing "argument that minority aggressiveness was responsible for white male backlash at the tail end of the 1960s," influentially critiqued by the historian Robin Kelley. He points out that this argument "masks the fact that the tragedy of most progressive movements in the United States has been white racism."[27]

By clarifying the terms of soft white backlash, we can separate industry retreatists from interventionists, the latter trying, with varying levels of commitment, to match their avowals of racial egalitarianism with equitable practices and concrete support for antiracist measures. In this book, a pair of close friends and filmmaking collaborators in the 1960s, Norman Jewison and Hal Ashby, capture these two faces of liberalism, evident in their different racial hiring practices and film-aesthetic priorities. As we shall see, retreatist Jewison and interventionist Ashby parted ways after a sustained period of film partnership because of their increasingly divergent creative and political visions. These two filmmakers stand as important actors in my story while at the same time serving semiallegorically to signal broader white racial positions in a realigning cinematic field.

Although there has been influential work on whiteness as a theme in film narratives—spearheaded by Richard Dyer's classic book *White: Essays on Race and Culture*[28]—there is very little work on white identity politics in the production and industry spheres of post–civil rights cinema. There is instead a strong tendency to examine filmmakers of color negotiating creative spaces within very broadly sketched institutional, commercial, and discursive white-determined landscapes. This tendency leads to arguments that strongly emphasize the role that marginalized individuals and groups play as the agents of racial change in cinema—and, by unintended implication, to a strong emphasis on minority *responsibility* when racial change doesn't happen. When aggregated across the subfield of race and film, the foregrounding of black creative activity and the sidelining of white practices, discourses, and structures have the effect of rendering highly important white racial attitudes and practices unsalient.

Because of this general underscrutiny of film-industry whiteness, critical race film scholarship on the post-1960s period by scholars such as S. Craig Watkins, Kara Keeling, Monica Ndounou, Judith Smith, and Maryann Erigha is crucial. They consider the intersections between white and black filmmaking discourses and activities, including a consideration and dethroning of "how whiteness is lived, constructed, and reproduced," in Watkins's words. These scholars insist on the need for work that sees all racial categories as inherently unstable, contested, and interconnected because, as Keeling states, invoking W. E. B. Du Bois, "neither [blackness nor whiteness] can exist unproblematically."[29] Without more such scholarship that attends closely to film industry whiteness, the subfield may inadvertently tend to reinstate rather than destabilize the implacability and therefore the dominance of whiteness. The aim of this study is not to fetishize whiteness as something to be extracted from broader race politics but instead, like the scholars mentioned here have done, to look at whiteness in relation to other racial identities.

Along with whites, this book's main focus is African Americans, the largest minority group in the United States in the 1960s and 1970s, when they emerged into new forms of mainstream cinematic visibility. There are already excellent accounts of black cinematic practice of this extraordinary time, providing insights that are crucial to the story I tell here.[30] My book takes particular cues from classic accounts of black film that foreground cinema's political economy: what Jesse Rhines calls "black film/white money."[31]

One consequence of framing my study of black film practice in terms of the white-determined industry is that it complicates the common narrative in scholarship on black film during these years that dichotomizes civil rights integrationism and black-power separatism: Sidney Poitier versus Melvin Van Peebles. This binary logic has given rise to dwelling on polemical black and left disputes, often waged over representation, in the rise-and-fall narratives of African American film in the 1960s and 1970s. What can get forgotten is the basic political common ground of antiracist projects as they extended into cinema and were met by strengthening forces of race reaction. As Ossie Davis states of Martin Luther King Jr. and Davis's friend Malcolm X, "Their tactics differed, but their goals did not."[32] Or as King's friend Harry Belafonte asserted, "I think the only area in which there was great conflict [between King and the Black Panthers] was the technique."[33] The primary research for this book repeatedly revealed shared basic objectives in the different strands of the movement in their engagement with the film industry.

By foregrounding the systematic rejection of these antiracist goals, often in the name of a specious white racial tolerance, this book finds continuing radicalism and collectivism but also mounting cynicism among some African Americans, reactions that found complex expression in black film culture. The early post–civil rights story told in this book thus traces the fading of a certain kind of collective responsibility in black cultural and labor politics. In the face of tremendous backlash against both organized antiracism and attempts to activate the new civil rights laws came not only tenacious and evolving black cultural alliances but also the forging of a new individualist politics and aesthetics. The latter would prove very marketable and ideologically powerful in the post–civil rights cultural industries to come.

The power of cinema to engage and animate debates over race, jobs, and representation stems from its dual role. Cinema's significance derives in part from its industry clout, big earnings, creative practices, political lobbying power, and prestige blue- and white-collar employment. But its significance also springs from its being an industry that, along with television, popular music, and advertising, produces cultural *texts* for large audiences. Film was one of the most influential cultural forms of the twentieth century, and through its powerful storytelling the film business made texts that participated in the reproduction of social meaning and feeling. Thus, this book contends that to gain a fuller understanding of racial-formation processes in cinema, we need to pay close attention to production relations, the films and, crucially, the complex interplay between the two.

Production/Text Reflexivity

The history of racial representation in American film is deplorable. People of color have been marginalized and misrepresented through stultifying images and narratives that have reproduced white-supremacist norms for audiences at home and abroad. Racist images of African Americans were first presented in the very earliest one-shot short films, such as *Dancing Dark Boy* (1895) and Thomas Edison's vignettes, including *Watermelon Eating Contest* (1896), and in the medium's many early blackface performances (roles that demeaned black people while also denying them jobs by being performed by whites). Film became a key symbolic arena in which white supremacy was consolidated—its "vicious and casual racism," in the film historian Jacqueline Stewart's phrase, legitimating a system of political and economic oppression.[34]

This shameful imagery was nowhere more evident than in Hollywood's biggest features. When the film scholar Linda Williams plotted her history of five preeminent racial melodramas across cultural platforms—starting with Harriet Beecher Stowe's novel *Uncle Tom's Cabin* (1852) and finishing in the 1990s with the O. J. Simpson murder trial—it was the two films *Birth of a Nation* (D. W. Griffith, 1915) and *Gone with the Wind* (Victor Fleming,

1939) that lined up most unequivocally on the side of white supremacy.[35] On its release, *Birth of a Nation*, an adaptation of Thomas Dixon's novel *The Clansman* (1905), was lauded as a landmark classic of American cinema and overshadowed all other productions well into the 1930s. Its epic account of American history before and after the Civil War depicted the virtues of slavery, slanderous stereotypes of blacks, and, in the words of the political theorist Cedric Robinson, the "horrifying unnaturalness of racial equality."[36] When *Gone with the Wind* was released at the end of the 1930s, it was the first to overtake *Birth of a Nation* as the most expensive and longest film ever made and, like the earlier film, was an "unapologetic celebration of the economic system of chattel slavery," as Williams details.[37] This epic blockbuster won eight Academy Awards and went on to become the inflation-adjusted top-grossing film of all time (a record it still holds in 2019).[38] By the early post–civil rights period, we might expect many viewers to regard *Gone with the Wind* as an oppressive throwback text. But this was not the case. It had been repeatedly rereleased and won a huge new audience in 1967, becoming the second-highest-grossing film of the year. As the film historian Peter Krämer points out in his book on the "golden age" of cinema from 1967 to 1977, dubbed the "Hollywood Renaissance"—associated with innovative hits such as *The Graduate* (Mike Nichols, 1967) and *The Godfather* (Francis Ford Coppola, 1972)—it is often forgotten that *Gone with the Wind* also featured prominently in renaissance-years American film culture.[39] The sustained popularity and critical standing of both *Birth of a Nation* and *Gone with the Wind* demonstrate the formidable marketability of racist melodrama, filmmakers' and distributors' willingness to produce and propagate white-supremacist imagery, and white audiences' eager receptivity to this imagery. Overall, these films' enduring popularity demonstrates how cinema has worked to reproduce and sediment racist mythologies at the heart of American popular culture.

Black Americans were, of course, well aware of the cultural damage inflicted by racist films and from the early days of cinema had sought to counter them with more complex and fulfilling portrayals of black life. In response to the racist propaganda of *Birth of a Nation*, for instance, the NAACP led protests that gave rise to the banning of the film in some states, and a group of black filmmakers produced the rejoinder text *Birth of a Race* (John W. Noble), released in 1918. By then, the black creative entrepreneurs William Foster and brothers Noble and George Johnson had already started producing "race films," which were made, cast, and in part funded by blacks.

Oscar Micheaux soon emerged as African America's first major film auteur. Many of the early race films foregrounded contemporary themes of employment and enterprise, often signaled in titles such as *The Railroad Porter* (William Foster, 1913) and *The Homesteader* (1919), Micheaux's first offering. This vibrant African American film sector, however, became unsustainable, and around the turn of the 1930s Hollywood started releasing its own black-cast films in the form of "plantation" dramas such as *Hallelujah* (King Vidor, 1929) and *Green Pastures* (Marc Connelly and William Keighley, 1936). As the film scholar Paula Massood has shown, these dramas tended to consign black people to a backward Old South pastoral idyll that disavowed the realities of black employment, migration, and modernity.[40] This film cycle was in turn superseded from the late 1940s on by Hollywood's production trend of liberal-reformist race "problem pictures," notably *Home of the Brave* (Mark Robson, 1949) and *No Way Out* (Joseph Mankiewicz, 1950), with mildly integrated casts.[41]

The potential for cinema to engage meaningfully with questions of racial justice during the midcentury decades was diminished not only by Hollywood's exclusion of filmmakers of color but also by its leftist purges. Many filmmakers, black and white, who might have been interested in making freedom-movement-inflected films had from the late 1940s on been barred or deterred from doing so by the House Un-American Activities Committee, which cast a corrosive shadow across the 1950s and 1960s.[42] The very slight integration of casts in the postwar cinematic landscape was supplemented in the early 1960s by a few lauded white-directed, black-themed, art-house productions, many with black creative input, such as *Gone Are the Days* (Nicholas Webster, 1963), *Cool World* (Shirley Clarke, 1963), and *Nothing but a Man* (Michael Roemer, 1964), starring Ivan Dixon and Abbey Lincoln—films that presented "the best of the liberal hope to change social conditions through knowledge and good will," according to the film scholar David James.[43] However, despite these rich individual contributions and the mounting pressure on the industry to respond to the black movement, racial exclusion in cinema remained the norm.

In my study of cinema in the years that followed this moment in the mid-1960s, I offer many film readings that emphasize the ubiquity and salience of racial stories about economic and employment relations. At the same time, I attend closely to industry and production questions—hence, my book title uses the terms *labor* to capture both creative and organized labor and *Hollywood* to designate the whole American film industry, controlled by a small oligopoly of companies based in southern California and encompassing many smaller studios and independent producers, with a second, large concentration in New York. While I explore film texts and the film industry discretely, I also develop an approach for unpacking the complex circuitry between the two. Thus, this book asks: To what extent did the social relations of race portrayed onscreen cohere with those existing behind the scenes? How did contestation in production relations over jobs and resources come to be staged and negotiated in films? How did key film narratives inform the industry's understanding of itself? How have race-themed films been mobilized to manage the public-relations image of the industry, particularly in moments of racial and labor crisis? Conversely, how have excluded communities used films to mobilize against economic exclusion? Have disjunctions between the levels of onscreen and behind-the-scenes racial representation led to moments of rupture? To what extent has the emergence of black filmmakers in Hollywood forced constructive renegotiations of film content? Or, by contrast, have such marginalized filmmakers found their "best fit" in films that further credentialize the industry's avowals of color-blind meritocracy (tolerance in principle but separation in practice)?

In answering these questions, this book shares the agenda of Anamik Saha when he asserts, "What is required is a theory of race and cultural production that illuminates the complex ways that the material shapes the symbolic—in other words, how the cultural industries make race."[44] Equally, drawing out such production/film interplay offers a specific analytical focus for understanding what the cultural theorist Herman Gray describes as "the constant articulations or linkages at play in the relation between representational practices and social locations."[45] Considering the interplay, or what I am calling "reflexivity," between the industry and its storytelling, between structure and signification, reveals cinema's immense ideological capability for shaping ideas and feelings about race across America and beyond.

My central premise—that reflexive relationships exist between the racialized production arrangements of cinema and the racial stories onscreen—differs from the two well-known paradigms of reflexivity in film and media studies. The first main application of reflexivity foregrounds aspects of theme and style that draw attention to the constructedness of the medium. Reflexivity is captured in those moments when a film, as Robert Stam puts it in his classic study, "calls attention to its own status as an artifact."[46] Rather than emphasizing self-conscious distancing techniques deliberately inserted into films, my concern is with the often inadvertent, socially and commercially (rather than primarily aesthetically) determined reflexive relationships between production and representation. I argue that film themes about work, enterprise, and race interact with production relations, as in the *Rocky* example, where the white ethnic revivalism of fictional unknown boxer Rocky Balboa is both underwritten and amplified by the publicity image of the self-made, first-time, white ethnic filmmaker Stallone.

The second key approach to reflexivity comes from the fertile subfield of production studies. A leading proponent of this subfield, John Caldwell, explores "industrial reflexivity" in cultural practice pertaining to the rise of metacommentaries and self-analyses by producers, particularly in the form of "behind-the-scenes" texts that have become in themselves "primary on-screen entertainment forms."[47] But whereas the Caldwell school tends to study production processes and self-reflections on their own terms, I consider them in relation to the resultant cultural output (in this case the feature film). For instance, I explore how the idealized staging of the integration of all-white workplaces in Sidney Poitier vehicles was ratified by the star's status as the lone black professional on Hollywood sets. I also examine how the repudiation of black power in William Styron's novel *Confessions of Nat Turner* (1967) and its planned film adaptation led to a proposed production without black creative input—a disjuncture between the white-determined project and the black struggle for self-determination in the historical source material that ultimately led to the film's derailment. In each case, such production/text racial reflexivity electrifies struggles over the unequal social relations of cinema. Screen stories are informed and authenticated by the complex conditions of their own determination.

Focusing on film's material and discursive linkages enables an examination not just of how cinema was shaped by historical forces but also, crucially, of how film practitioners and organizations actively positioned themselves within racial politics at this pivotal conjuncture. My book insists that individuals and groups had different options at their disposal—they made political decisions that we should not prejudge but that, I argue, can and should be subject to judgment. This focus on explanation and evaluation follows cultural-industries approaches forwarded by David Hesmondhalgh, who calls for more work that poses "ethical questions regarding questions of power and social justice in relation to cultural production."[48] By excavating and evaluating film practices and discourses of the post–civil rights period, I try to avoid imposing today's racial knowledge on history but instead seek to access and re-create a sense of the kinds of political alternatives that were then available. I do so in part to emphasize that none of what occurred during this transitional decade was predetermined. Sweeping, pessimistic scholarly accounts of racism in the cultural industries—which sometimes seem to view bad outcomes as foregone conclusions—may be broadly persuasive, but they need to be accompanied by close examinations of how things came to pass and how they were contested on the ground. My book stands as part of media scholarship that emphasizes the clash among competing, unstable, and uneven political alliances, tracing cinema's contradictory racial role during a period that saw some constructive change but also continuing exclusions and new legitimations of its racist order.

A Piece of the Action

The story told here chronicles how cinema negotiated racial and labor politics in a moment of high-stakes mobilization, polarization, and containment, moving roughly chronologically through this extraordinary period. Chapter 1 describes the film industry's overwhelmingly white racial demographics in the mid-1960s, propped up by racist discourses on- and offscreen that protected the industry from racial self-awareness and meaningful reform. I then illustrate how these industry employment practices and discourses played out in the film In the Heat of the Night (1967). Starring Sidney Poitier and Rod Steiger and directed by Norman Jewison, it was deemed by mainstream critics to be a landmark film of Hollywood racial liberalism. How did the white men who made this film position themselves within the volatile racial politics of the period? How did its African American star? The chapter shows how Poitier—under enormous symbolic pressure and assiduously working his raced identity—became the embryonic "postracial" black star, long before that term entered critical parlance.[49] Given the industry's racist structures, Poitier's advancement was breathtaking. However, through an account of the film and its production, I chart the industry's early adoption of incipient post–civil rights discourses of anti-interventionism and racial meritocracy, which Poitier's screen image warranted. This well-regarded film helped propagate a retreat from jobs and justice by many white liberals at the critical moment when the black freedom movement was stepping up its calls for concrete change in Hollywood.

Following Poitier's brief emergence as the first full-blown A-list black film star, a few African Americans finally broke into mainstream filmmaking (1969–1970). Chapter 2 charts this entry of the directors Gordon Parks Sr., Ossie Davis, and Melvin Van Peebles, the writer Bill Gunn, and the producer Harry Belafonte into a still intransigently white industry during a period of social unrest, politicoaesthetic experimentation, and industry reconfiguration. In the vast scholarly literature on the Hollywood Renaissance, which coincides with the transitional decade, black filmmakers tend to be treated either separately from white filmmakers or, more usually, not at all. Chapter 2 instigates this book's argument that black filmmakers were integral to the widely extoled Hollywood Renaissance. The new black film entrants were often steeped in experiences of race and labor politics that stretched back to earlier decades and also drew on the extraordinary creative and political energy of the years of the Black Arts Movement, black power, and soul-funk music. The cultural-political ferment of this period pulled black "symbol creators" into film production, and it tested those white filmmakers who could see the new marketability and political salience of racial content.[50] Although some whites balked at the period's political mobilizations, seizing on topical racial themes while rebuffing calls for more black creative self-determination, others, including the left- and counterculture-oriented Hal Ashby, John Cassavetes, and Kenneth Hyman, engaged with and enabled the new black film culture.

Chapter 3 opens out further into institutional politics. It examines the extraordinary face-off between the federal government and the film industry (1969–1972) that ran in tandem with the arrival of the first batch of black Hollywood directors. Following its hearings in Los Angeles, the EEOC, tasked with implementing the new civil rights laws, identified an industry-wide pattern of discrimination in motion pictures. It extraordinarily called on the U.S. Justice Department to file suits against practically the whole West Coast industry. The chapter reveals how Hollywood management—above all, the industry's most powerful spokesperson and lobbyist, Jack Valenti—fashioned budding neoconservative racial discourses and policies to discredit those seeking structural change. The import of the dispute between

Hollywood management and the federal government over film jobs traveled beyond the industry and into politics at the highest level as the national mood turned, leading to the toppling of the EEOC head, Clifford Alexander. The chapter then turns to the response of the technical-craft labor force overseen by IATSE. Many—though by no means all—of film's below-the-line workers were not even willing to pay lip service to racial amelioration. Calls of "reverse discrimination" started to resound in some of the industry's union locals, with experienced technicians refusing to train or work with new minority recruits. Cinema was, as I suggest, both an early adopter and a significant incubator of corporate and labor reaction to demands for racial job redistribution, its pro-corporate lobbying and communicating sharpened by industry instability, falling profits, and underemployment across the 1960s.

In the face of failed top-down, federal reform efforts, black symbol creators turned to more self-sufficient, radical, and entrepreneurial strategies in the early 1970s. Chapter 4 investigates the entry of black film producers behind the scenes and the concomitant rise of stylish underground black entrepreneurs onscreen. It starts by looking at politicized film producers such as Ossie Davis (collaborating with Hannah Weinstein), Sidney Poitier, and Harry Belafonte, all of whom were part of a long-standing New York black and left arts community and had a sophisticated grasp of cinema's political economy. These film performers tried to become producers to cut deals and achieve greater financial, organizational, and creative control. I detail how in different ways they sought an alternative and more equitable production model for cinema. The chapter then traces the turn to the more individualist, subcultural, masculinist, but still politicized priorities in the emergent ghetto action-film cycle. The new street-identified enterprising heroes onscreen in iconic films such as *Sweet Sweetback's Baadasssss Song* (Melvin Van Peebles, 1971), *Super Fly*, and *The Mack* were energized and legitimated by black subcultural histories and creative workers.[51] The glamorized hustler as screen hero was the site of heated black and left contestation within a climate of persisting radicalism but also mounting social cynicism, state withdrawal, and market-driven thinking. Along with the powerful legacy of Poitier's postracial stardom (black screen heroes exuding professionalism, forbearance, and palatability), the macho, street-smart, entrepreneurial creative (or what I am calling the "hustler creative") was the other preeminent black figure to emerge at this moment as a far-reaching post–civil rights pop-cultural archetype. These film projects led to unprecedented jobs and training for black workers and high revenues for individual black symbol creators, but almost all of them made more money for industry whites, thus frustrating the ambitious goals of the more collectivist black film producers.

The early ghetto action films that mesmerized black and cross-racial youth audiences—*Cotton Comes to Harlem*, *Sweetback*, *Shaft* (Gordon Parks Sr., 1971), and *Super Fly*—launched a black-oriented film wave that lasted from 1972 to 1976, explored in the final chapter. I emphasize the breadth of black-themed stories during this period, which often revolved around narratives of racialized work and economic relations and included substantial leading roles for black women (which is noteworthy in a wider moment of well-documented heightened masculinism in the film culture of the 1970s). Nonetheless, some of the films of the black film wave (produced mostly by whites) were carelessly made and marketed, heavily laced with melodramatic racial antagonism, and screened in largely segregated theaters. Thus, the widely used new label *blaxploitation*, coined in 1972, resonated as both a term of critique and a basis for protest. The second half of chapter 5 considers how this film wave and the "blaxploitation" protests sat within broader industry politics. It considers how Hollywood management moved to suppress blacks' participation in the production of films through the consolidation of racially laissez-faire corporate discourses as the industry made a quiet retreat from racial justice. As the 1970s progressed, studio management rejected critiques of institutional discrimination by the Coalition Against Blaxploitation and others by characterizing the film sector as having meritocratically moved beyond racial hierarchies. At the same time, the industry was ironically profiting from the reification of racial difference through its often hyperracialized texts and target marketing strategies. Charlton Heston and Ronald Reagan, along with Jack Valenti, were important postracial and "postlabor" management players of the new Hollywood consensus that I consider here. This chapter closes with a consideration of the state of the quest for employment and representational justice in American cinema at the end of the transitional decade as African American filmmakers and black-oriented stories all but disappeared.

The conclusion starts with my final case study: the film *Blue Collar* (1978), starring Richard Pryor and Harvey Keitel and directed by Paul Schrader, which once again reveals complex and charged racial negotiation between production and storytelling. Through this film example, I suggest that the transitional decade set many of the terms for what has come since. Focusing on practitioners, activists, and film texts of the 1960s and 1970s, many of them steeped in race and labor-movement politics, helps sharpen our attention to the contemporary possibilities for and constraints on racial change in and through cinema. During the transitional decade, black filmmakers and performers started to grasp the sheer intractability of white structures of advantage and exclusion, notwithstanding the civil rights legislation. In part as a result of this knowledge, they developed new, more individualist and networked strategies to try to leverage the mainstream's interest in images of blackness. Some black filmmakers have managed to pry open all-white cultural-industries workplaces on an ad hoc basis, often bringing other black creatives along with them. In so doing, they used a reflexive lever that other marginalized groups, with much less symbolic purchase on screen, were not (and still are not) fully able to pull. Mainly, though, the period that followed continued with the closed ideological circuitry of white-dominated productions making sincere-fiction racial dramas. Thus, the conclusion suggests how the model of production/text reflexivity developed in this book can help explain some of the complex, co-opting, and controversial racial trends in recent American cinema.

The title of my book signals many of the concerns discussed here. *A Piece of the Action* is the title of a successful black-cast comedy film, with a score by the leading soul artist Curtis Mayfield, released in 1977, at the end of the transitional decade, and directed, produced, and based on a story by Sidney Poitier, who also stars in it. By foregrounding this film project in my title rather than one of Poitier's iconic "Saint Sidney" screen roles, I signal this book's strong focus on black production and creative labor. Where Poitier has often been reduced to a white-ingratiating "effigy" through his civil rights screen image,[52] his film career as director and producer is often overlooked. Keenly focused on wresting black financial and creative authority from a racist film industry to create employment opportunities for black workers and to cater to underserved black audiences with tailored content, he became the most commercially successful African American director and producer (a record he held for more than a decade).[53] Poitier's black-cast family comedies distributed by major companies—which, along with *A Piece of the Action*, include *Uptown Saturday Night* (1974), *Let's Do It Again* (1975), and the fully crossover, interracial *Stir Crazy* (1980), produced by white radical filmmaker Hannah Weinstein—may not be critically well regarded. But they stand as showcases of black-determined comedic talent and demonstrate the potential of gaining a crossover audience for big-screen family entertainments made by, about, and primarily for black people. My title phrase thus indicates this book's exposition of how black film creatives, as performers and producers, ably tried to install viable filmmaking practices in a structurally racist movie business.

However, as a pragmatic, business-friendly, and vernacular phrase, "a piece of the action" also serves to indicate, perhaps inevitably, a sense of capitulation. Many black cultural workers were excluded from filmmaking as the 1970s progressed; those who remained were forced to bid for (and very occasionally win) a portion of the extant white- and corporate-determined dividends, having been blocked from their ambitious attempts at transforming racial and labor conditions in cinema. This note of capitulation also sounds in the politically quiescent and patriarchal uplift themes in the film narrative of *A Piece of the Action*, in which Poitier schools unruly black working-class adolescents in a role that recalls and revises *To Sir, with Love* (James Clavell, 1967). When he counsels them that everyone needs to find their "own piece of the action," he seems to be suggesting that they must develop their human capital in quite individualist, opportunist terms. Thus, the film title captures the narrowing of political possibilities in the long decade following the Civil Rights Act and the birth of black power—a period that saw not only some dramatic racial gains that have had lasting consequences but also white racial containment amid dawning neoliberal inequality. In this hardening climate, African Americans increasingly found themselves forced to work within the existing racist profit and image structures or not to work at all. Thus, the phrase "a piece of the action" signals both the arrival of a collectivist black creative, political, and financial dynamism in film mapped in this book and the curtailment of a black-left political agenda during a decade of struggle against recalcitrant power structures— the latter felt keenly by many of the symbol creators who feature in this book, including Sidney Poitier.

1

"THE SCREEN SPEAKS FOR ITSELF"

Institutional Discrimination and the Dawning
of Hollywood Postracialism

W hen Sidney Poitier was voted the most bankable star in
America in 1968, it was an unexpected and exhilarating
racial achievement. Poitier's star had been rising ever since
1950 with his breakout film role as a doctor in *No Way Out* (Joseph Mankiewicz), his screen image encapsulating and fueling the production trend of
liberal-reformist race "problem pictures." By 1967, he became the first African American to appear on Quigley's star rankings of top-ten box-office
attractions as voted by exhibitors. In a *New York Times* cover story, veteran
critic Bosley Crowther identified him as "the most conspicuous and respected
exponent of the American Negro on the screen."[1] Then, following the success of his three hits that year—*Guess Who's Coming to Dinner* (Stanley
Kramer), *In the Heat of the Night* (Norman Jewison), and *To Sir, with Love*
(James Clavell)—Poitier came to top Quigley's chart in 1968, taking over
from musicals star Julie Andrews to become the year's highest-grossing
actor.[2] That an African American, however fleetingly, achieved this level of
national, mainstream acceptance was in itself remarkable. However, part of
the strategic significance for the film industry of this most conspicuous
"exponent of the American Negro on film" was that it drew attention away
from the industry's own pervasive behind-the-scenes employment exclusions, just as the federal-backed antiracist challenge gathered pace.

In the film business of the 1960s, minorities were pervasively absent or
marginalized on all but the lowliest employment levels. As minority workers increasingly sought entry into film work, white symbol creators, studio

executives, and film technicians had to consider, perhaps for the first time, their own racial workplace assumptions. Some continued with old-style racist exclusion—there were, to be sure, many overtly discriminatory personnel, who made no effort even to pay lip service to racial tolerance (see chapter 3). But my main focus in this first chapter, as indeed in this book as a whole, is on industry personnel with more centrist, hegemonic perspectives and the way in which they negotiated racial change. After setting out the industry's institutional and discursive racial employment dynamics, I turn to how these dynamics played out at the microlevel of an individual film project: *In the Heat of the Night*. Released by the Mirisch Corporation for United Artists and directed by Norman Jewison, this detective film enjoyed by far the highest standing of Poitier's three vehicles in 1967, winning the New York Film Critics Circle Best Picture award and landing five Oscars, including Best Picture. I first explore how this flagship racial drama engaged with employment themes onscreen in the immediate post–Civil Rights Act moment, and then I examine its production relations as a site of racialized creative labor. Finally, I turn to its top-billed actor, Sidney Poitier, and his performance of Virgil Tibbs. I want to capture the contestedness of microlevel racial negotiations in order to emphasize a point made in the introduction: different choices were possible at this moment of crisis and possibility.

This case study is by far the most detailed discussion of a movie in this book, and its purpose is to showcase in detail my approach of looking at the interplay between production history, film content, and industry public relations. In this film and his other vehicles in 1967, Poitier was an isolated black creative in overwhelmingly white production contexts, and these racial employment relations were mirrored by his predicament onscreen as an isolated black professional in a white world. This reflexivity between production and film helped validate the film's racial politics and Poitier's star image, but it also pointed to new and far-reaching post–civil rights dynamics of racial containment in film-industry employment and symbolic relations.

Industry Discrimination

From the forced labor of slavery through sharecropping and on to the material exclusions of Jim Crow, African Americans had been consistently locked out of full economic citizenship in a system that enforced white advantage. Cumulative confinement to inferior jobs led to economic marginalization for black people: lower living standards, poorer life chances, and chronic financial insecurity. The resultant wealth disparities were compounded in the twentieth century by racist government policies, business enterprises, institutional norms, and private actions. This "possessive investment in whiteness," to use George Lipsitz's enduring term, persisted in the arenas of employment, business, pensions, land acquisition, and real estate, all propping up the fiscal dimensions of white supremacy.[3] By the mid-1960s, unemployment rates for blacks hovered around double the rate for whites, with many African Americans concentrated in the least-desirable and lowest-paying jobs.[4] Los Angeles County, the headquarters of the U.S. film industry, was home to around 650,000 black people by 1965, and they experienced an unemployment rate of about three times the rate for whites. As a result, 30.7 percent of black and minority ethnic families were below the poverty line, as compared to 8.8 percent of whites.[5] The lack of wealth had, among other things, "a devastating impact on the ability of blacks to build and maintain successful enterprises," as Melvin Oliver and Thomas Shapiro explain,[6] and this impact encompassed cultural enterprises, including, to be sure, the capital-intensive, segregated realm of film production, distribution, and exhibition.

Despite deep economic barriers, a sizeable black independent film sector had emerged as early as the 1910s, headquartered in Chicago.[7] As already mentioned in the introduction, "race films" were controlled mainly by blacks: made by and for African Americans with all-black casts and usually cofunded by blacks and whites. However, following a final spurt of productions in the late 1930s, this era of black independent filmmaking petered out, squeezed by the soaring costs of feature production, the move by the major studios into some black-cast musical productions, and, particularly following the propagandist drive of World War II, into some mildly integrated but still predominantly white-cast productions.[8] In the postwar period, race advocacy groups, led by the NAACP and its head Walter White, downgraded the importance of black-made productions and critiqued Hollywood's all-black pastoral musicals, advocating instead for integrationist, mainstream dramas that were seen to uplift the image of African Americans.[9] This advocacy gave rise to a relative improvement in the profile of roles, according to the film scholar Anna Everett, facilitating the emergence of black film stars such as Lena Horne, Dorothy Dandridge, Harry Belafonte, and of course Poitier. However, it also precipitated a decline in the number of acting roles for

African Americans.[10] Moreover, despite the film industry's liberal screen ges-
tures, as of the mid-1960s no major-studio picture had ever been directed
by an African American. As the film scholar William Grant summarizes,
"Between 1915 and 1969 not a single film out of more than ten thousand
motion pictures produced by the majors . . . was under the creative control
of a black person."[11]

The pervasive exclusion spread well beyond film directors and into practically all the coveted jobs in the industry. In terms of film exhibition, out of
about fourteen thousand movie theaters nationwide in the 1960s, less than
twenty were black operated or owned.[12] In terms of the studios, there were
no black, Latino, or Asian American senior executives at any of the majors
in the late 1960s. Overall employment of minorities at the studios was well
below the average rates for industries in the Los Angeles area, including other
cultural industries.[13] The patchy employment data detailed here are based
on self-reporting by the industry and are thus far from reliable, but they give
a clear indication of pervasive underrepresentation. Six of the seven major
film studios—Twentieth Century-Fox, Warner Bros.–Seven Arts, Columbia,
Walt Disney, Metro-Goldwyn-Mayer, and Paramount—employed, on average,
only 2.1 percent blacks in 1967 (well short of the 7.4 percent black workforce
in the Los Angeles area). The situation was little better for other minority-
ethnic groups. Latinxs, who represented 10.1 percent of the area's workforce,
represented 4.2 percent of all studio employees, and Native Americans and
Asian Americans, notwithstanding their much smaller overall workforce
numbers, were also very underrepresented.[14] Even more discrepant than the
raw numbers was the fact that the industry's minority employees usually
worked the most low-pay, low-skill service jobs—a large proportion of the
studios' black and Latinx employees were janitors and messengers.

Cinema's technical workforce was also overwhelmingly white. In terms
of union membership in the technical crafts in the Los Angeles area, blacks
represented 2.9 percent, and Spanish-surnamed Americans 5.3 percent, again
well below their overall workforce numbers.[15] The prestigious areas of sound,
camerawork, and illustration were almost exclusively white, with some union
locals having no minority members at all, including, for instance, the fifty-
member Illustrators and Matte Artists Local in Los Angeles. Even the lower-
skill crafts were heavily exclusionary. In the late 1960s, for example, the
four-thousand-member Set and Propmen Local in Los Angeles had just eight
black members (0.2 percent).[16] In New York, the nation's other main filmmaking center, the *New York Times* reported that there were only twelve

blacks and six Latinxs in a motion-picture technical workforce of approximately six thousand members (0.3 percent nonwhite) in 1969.[17] Most of film's craft unions were thus basically white enclaves, built on a seniority structure known as the "experience roster" that all but excluded minorities.

The craft rosters were overseen by the all-white Association of Motion Picture and Television Producers (AMPTP)—run by the powerful Lew Wasserman, who represented the interests of studios and major producers in labor negotiations, and maintained through collective-bargaining agreements (see chapter 3). Thus, both studios, under the auspices of the AMPTP, and unions—represented by IATSE, which had no black board members—were responsible for the rosters' organizational arrangements. Together the studios and unions maintained a system in which everyone in the union must be employed or offered a job before an outside recruit could be hired. Yet in what commentators called a "double refusal," an individual first needed a studio job to join the union.[18] Black cameraman Robert Grant explained, "You go to a place like Columbia and they say go get into IA [IATSE], you go to IA and they say get a job first. I know it happens to almost everyone, but white cameramen get in somehow, don't they?"[19]

The guilds, which represented the above-the-line film-industry positions of directors, scriptwriters, publicists, and actors, were in many cases not subject to the protectionist experience roster but were scarcely less exclusionary. This was nowhere more evident than for the Directors Guild of America, which had failed to produce or include a single African American feature-film director. A celebrated new exception to this pervasive whiteness was the Publicists' Guild, which became in 1967 the first Hollywood labor organization to be headed by an African American when it appointed Vincent Tubbs.[20] But Tubbs was very far from representative of the workforce he represented, and it is perhaps no coincidence that the one black union boss to emerge was the figurehead for the Hollywood organization concerned with marketing and image management.

Following the Civil Rights Act of 1964, which came into effect in July 1965, the studios had the legal power to begin forcing the labor organizations to include minorities when presenting their lists of applicants for jobs or, when that failed, to look beyond the unions for personnel. But studios, with the partial exception of Universal City Studios (see chapter 3), did not start to intervene in these processes that afforded systematic advantages to whites. Things were not improving. The most complete minority job figures were produced by the Screen Actors Guild in the category of film extras, which actually showed some decline across the mid-1960s, after peaking at 2.3 percent in 1963 (a year of heightened activism).[21] Though voluntarily submitted figures of minority employment at the studios and guilds in the mid-1960s do not make for solid comparative data, they suggest no increase in blacks on the payrolls.[22] After a meeting with representatives of the AMPTP in summer 1965—another peak year for movement activism, state repression, and public outcry—the labor-industry chair of the Hollywood–Beverly Hills NAACP, Davis Roberts, expressed "disappointment" with the "negligible results" achieved by "regular confabs with the AMPTP, despite consistently pleasant relations and accord."[23] According to the *Los Angeles Times* staff writer Dan Knapp, who wrote several prominent features on race in the cultural industries in the late 1960s, "Even among those with their hearts in the right place, there is a tendency to over-estimate the progress that has been made, and to see clearly with one eye but not the other."[24] To explain why many industry whites perceived progress despite continuing pervasive underutilization of minority workers, we need to look more closely at the industry's discursive explanations of its racist division of labor.

White Self-Fictions

Minority film workers were only too aware of the overestimation of progress by many industry whites. Actors Diana Sands and Robert Hooks, who gave evidence at a New York State civil rights hearing in 1968, explained that "progress made in the past few years has not been nearly up to the level generally surmised by the white community."[25] Commentator Leonard Feather pointed to the same perceptual schism: "Although both the companies and the union deny that they are responsible for any discrimination, they have not convinced many members of the black community."[26] The industry had responded to the antiracist movement mainly by paying lip service to liberal principles by having "regular confabs" in the form of meetings, fundraisers, and luncheons and by hiring a few more minority studio messengers and, at flashpoint moments, minority actors and extras.

To be sure, in an industry where hiring is normally done through friendship networks and known experience, bringing minorities (and women) into almost exclusively white (male) film workplaces presented challenges. When assembling a team for a project, many of film's symbol creators and executives look for "a personal comfort zone with someone of the same ethnic group, and reassurance from prior experience that that individual has the professional talent and/or personal style to function effectively," as John Downing and Charles Husband explain in their important book on race and media. The film business writer Vance King pointed out in 1969 that the industry "hires mostly through friendship and acknowledged skill. It hires because of proven records. It hires because of whim and fantasy." Labeling these entrenched practices a form of "cronyism," Downing and Husband show that they play a central role in perpetuating racial inequalities in the industry.[27] The organizational arrangements in this high-risk, short-termist industry, where deals are put together and talent packages assembled in ad hoc ways, militated against consideration of and remedies for structural discrimination. Compounding these difficulties, good jobs in the cultural industries were highly prized (despite many of them being insecure and quite badly paid). Because of the high levels of perceived self-determination, creativity, and prestige as well as, in some areas, good wages and conditions in this sector, there was an oversupply of potential workers, and those who held these coveted jobs hoarded them.[28] Many minority workers, whose employment expectations had initially been buoyed by the Civil Rights Act, found that they had to contend with both class- and race-based impediments. Given the manifold barriers, some minority members preempted rejection by choosing to pursue careers in less structurally exclusionary fields because, as African American media organizer Cliff Frazier of the Community Film Workshop explained, "most blacks have been conditioned not to think of the film industry as a possible area."[29]

But whatever the complexities of opening film jobs to nonwhite workers, the driving force for exclusion remained white inertia and job hoarding, about which, as Diana Sands and Robert Hooks stated at the New York State civil rights hearing in 1968, whites were largely in denial.[30] Opinion surveys of white attitudes across the country showed that white people were moving toward an outward rhetoric of racial tolerance during the 1960s—an improvement on their previous widespread public acceptance of overt racism. Before the racial break, "segregation, discrimination, and openly verbalized prejudice toward minorities of all kinds were entirely acceptable throughout much of the US," as the race sociologist Howard Schuman and his colleagues explain. This open prejudice then gave way to "norms calling for equal treatment regardless of race," such that by 1972, at least in one large public-opinion survey, the vast majority of whites had rejected the principle of explicit discrimination against blacks in employment. However, although some whites had made the new norms an integral part of their belief system and tried to live in accord with them, for many whites these new norms acted more as "an external constraint."[31] The many whites for whom equal treatment was nonintegral to their belief system were willing to espouse liberal principles of equality when directly asked, but their private attitudes and actions were far from egalitarian.

A salutary reminder of how little many whites were actually internalizing the new norms came in 1964 with Proposition 14 in the film industry's home state, California. This law overturned the Fair Housing Act passed the previous year, which protected minorities from racist property owners and landlords who refused to sell or rent property to them. Proposition 14 proved very popular, winning fully 65 percent of the vote, crystalizing early civil rights backlash politics, which intensified in Los Angeles after the Watts uprising the following year.[32] By publicly professing egalitarian norms that had not been internalized, many whites developed powerful new assessments of themselves as racially magnanimous. As already noted in the introduction, Feagin, Vera, and Batur call these self-perceptions "sincere fictions of the white self," which are "personal ideological constructions that reproduce societal mythologies at the individual level. In such personal characterizations, white individuals usually see themselves as 'not racist,' as 'good people,' even while they think and act in antiblack ways."[33] Such discourses are "sincere" because they are often heartfelt but also "fictions" because they deny that there is discrimination in the face of persisting practices of structural racism and of white practices of separation.

Though Feagin, Vera, and Batur identify such sincere fictions in whites' attitudes of the 1990s, these fictions were already in evidence in the film industry of the late 1960s and 1970s as it started to fend off challenges to its employment practices. One notable fiction the sociologists pinpoint, that "whites are more insightful about or active in racial change than blacks,"[34] was a repeated claim made in the statements by film-industry personnel. The idea that well-intentioned whites were working assiduously to help minorities is evident, for instance, in the avowal by one anonymous "white executive," quoted in the *Hollywood Reporter* in 1968, that "there is a conscious effort on the part of the people in the industry who do the hiring to consider as many Negroes as possible. There was a great move in that direction in 1963. By 1965, it seemed we had done about all the assimilating we could. Now, however, the efforts continue but it's getting harder to find qualified people."[35] This executive drew attention to the upsurges in civil rights activity in the years of the March on Washington and Selma. The industry responded apparently with "a conscious effort" and "a great move," and its "efforts continue[d]." AMPTP vice president Charles Boren offered another example of this rhetorical emphasis on heightened industry efforts: "There has been a run on the minority manpower market in Los Angeles."[36] Labor-market demand for black and Latinx workers, he intimated, was far outstripping supply.

The labor-relations head at Warners, Arthur Schaefer, also tried to forward this rhetoric of magnanimous white activity, complaining about his "trouble finding minority people." But when asked if he had made any contact with the Urban League to assist in the search, Schaefer was forced to reveal that his actions predictably amounted to "[going] to a number of lunches."[37] The implication of this dubious insistence on white activity in bringing about racial change is that when change doesn't come, responsibility for continuing underrepresentation rests with minorities themselves. A public-opinion survey in 1968 found that although whites were moving away from explanations of black disadvantage based on lack of innate ability, they were also moving away from classic liberal explanations based on structural discrimination. A large majority of whites instead "attributed black disadvantage to lack of motivation (for example, 'not trying')." This lack of motivation compared very unfavorably to whites' supposed "conscious effort," noted earlier. As Schuman and his coauthors explain, "[Black under-motivation] was offered by respondents as a self-sufficient explanation, one that in effect assumes 'free will' as the main source of success in America."[38]

Indeed, many in Hollywood, unwilling or unable to take practical steps to reach out to black organizations and networks for assistance, overestimated blacks' agency to enter and progress in the industry. Foregrounding a rhetoric of individual agency while failing to take concrete steps to develop pipelines, industry spokespeople encouraged the public to rely on cultural and media imagery as a social reference point instead. AMPTP vice president Charles Boren encouraged a reliance on cinematic images to inform perceptions of apparent racial employment amelioration in cinema: "The best evidence of improvements is up on the screen. The public can see what has been done. The screen speaks for itself."[39] Sociologists explain that whites' tendency to use media and pop-cultural imagery to form their racial attitudes is exacerbated by their lack of contact with people of color. Feagin, Vera, and Batur describe an "encapsulated white bubble" within which the least racially integrated group (white people) lives. In the 1960s, racial disconnection in everyday life and in concrete workplaces such as the film industry compounded the influence of media imagery on people's attitudes and beliefs. As the film scholar Mark Reid remarks, "Most whites did not socialize with blacks. . . . Thus, they naively formulated their ideas about Afro-Americans from white literature, television, and the movies."[40] A detailed reading of a key film, its production history, and its black star demonstrates the beguiling dangers of letting "the screen speak for itself."

Representing Race and the Workplace: *In the Heat of the Night*

Sidney Poitier's three film hits of 1967, which propelled him to A-list stardom, fed topical race-relations themes into classical Hollywood narrative formulas: a romantic comedy (*Guess Who's Coming to Dinner*), a rite-of-passage school drama (*To Sir, with Love*), and a detective story (*In the Heat of the Night*). Media scholar Christine Gledhill has looked at how pop-cultural texts combine both melodramatic and realist modes, working "both on a symbolic, 'imaginary' level, internal to fictional production, and on a 'realist' level, referring to the sociohistorical world outside the text." The complex negotiation between these two modes has extra charge, she argues, in popular culture that features protagonists from subordinated groups.[41] Although both *Guess Who's Coming to Dinner* (grossing $57 million at the domestic box office) and *To Sir, with Love* (grossing $42 million) were more successful than *In the Heat of the Night* (grossing $24 million), they were seen in the context of the racial volatility of the late 1960s to refer much less meaningfully to the sociohistorical world beyond the text. Bosley Crowther described *To Sir, with Love*, for instance, as "a cozy, good-humored, and unbelievable little tale."[42] By contrast, both industry and mainstream commentators interpreted the detective story as working powerfully on Gledhill's realist level. Reviewers made very strong truth claims about it and in so doing imbued it with a sense of social salience. In the *New York Times*, Crowther stated that *In the Heat of the Night* possessed "the look and sound of actuality and the pounding pulse of truth"; Richard Schickel pronounced it in his *Life* review "a sound, serious, and altogether excellent film." The *National Observer* suggested that it struck a perfect balance between its symbolic and realist registers and applauded "a melodrama with the taste, the feel, and the smell of absolute authenticity."[43] The film also enjoyed industry acclaim, winning Oscars not only for Best Picture but also across the key areas of Best Actor, Best Editing, Best Screenplay, and Best Sound. Although there was heated criticism in black political and intellectual circles about Poitier's "super Sidney" image at this time (which I discuss later in this chapter), *In the Heat of the Night* was rarely singled out for particular opprobrium and also emerged as a black audience favorite.

Some scholars have tended to reproduce—albeit with more nuance—the sociohistorical credibility claims about *In the Heat of the Night*. In their study of race and film, Hernan Vera and Andrew Gordon contend that the film "represents the best that Hollywood film could do in 1967 in the treatment of race relations. It was made by a group of earnest white activists. They had the best pedagogical intentions. Jewison wanted the film to make a difference at the time."[44] In a somewhat similar vein, the historians Emma Hamilton and Troy Saxby contend in their insightful reading of the film that it credibly captured radicalizing freedom-movement trends as the 1960s progressed. The film "reflects the context of production," offering "examinations of institutional disadvantage, the rise of black power, and issues of separatism."[45]

I agree that the film engaged with racial politics of the time, but I also argue in opposition to this scholarship that the film narrative tended to deny rather than to expose institutional workplace disadvantage and was undergirded by discourses of informal white (rather than black) separatism. As Howard Winant writes in *The World Is a Ghetto*, "The unity of the civil rights movement eroded rapidly after the mid-1960s. Its mainstream liberal supporters—and most of its white adherents—congratulated themselves on the victory of the enactment of civil rights reforms. But many movement activists, and much of its black membership, wondered how much change civil rights could bring, absent significant redistribution of income."[46] This well-loved film, though assuredly an ambivalent and overdetermined text, advanced this politics of white racial retreat from economic justice. It served to consolidate "sincere fictions" at the beginning of the transitional decade when many, though not all, white liberals congratulated themselves on the "culmination" of civil rights and recoiled from the implications of the black movement, particularly in wealth and employment redistribution.

The film begins when a black northerner, Virgil Tibbs (Sidney Poitier), is wrongly arrested as a suspect in a murder case while traveling through the small Mississippi town Sparta to visit his mother. Tibbs, who turns out to be a top homicide detective from Philadelphia, soon teams up with the town's white sheriff, Chief Gillespie (Rod Steiger), and helps to solve the murder case. The film sets up dramatic binaries between the working environments of the apparently modernized and integrated North and the benighted South. An iconic early scene, when Tibbs first meets Gillespie, stages white southern workplace dysfunction: the sweaty police station with its comically inept officers and faulty air-conditioning unit. Gillespie interrogates Tibbs, demanding to know where he came by the $200 in his wallet. His resentment grows when he learns that Tibbs earns "$162.39 a week": "Now just what you do up there in little old Pennsylvania to earn that kind of money?" The sheriff is astonished to discover that Tibbs is, like himself, a police officer— the long reaction shot dramatically captures Gillespie (and presumably the white viewer) coming to terms with the news. The scene suggests that workplaces in an enlightened North, such as Philadelphia's police department, are already well integrated by 1967, with blacks getting hired, promoted, and well remunerated without facing individual and institutional discrimination.

The idea of the color-blind northern workplace is further substantiated by the film's other nonsouthern protagonist: Mrs. Colbert (Lee Grant) from Chicago. Her husband, the murdered Mr. Colbert, was a prominent white industrialist who had sought to modernize and bring jobs to the small Deep South town by building a factory that would employ an integrated workforce. Mrs. Colbert, his widow, wants to continue this mission, and she seems totally free of racism when she insists that Tibbs is kept on in the murder case: "I want that Negro officer on this case. . . . If not, I will pack up my husband's engineers and leave you to yourselves." Mrs. Colbert's moral authority as a northern progressive is enhanced by the leftist credentials of screen actor Lee Grant, who had been blacklisted under McCarthy. Thus, northerners (Virgil Tibbs, Mr. and Mrs. Colbert) consistently bring enlightenment to the backward southern town, and their enlightenment is demonstrated mainly in their racial attitudes toward and practices of employment.

As the complex task of implementation of civil rights legislation was just grinding into gear across the nation, how did the key race movie of the year engage with the quest for jobs and justice? Enforcement of the new Civil Rights Act was cast as unnecessary for the hiring and promotion practices of Philadelphia's police department: Tibbs had already scaled its heights through sheer merit and hard work. This logic is further substantiated by the Colberts and their already-integrated northern factories: no need for interventionism. The film thus promotes values of employment laissez-faireism among centrist and northern whites—values at loggerheads with the calls among contemporary antiracist activists for deep-seated change to address the endemic nature of race privilege and employment discrimination across America.

In John Ball's source novel, the murdered man is an Italian music conductor rather than a northern industrialist.[47] It was the screenwriter Stirling Silliphant who first inserted into the screenplay's subplot the North/South employment theme. In doing so, Silliphant was tapping into liberal-consensus ideas about the significance of jobs to racial integration and economic development, which were prominent discourses in the mid- to late 1960s and at the heart of President Lyndon Johnson's Great Society and War on Poverty programs. However, though the film's race-employment modernization themes were well intentioned, the way they played out risked legitimating laissez-faireism.

Most critics did not deem problematic the film's dramatic suggestion that continuing racism was confined to the South, whereas the North was embracing both white-collar and blue-collar black workers. Crowther's *New York Times* film review was the only one I identified from the mainstream press to note that "the hot surge of racial hate and prejudice that is so evident and critical now in so many places in this country, not alone in the traditional area of the Deep South, is fictionally isolated in an ugly little Mississippi town in the new film."[48] However, even he did not see this misleading geographical isolation of racism as diminishing the film's "pulse of truth." One northern reviewer suggested that the film was actually "an educational showpiece" for "Northerners [who] don't understand the degradation involved" in a racist "Southern attitude, still not eradicated."[49] Such framing of the film as racial pedagogy for progressive northerners flies in the face of a black movement that was then insisting on endemic racism across America. By 1967, King had taken his campaign from the South to Chicago. What he found there aligned him with what Malcolm X had been insisting on in 1964 when he repeatedly told black audiences in his "The Ballot or the Bullet" speech, "If you black, you were born in jail, in the North as well as the South. Stop talking about the South. As long as you south of the Canadian border, you South."[50]

In the Heat of the Night's sincere-fiction notion that northern whites were instruments of progressive social change finds a correlative in some of the scholarship about the film, which tends to read it in terms of growing black separatism. The literary scholar Andrea Levine interprets *In the Heat of the Night* as the "white male's aggrieved response to his diminished importance in the arena of racial politics and, in turn, his rejection by black male activists" during the period of the Student Nonviolent Coordinating Committee and deepening radicalization. Hamilton and Saxby, who rightly critique the film for its misleading confinement of nationwide racism to the South, nonetheless concur with Levine when they explain the resonance of the film in terms of a new black leadership that "rejected integration and white coalitions."[51] These readings are representative of trends in scholarship that foreground the black movement's aggressive repudiation of whites. However, the racial dynamics circulating in America at this time and reflected in this film surely had more to do with the continuing separatism of whites avowing tolerance (including on screen) while generally rejecting the demands for concrete change demanded by black people and their allies. As such, white men did not have a diminished role in the arena of racial politics, as these scholars suggest, but rather an augmented one.

If the film's romanticized representation of northern workers and workplaces as already integrated has been underacknowledged, even more neglected is its romanticized construction of the South. Again, mainstream journalists at the time tended to laud the film's verisimilitude. According to one northern white reviewer, the film was "a biting portrait of today's South," and another declared that "the portrait of the South that emerges is the most realistic of any recent American feature film." Ann Faber at the *Seattle Post-Intelligencer* endorsed the "mythical but real-as-touch town called Sparta, Mississippi," which is "totally believable."[52] Certainly, the quasi-documentary moments and grainy filming by cinematographer Haskell Wexler enhanced the drama's vérité aspects. Although there were resonant elements of documentary realism in the film's style, the truth claims about its depiction of small-town Mississippi are dubious (and hardly any of the film was actually filmed in the South). Perhaps most egregious is the character of Chief Gillespie, who was widely described in the contemporary white press reception as the very embodiment of the southern racist police chief. His red-neck cop "fairly oozes sweat and hate," asserted Crowther, and *Daily Variety* described the chief as "a diehard Dixie bigot."[53] Jewison had certainly intended this referential frame: "I wanted him to look like the stereotype of every beefy, bigoted police chief in the South."[54]

However, from the beginning, Gillespie is a remarkably benign rendering of the southern sheriff. As James Baldwin pointed out in his book-length critique of race representation in cinema, *The Devil Finds Work* (1976), which includes a critique of *In the Heat of the Night*, "We are asked to believe that the Sheriff imagines that he needs a confession from this black Northern vagrant, and so elects to converse with him before locking him up, turning him over to his deputies, and closing the case."[55] Beneath Gillespie's paunchy southern front, he is shown to be intuitive and empathetic, the resilient white male underdog in many workplace scenes in which he faces off with the hyperprofessional Virgil Tibbs. In Schickel's admiring terms, Gillespie "is a man learning and changing in a tense situation and under the impact of Tibbs's exasperating skill in their shared profession."[56] In a piece of dialogue used in the film's promotional ads, Gillespie propositions Tibbs: "Now listen, they pay you $162.39 a week to look at dead bodies. Why can't you look at this one?"[57] The supposed entrenched racism of the diehard Dixie bigot melts away to uncover an able and underpaid professional with racial humility. In most of the press reception of the time there was a failure to recognize the romanticized nature of this portrayal, and this failure once again risks being reproduced in scholarly readings. In Hamilton and Saxby's view, the portrayal is evidence that "an enlightened Southern sheriff had become implausible, and the stereotype of the ignorant Southern racist took precedence."[58] But the enlightened southern sheriff did take precedence: Gillespie emerges as an early example of beset post–civil rights white masculinity being forced to give up racial privileges in the workplace and doing so quite graciously. Even the southern sheriff turns out to be basically "not racist" and "good people." Gillespie is thus a prototype for what Hamilton Carroll calls "affirmative reaction" in his book on the pop-cultural representation of post-1960s white masculinity.[59] Carroll looks at how iconic portrayals of white men found new ways of maintaining privilege ironically by reproducing a sense of its erosion. Even though white men still held onto nearly all the good jobs in America, this film plausibly takes for granted the idea that the white man is the occupational subordinate for whom the viewer can root in a scene-stealing role for which Rod Steiger won a Best Actor Oscar.

The sheriff's recuperative southern portrayal finds a correlative in the wealthy plantation owner Endicott (Larry Gates), who is also ultimately a surprisingly benign portrayal of the southern white gentleman. Tibbs's suspicions that the agrarian Endicott is behind the killing of the northern industrialist Colbert proves to be wrong-headed, built on the prejudices not of whites, but of the black detective himself. When Tibbs famously returns Endicott's facial slap with a counter slap, the white power brokers do not retaliate (again, hugely implausible). Rather than the sheriff and the plantation owner being archracists, it is actually the poor and working-class white southerners who emerge as the demonized others. As the historian Allison Graham argues in *Framing the South*, "All ends up right with the system: the fat cat is blameless, . . . and the white rural police chief, himself a lonely outsider as it turns out, joins forces with the urban black man to unveil the real criminal in Sparta, Mississippi: white cracker Ralph Henshaw, night worker at the diner."[60] Thus, those who preside over the archly racist and classist economic system are ultimately on the side of stability and compromise, while the low-class whites emerge as abject, incestuous, underemployed, and murderous. This portrayal of the South may help to explain the healthy returns the film enjoyed in southern cinemas and from whites, approval that was captured by a "fan letter" to screenwriter Stirling Silliphant "from two Southerners who think you did a thoroughly honest job with 'In Heat of the Night.'" Watching the film in Birmingham, their white "Southern eyes and ears were never offended by your treatment of the script."[61] The film consequently "played very well indeed and virtually without incident in the South," reported the *Los Angeles Times*.[62] White self-fictions in this text thus interpolated both northern whites and (aside from its white-trash others) southern whites.

The problem is not only that the film narrative is at odds with sociohistorical reality—and it would of course be a mistake to expect Hollywood's classical storytelling to be attempting verisimilitude—but also that the film affirms a certain kind of *racial project* through its content and reception. As the race scholars Michael Omi and Howard Winant explain, the discourses and policies in any racial project are correlated and mutually reinforcing.[63]

If one thought that America, despite pockets of racism (such as Sparta, Mississippi), was basically moving beyond racial hierarchies in 1967 and that Tibbs as top detective was evidence of actual racial meritocracy following legislative victories, then one might indeed consider policies that worked toward the implementation of civil rights unnecessary and actually discriminatory toward whites (including the beleaguered and underpaid Gillespie). *In the Heat of the Night* presented a dangerously misleading image of the racial division of labor in America's workplaces, which served to discredit the mounting race/class critique of the period and its attendant policy solutions. In opposition to the scholarly view that this film was the best that could be achieved by whites at the time, I suggest that *In the Heat of the Night* was, by contrast, injected with white liberalism in racial retreat. It represented a move away from an awareness of structural racism and back toward individualized narratives of intolerance overcome. This is likely what James Baldwin was pointing to when he remarked that "the effect of such a film is to increase and not lessen white confusion and complacency."[64]

This argument becomes more powerful when considered in relation to the film's own racialized production history. Its representations of race and employment onscreen emanated from its production politics, and, in turn, the movie shaped racial attitudes within and about the film industry.

Producing *In the Heat of the Night*

In the Heat of the Night employed no black workers behind the scenes. Black musicians were brought in for the soundtrack—Quincy Jones wrote the universally lauded score, and Jones got his friend Ray Charles to sing the famous title song (composed by Jones, with lyrics by white duo Marilyn Bergman and Alan Bergman). Notwithstanding discrimination, black performers and producers were starting to have more of a footing in the music industry in the late 1960s. Quincy Jones was a pioneer, having worked on a number of scores, including his acclaimed work on Sidney Lumet's *The Pawnbroker* (1964), with a cast that included Brock Peters and an uncredited screen debut by Morgan Freeman, and on Sydney Pollack's *The Slender Thread* (1966), which, like *In the Heat of the Night*, was scripted by Silliphant and starred Poitier.

But, beyond music, there was no sense on the part of producer Walter Mirisch or director Norman Jewison that they had a responsibility to employ any blacks for the film production of *In the Heat of the Night*. At the time, the Mirisch Corporation was the most successful packager of independent productions for United Artists, which by 1967 was the largest producer-distributor in the world, as the film historian Tino Balio has explored.[65] The United Artists roster held many creative producers, including Stanley Kramer, who had carved out a niche by developing a distinct brand of social problem films exemplified by the early integration drama *Home of the Brave* (Mark Robson, 1949) as well as by Poitier films *The Defiant Ones* (Stanley Kramer, 1958) and *Guess Who's Coming to Dinner*. Unlike Kramer, Walter Mirisch was not a creative producer, nor was he pursuing a liberal-reformist project. He occupied a different part of the United Artists roster, simply offering legal and business services to a range of independent filmmakers. According to Mirisch, his company's films spanned a "diversified diet" of genres, with no particular connection to problem pictures or to race as a theme beyond seeing its marketability as the 1960s progressed. Mirisch did "not necessarily [want] to make a social statement" when his company signed on to produce *In the Heat of the Night*.[66] Even though workplace integration is a major theme in the film—the white South painfully coming to terms with a changing racial division of labor—there was no equivalent impetus behind the scenes from the production company.

What about the racial politics of the key white symbol creators on this project? The central creative force was Canadian director Norman Jewison, one of the new-generation Hollywood filmmakers who had aggressively lobbied Mirisch for the job after Silliphant and Poitier were already signed up.[67] Jewison had gained some experience of producing race-themed content on Harry Belafonte's celebrated television variety show *Tonight with Belafonte* at the turn of the 1960s, and, indeed, Belafonte, a frequent critic of Hollywood personnel, speaks well of Jewison in his autobiography (calling him "a stand-up guy").[68] However, the processes of script development and editing on *In the Heat of the Night* suggest that Jewison, though certainly supportive of racial liberalism in principle, was a filmmaker in retreat from actual race parity. In order to highlight the exhilarating racial exceptionalism of Virgil Tibbs, Jewison, once on board, deleted scenes from Silliphant's early drafts in which the detective befriends a black family in Sparta with whom he lodges. Expunged material from Silliphant's early screenplay include Tibbs being offered advice by the father, Jess, about how to survive in racist Sparta and befriending the young son, who is intrigued by the northern detective.[69] In his "character notes," Silliphant had written of his intention to "write a larger sense of the [Negro] community and Tibbs within it."[70] It was Jewison, working on script revisions, who excised this material, and in doing so he cut not only representation of blacks but also jobs and screen time for black actors. Assisted by the film's editor, Hal Ashby, Jewison cut even more material of Tibbs with the black family during the editing process, until next to nothing of that relationship remained.[71] Leading black commentator Nelson George remarks: "The dark side of the film was how disconnected Sidney's Tibbs was from the black community. . . . In real life a big-city black detective in a Mississippi town would have received tons of support from its black citizens."[72] Indeed, in a regressive, postracial step, Tibbs emerges as more isolated than Poitier's character had been in *No Way Out* in 1950, which included parts for Ossie Davis and Ruby Dee as his family members.

Although Jewison cut out black solidarity in pre- and postproduction, he insisted on making room for extended long-shot vistas of black plantation workers: "I wanted [a cotton field] in the movie, the part of the landscape that had been central to my mental picture of the South ever since my hitchhiking tour years earlier, a cotton field populated with black farmhands bent over their work."[73] The white Canadian's racial imagination—formulated as a young tourist and also no doubt by plantation film tropes—was determined to portray anonymous superexploited black laborers as part of the pastoral "landscape" and to set them against Tibbs's northern, urban, integrated heroism, with next to nothing in between.

Early drafts of the outline and script, which Silliphant had begun working on in 1965, had also emphasized the theme of structural racism in the South, which was apparent in Ball's novel (both early drafts and the novel included, for instance, the "colored" sign on the "dingy" door of the waiting room in which Poitier is arrested in his introductory scene).[74] Once taken on as director, Jewison did not like this insistence on institutional discrimination, and so he cut out the sign. The director also excised other direct references to white racism, including scenes Silliphant wrote in which Tibbs has trouble gaining access to a hotel to see Mrs. Colbert and is unable to get something to eat because the only restaurant in town that will serve him is far from the train station.[75] Furthermore, Gillespie is more racist in the source novel, insisting, for instance, on segregated facilities in order to denigrate Tibbs (he directs the Philadelphia detective to "the colored wash room" in the police station, which has "no soap or towels").[76]

As Jewison worked on the script with Silliphant, Gillespie, even before he evolves over the course of the film, was cleansed of such white bigotry. Commercial and generic determinants assuredly played a role in such creative decisions. Jewison wanted his film to reach a wide (predominantly white) film-going audience and of course to make money. He had negotiated, on top of his fee, an unusually generous 25 percent share of the profits, and this no doubt spurred some of the decisions to cut structuralist comment that might have discomfited or bored white audience members.[77] Classical Hollywood narration, of course, tends to focus on individuals and revolve around their goals to drive the narrative forward, staging personal-political dramas much more than sociostructural ones. It is this psychological causality that "gives the classical film its characteristic progression," as the film scholars David Bordwell, Janet Staiger, and Kristen Thompson put it.[78] Nonetheless, given the fierce debate at the time over the causes of continuing racial inequality and the new rallying cries over institutional racism, Jewison's vision is striking: rejecting almost all structural racial critique, even in the Deep South, and devoting screen time to a liberal-individualist drama about the decisions of two flawed but ultimately honorable men.

The film's denial of the South's overt segregationism was perhaps abetted by its being shot in Illinois for the most part, far away from its Deep South setting. While *In the Heat of the Night* was re-creating a sanitized South in the Midwest, another film, the interracial drama *Hurry Sundown* (Otto Preminger, 1967), which centered on race and land ownership in the South, was filming on location in small-town Louisiana. The black actors in this film starring Michael Caine, Jane Fonda, and Diahann Carroll were terrorized with racial threats of violence. From the set, Carroll stated, "You can cut the hostility here with a knife." While fictional Chief Gillespie is willing to put his job on the line for Virgil Tibbs and for racial comity, during the making of *Hurry Sundown* the local Louisianan cops, reported the press, were not inclined to protect the black cast and crew from the threatened violence, which was so acute that they were "housed in a section of the motel, like an army encampment, that is guarded 24 hours a day by armed state troopers," described Carroll.[79]

Filmmaking is of course a group endeavor, and, complicating matters in the production history of *In the Heat of the Night*, evidence suggests that the dynamic white creatives around the director—its writer Stirling Silliphant and cinematographer Haskell Wexler (and editor Hal Ashby, discussed in the next chapter)—were not, like him, retreatist liberals. By the time all the changes had been made to the script of *In the Heat of the Night*, Silliphant, who had been part of the project from the outset, "didn't care for [the film] because it was not an honest portrayal of blacks," recalled Poitier. In a *Daily Variety* interview in 1969, Silliphant would state that in terms of the rise in race-themed filmmaking, "I fear there is more tokenism than atonement, more exploitation than compensation. . . . All this genial and impenitent commercialism is being carried on by friends of mine and yours who are blithely self-persuaded they are doing the blacks a jolly good turn."[80] This description resonates with the sincere-fiction idea of industry whites celebrating their own sense of enlightened racial generosity even while acting in self-interested, pro-white ways.

The film's cinematographer, Haskell Wexler, was a left-liberal activist who had made his own documentary film of the March on Washington, *The Bus* (1965), about a cross-racial group of San Franciscans heading to D.C., self-funding the film's cost of $20,000.[81] Jewison, who didn't attend the march, remarks in his autobiography that he and Wexler "shared the same liberal political beliefs."[82] But this is not true. Wexler followed the success of *In the Heat of the Night* by working on John Cassevetes's independent film *Faces* (1968) and then directing his own experimental classic *Medium Cool* (1969), about the explosive politics of the late 1960s. The latter film, of which he is "most proud," is about "the people of Chicago, the Appalachian people, black people, people who we didn't ordinarily see on TV"—Chicagoans who bear little resemblance to Mrs. Colbert.[83] In 1976, Wexler would be ordered to appear before a federal grand jury because of a documentary he was making on the Weather Underground.[84] He continued to insist on the deep connections between the antiwar movement and the black freedom struggle (in 2014 describing both foreign wars and black domestic oppression as "part of racism" and about "othering"[85]), and he combined activism on civil rights with activism on labor rights, participating in campaigns to restrict the extreme working hours on film productions.

In his landmark book *White*, the film scholar Richard Dyer uses *In the Heat of the Night* to exemplify Hollywood's inferior lighting and framing of black actors. He argues that Poitier was less well lit than Steiger in key sequences—above all the famous male-bonding scene at Gillespie's house, when the two drink bourbon. For Dyer, the cinematography here exemplifies

the tendency toward "the white face as the norm." Through Wexler's camerawork and lighting, Steiger "not only is more fully visible to us but he can
display a range of modulations of expression that indicate the character's
complex turmoil of feelings and reminiscences. Poitier, by contrast, remains
the emblematic, unindividualized, albeit admirable, black man."[86] Although
this description holds true in this important scene and furthers the notion
of the white underdog sheriff's emotional growth, it fails to account for
Wexler's innovative techniques in lighting Poitier on this moderately budgeted production in other key sequences. In the pivotal police station scenes,
the light is bounced off the ceiling and down onto the set in the manner of
still photography, illuminating the actor's face, and in the iconic Endicott
greenhouse scene an umbrella light sends rounded rays of light that enhance
Tibbs's expression as he slaps back. In both scenes, the dark-skinned Poitier's facial modulations are on display, using innovative techniques that later
became standard. Nelson George, recalling the film's affective power over
him as a child, points precisely to Tibbs's expression: "That face full of character and intelligence and confidence made him the man I wanted to be."[87]
While Dyer's intervention shows how the film apparatus and white cine-
matographers contribute to white normativity—drawing attention to "the
specificity of whiteness, even when the text itself is not trying to show it to
you"[88]—such readings may risk underestimating innovative attempts by
some whites to give thought to sensitively light or frame black actors. Thus,
it was in part the input of the race-conscious scriptwriter and cinematographer that lent *In the Heat of the Night* some of its aesthetic and narrative
credibility, which was praised by commentators and which somewhat miti-
gated but also seductively masked its elements of soft race reaction.

Race scholars such as David Roediger state that "white views on race are
quite heterogeneous,"[89] a point that might seem obvious but that needs
emphasizing because film studies scholarship usually talks about white racial
liberalism in the transitional moment in totalizing and vague terms (as
discussed in the introduction). This collapsing of different positions into
white liberal centrism can be explained by the emerging supertrend in which
many whites started to *claim* to be racially tolerant. But this is precisely why
the difference between the actions of retreatist liberals and the actions of
social activist liberals is crucial.

Although an increasing majority of whites in the late 1960s were hostile
to a black freedom struggle that was demanding concrete action, a sizeable minority of whites remained sympathetic to it.[90] The film industry

encompassed both groups, and the making of *In the Heat of the Night* was a site of testy negotiation. A closer look at this film—which I am using emblematically to shed light on wider patterns—shows that although some so-called liberals were affronted by and resistant to the mounting calls for structural change, others—with whom the former were often friends and collaborators—actively supported constructive change. In truth, individuals probably harbored contradictory beliefs and acted in uneven ways in this immensely fluid period.

The overriding impetus in this film project, with strong directorial authority from Jewison, was an incipient postracialism. In the new racial landscape, it became possible, in Howard Winant's words, "to uphold the principle of racial equality while simultaneously steadfastly opposing such practical antiracist policies as income and wealth redistribution or positive antidiscrimination."[91] Whites did not have to relinquish any of the structural, unspoken privileges to find reassuring points of investment in *In the Heat of the Night*. Its textual relations, staging a narrative about workplace integration, stood in disjunction with its largely white-separatist production relations. Day-to-day engagement with black and Latinx people for most white film personnel in the mid- to late 1960s amounted to, at best, a casual exchange with a studio janitor, messenger, or perhaps a rare actor or craft-union employee, and the set of *In the Heat of the Night* did next to nothing to burst this white industry bubble. Little had changed since Ossie Davis first arrived in Hollywood in the late 1940s to do a small role in the Twentieth Century-Fox film *No Way Out* (Poitier's starring debut) and found that "at the studio, we were immediately struck by the fact that we didn't see any black people working anywhere. No technicians, no grips, no electricians, no props people. We didn't see any dark skins in the makeup and wardrobe depts or as hairdressers. From the minute we entered the gate in the morning till the time we left, we were in an all-white world, and that reality was hard for us to ignore."[92] *In the Heat of the Night* seemed to be showing that outside the South the country had already confronted and overcome its employment exclusions when, in fact, the film industry (sited in the North and West) had yet to really begin its own struggle to integrate its all-white world, with the first big showdown coming in 1969 with the EEOC committee's hearings (discussed in chapter 3).

Facing difficult questions about the lack of black creative input on his next race-related film project, *The Confessions of Nat Turner*, in 1968 Jewison would assert: "I think *In the Heat of the Night* speaks for itself as far as my feeling toward social problems in this country."[93] This statement echoes "the screen speaks for itself" corporate fiction expounded by AMPTP vice president Charles Boren. Without the movie business giving up its white privilege in behind-the-scenes workplaces, Jewison, like Boren, was able to racially credentialize himself through a reliance on fictive images, gaining legitimacy and profits by tapping into the antiracist movement's moral capital.

The ideological work of this film release, at a moment of realignment, is further evident in the way the industry created a discursive linkage between Sidney Poitier and Martin Luther King Jr. in the year that the actor became America's top star and the civil rights leader was assassinated. Gregory Peck, film star and then president of the Academy of Motion Picture Arts and Sciences, opened the Oscars in April 1968, which had been postponed by several days because of the killing of King and at which *In the Heat of the Night* won Best Picture, by paying tribute to the slain leader. King's message, asserted Peck, was that "we must unite in compassion in order to survive." The best cinematic memorials, he continued, were films such as *In the Heat of the Night* that "celebrate the dignity of man."[94] Jewison would later echo these sentiments, asserting that "the success of the movie was more than what such things tend to be: it was a confirmation that America was ready for our message. That it was ready for MLK's message of hope."[95] But the "King" whom the industry constructed, discursively correlated to the film, was far removed from the Southern Christian Leadership Conference leader at the time of his murder—and for that matter from Sidney Poitier the actor. In 1968, King was not foregrounding the liberal "hopeful" "dignity of man" message but was positioning himself in diametric opposition to it as he mobilized on the basis of a formidable critique of racist, imperialist, and class-ridden America.[96]

As Downing and Husband remind us, "The discourse of tolerance as employed by a majority tends to seek to obscure the fact that there are fundamental conflicts of interest between the oppressor and the oppressed,"[97] and it was this obscuring discourse that the film industry mobilized on that night in April 1968 and that was animated by *In the Heat of the Night*. King had been part of a movement that was exposing rather than obscuring fundamental conflicts of interest, calling for transformative economic redistribution: "The Movement," he said, "must address itself to the restructuring of the whole of American society." As his close friend Harry Belafonte remarked, "At heart, Martin was a socialist and a revolutionary thinker."[98]

FIGURE 1.1 *In the Heat of the Night* winners backstage at the Academy Awards ceremony in April 1968, postponed by several days because of the murder of Martin Luther King Jr. (*left to right*): Hal Ashby (Best Film Editing), Norman Jewison, Rod Steiger (Best Actor), Walter Mirisch (Best Picture).

Source: Courtesy of the Academy of Motion Picture Arts and Sciences. Copyright © Academy of Motion Picture Arts and Sciences.

Hollywood's containing rhetoric would come to be powerfully adopted by film-industry management in the battle to reframe King's legacy along neo-conservative lines (as discussed more fully in chapter 3).[99] When scholars map the history of black film in these years by aligning Poitier vehicles and Martin Luther King Jr. as totems of tolerance and assimilationism (in opposition to correlated black-power and black action films), they risk reinforcing Peck and Jewison's retreatist rhetoric. *In the Heat of the Night* and its reception became part of the propagation of the incipient discourses of post–civil rights white privilege that started proving "itself capable of absorbing and adapting much of the 'dream,' repackaging itself as 'color-blind,' non-racialist, and meritocratic," as Winant argues.[100]

Overall, then, the film's onscreen relations presented a very misleading image of the racial division of labor within the industry. Bringing Poitier the performer and his Tibbs role—representing individual black agency and high-visibility black employment—back into the center of the frame both continues and complicates this argument.

Poitier/Tibbs as Racial Exception

Black commentators of the late 1960s, many of whom were critical of Poitier, pointed to the dangers of these liberal-reformist narratives, in line with the argument I have developed about *In the Heat of the Night*. Indeed, by this time Poitier's screen image gave rise to lambasting criticism by black intellectuals and artists, telegraphed in two articles published in the *New York Times*, as film scholar Ed Guerrero has compellingly chronicled.[101] In 1967, playwright Clifford Mason published the arch but nuanced critique "Why Does White America Love Sidney Poitier So?"—explaining how Poitier's star image was comforting to whites in ways that militated against change. The "Poitier syndrome: a good guy in a totally white world" is representative of "gradualism," which "in art . . . just represents a stale, hackneyed period, to be forgotten as soon as we can get on to the real work at hand." In 1969, black nationalist Larry Neal went further in personalizing the attack on Poitier in his article "Beware the Tar Baby," in which he used African American folktale allegories to suggest Poitier was the prime totem (a sticky tar mascot) of racially containing Hollywood norms.[102] These critiques had deep explanatory resonance in a moment of growing mobilization for antiracist action, and as this chapter has argued, they are only more legible when we foreground how Poitier vehicles obscured white double standards in the film industry.

However, the tendency of such critiques and in scholarship since then to focus narrowly on Poitier's star image at the expense of the white men and milieus that produced these films had and has the unintended effect of displacing attention from the white creatives and institutions and onto the black screen image and black performer as the main bearer of the racial burden of representation. Moreover, because the force of this critique centered on Poitier, there was little acknowledgment at the time, nor has there been since then, of why and how the star's screen image was so pleasurable and meaningful to many black viewers. And this identificatory pleasure and meaning should not be peremptorily confined, as it often is in the scholarship, to a conservative *Ebony*-reading black bourgeoisie or simply to false consciousness. While registering that Poitier's image mollified whites, his friend James Baldwin also insisted on the star's landmark representational value for blacks in his *Look* magazine cover story published in July 1968: "The *presence* of Sidney, the precedent set, is of tremendous importance for people coming afterward." And as another of Poitier's friends, Ruby Dee, said to him in interview, "To many people . . . you represent a fulfillment, a satisfaction. They take great pride in what you have accomplished."[103] She intimated her own distance ("they" rather than "we") as a black radical creative for whom Poitier's screen image in the 1960s was assuredly not a fulfillment, but she nonetheless invoked important affective registers for black viewers in their responses to Poitier's complex stardom.

It is salutary to remember that none of Poitier's three vehicles in 1967 made as much money as the rereleased *Gone with the Wind* that year (which returned $36 million to the industry, $10 million more than Poitier's highest-earning film, *Guess Who's Coming to Dinner*, with $26 million in returns).[104] Though Poitier had formed his career in the New York black left community (see chapter 4), he became the black actor who chose and was able to operate most deeply within the mainstream Hollywood system. This decision to inhabit a conservative cultural sector meant that his screen image could not be very provocative, and there was a clear discrepancy between his white-conciliatory screen image and his more critical publicity statements and political activities. As Poitier tried to wrest some control over his parts, he positioned his screen image quite deliberately at that moment in relation to what Stuart Hall would later call that era's black positive-image canon, installed in opposition to the baldly racist images and racial marginalization that were still widely prevalent in cinema.[105]

As Clifford Mason vividly pointed out, dramatic tension in Poitier vehicles rested on his protagonists being lone African Americans inserted into predominantly white worlds. And, as we have seen, white filmmakers such as Jewison purposely stripped Poitier heroes of black peers (on- and off-screen), resulting in actor Sidney Poitier being an isolated black performer within all-white crews and white-dominated casts. Poitier's racial isolation behind the scenes in his star vehicles in the 1960s thus paralleled onscreen dynamics, which revolved around the newfound status of an occupational "racial exception." Bosley Crowther described how Poitier "first came to attention and established his name in films where he played an individual Negro fighting for position among whites," and, notwithstanding exceptions that worked against type—such as the important role in *A Raisin in the Sun* (Daniel Petrie, 1961)—this position was absolutely central to his screen image and appeal.[106] Such integrationist narratives marked a sharp turn away from the all-black musical and plantation features of the 1940s, a trajectory that Poitier had himself followed. From his unhappy starring role in *Porgy and Bess* in 1959 (Otto Preminger and Rouben Mamoulian), an Old South black-cast nostalgia narrative, in the 1960s he came to find his perfect fit in these mainly white-cast films.[107] His "fighting for position among whites" was not always in work environments (for example, the role of a black convict fleeing from prison shackled to a white convict in *Defiant Ones*). But usually it was: the black doctor facing professional pressure because of his race (*No Way Out*); the black high school student among the group of white delinquents (*Blackboard Jungle*, Richard Brooks, 1955); the frustrated black construction foreman building a chapel for a group of white immigrant nuns (*Lillies of the Field*, Ralph Nelson, 1963); the sole black prison clinician coping with a psychologically disturbed white racist inmate (*Pressure Point*, Hubert Cornfield, 1962); the black psychologist deploying his professionalism to help a white suicidal girl (*Slender Thread*); the lone black schoolteacher (*To Sir, with Love*); and, of course, the black detective helping a white police force.

In the rest of this final section, I engage closely with Poitier's experiences as a film creative and his screen image in this highly regarded role as Virgil Tibbs. As Nelson George recalls, "This was the film that really made me fall for Sidney."[108] Looking at both tensions and parallels between Poitier's performance and screen character in *In the Heat of the Night* reveals the role's surprising credibility, which is both exciting and problematic. Indeed, it signals, I argue, the dawning of postracial discourses of blackness.

As the ace Negro detective, Tibbs stands as a misleading departure from actual black experiences of employment in the North and in Hollywood. But he *is* representative of Sidney Poitier—occupying the exciting yet burdensome and precarious role of being the singular, immaculate black film star in a white world. Poitier's dramatic aloneness is slightly tempered by the artistic authority of actor Beah Richards in *Guess Who's Coming to Dinner* and *In the Heat of the Night*, in which she plays a small role as Mama Caleba, the town abortionist.[109] But in most scenes the heroes he plays remain racially isolated. Thus, although these Poitier heroes are clearly inauthentic

FIGURE 1.2 Publicity still from *In the Heat of the Night* (Norman Jewison, 1967). Mama Caleba (Beah Richards) and Virgil Tibbs (Sidney Poitier). Aside from this scene, Tibbs almost exclusively interacts with white people.
Source: Courtesy of the Academy of Motion Picture Arts and Sciences.

symbols of black working life in the mid- to late 1960s, the linkage between screen role and publicity image helps to explain his performative credibility. There was an important *conjunction* between the racial isolation of Poitier's hyperprofessional protagonists and his own privileged yet isolated workplace position.

These reflexive parallels between racial-exception Poitier and racial-exception Tibbs elucidate why critics repeatedly described his unrealistic roles as nonetheless believable. At the time, one reviewer identified Poitier's "sincerity that validates the most unlikely of circumstances," while another asserted that "his pictures have a way of seeming to be better than they actually are, made so by the conviction he establishes." According to James Baldwin, "Sidney was beautiful, vivid and truthful" and somehow escaped the framework of his films by "smuggling in a reality that he knows is not in the script." Nelson George later concurred: "As inhumanly unrealistic as Tibbs was, Sidney made him work."[110] Stuart Hall's classic article "What

Is This 'Black' in Black Popular Culture?" sheds light on the basis of this popular-cultural vitality: "The role of the 'popular' in popular culture is to fix the authenticity of popular forms, rooting them in the experiences of popular communities from which they draw their strength, allowing us to see them as expressive of a particular subordinate social life that resists its being constantly made over as low and outside."[111] As many have pointed out, Poitier's portrayals are far from being "rooted in the experiences of popular communities"; however, they instead "draw their strength" from their genuine rooting in the possibilities and perils of working as black top talent within the white-dominated, racist film industry. Poitier's influential protagonists—consummate professionals precariously positioned in white work environments—were electrified by the difficulties and double binds of operating as a high-end yet racially subordinate worker. As the race theorists Devon Carbado and Mitu Gulati suggest, blacks in all-white workplaces have to perform a certain version of their raced self in costly "identity transactions" that appease their white colleagues.[112] At its best, Poitier's power, more than scholars allow, stemmed from his self-conscious onscreen staging of these onerous and appeasing racial transactions, which were warranted by his experiences in the film industry.

Poitier's "conviction" stems from two competing reflexivities between protagonist and performer. The first is their shared, exhilarating black success. The implausibility of Tibbs being the "number one homicide detective" in Philadelphia of the mid-1960s is tempered by the extraordinary fact of Poitier as number-one bankable star on Quigley's list. Poitier in 1968 was also, even more exceptionally, the highest-paid actor in the world (signaling him as an adept creative entrepreneur, a topic explored later in this book).[113] When Chief Gillespie exasperatedly complains within the diegesis, "Coloreds can't earn that kind of money, boy, hell that's more than I make in a month!" his statement chimes with the white actor's actual lower remuneration. Rod Steiger had signed on to the film for $100,000, about half of what Poitier received.[114] Despite constraints, Poitier, unlike most black cinema actors at the time, did have some agency in the development of his screen image, including in the genesis of the Tibbs role. Poitier, as one industry journalist put it, was "constantly reading novels, plays, short stories and originals in quest of suitable material for himself," and he and his agent-manager, Marty Baum, were increasingly able to insist on some fuller characterization.[115] It was Baum, his manager of fourteen years by 1967, who first spotted the potential of the *In the Heat of the Night* source novel, leading them to approach Walter Mirisch.[116] Poitier had input in the development of the role during the early screenwriting process, having worked well with Silliphant previously. The unlikely performative credibility in Poitier's idealized roles thus derives in part from his being the well-remunerated and precariously empowered professional working within white structures both on- and offscreen.

By contrast, the second source of "conviction" in Poitier's better performances, allowing him to "smuggle in reality," had little to do with indexing exhilarating new black cultural industries' mobility. It instead sprang from his self-conscious staging of racial anger and constraint. In conditions largely not of his own choosing, he channeled the frustrations and difficulties of being a racially isolated worker into his performances of roles like that of Virgil Tibbs. Poitier was, more than is often recognized, quite candid about Hollywood's racist politics. Responding to a recurrent question about his assimilated "Saint Sidney" image, he pointed to the pervasive lack of minority creative and economic power in cinema: "The guys who write these parts are white guys, more than not; they are guys in a business and they are subject to the values of the society they live in. And there are producers to deal with who are also white. And a studio with a board of directors, also white."[117] He staked out the political-economic constraints on mainstream black image making, and the veiled anger in such pointed critiques chimed with the restrained ire in his screen image.

Poitier's performance of professional isolation as Tibbs in this angriest of his super-Negro roles was no doubt augmented by the conditions of the film's making and particularly by his costar Rod Steiger's famed immersive acting technique. Poitier recalls that, from the beginning to the end of the shoot, Steiger stayed in role as Gillespie: "On weekends when we ventured out to a movie or dinner . . . he would remain completely immersed in the character of the southern sheriff. . . . I was astonished at the intensity of his involvement with the character." An indulgently improvisational Steiger goaded the lone black actor off camera. According to assistant director Terry Morse, he would call his costar a "nigger" (a term mainly expurgated from the film) during Poitier's close-up filming, apparently to draw Poitier out ("just to get his eyes popping"). Rattled by Steiger's unrestrained and intimidating approach to acting, Poitier, according to Jewison, asked the director: "Are you gonna let him do that?!"[118] By all accounts, Jewison not only let

Steiger do that but also relished his technique, as recounted in Mark Harris's illuminating production history, which also chronicles an episode during a dinner break when Poitier overheard an actor using the *n* word and was "very offended" (though it was apparently "a misunderstanding and was cleared up easily"), in the recollection of the white actor William Schallert, who played the town's mayor. What emerges is a picture of an isolated Poitier being racially taunted in the workplace—what sociologist Remi Joseph-Salisbury calls "racial microaggressions" targeting "black bodies out of place."[119]

Yet in film history accounts—including Harris's and also, it must be said, even Poitier's tame autobiography—the microaggressions are construed as creatively generative, allowing Poitier to grow as an actor particularly from Steiger's provocations. Jewison and Harris stress that it was Poitier who prevented *In the Heat of the Night* from being filmed mainly in the Deep South, refusing to spend sustained time there. What is rarely if ever mentioned, though, is that his northern "liberal" cocreatives in any case set about reproducing "southern-style" racist intimidation during production in the Midwest. As a result, Poitier increasingly retreated into his own company. With Steiger, according to Poitier, speaking "with the same accent and walk[ing] with the same gait, on and off camera," the distance between production and text collapsed. Poitier enacted onscreen the performative pressures of being an isolated African American in a supposedly benign but insidiously racist workplace situation offscreen. In candid conversation with Ruby Dee in 1969, Poitier stressed the difficulty of and constraint on his black film labor within Hollywood's web of whiteness: "What I have done in Charlie's community, what I have carved out, took a lot of energy, a lot of just plain stubborn stick to it ness. I took a lot of beatings."[120]

Carbado and Gulati have explored how black workers in predominantly white contexts perform their raced identities in relation to both white and black norms, and in this film Poitier offers a heightened charismatic performance of such costly identity transactions in the workplace.[121] His screen image deliberately projected a raced identity in relation to white norms. He explained in 1980: "What I did choose to do as an actor was to make selections that would not only please me as an actor, but yield positive impressions to people who had negative attitudes toward minorities."[122] Nonetheless, in his best roles Poitier gave heightened performances that in foregrounding emotions generated by these onerous racial transactions of workplace mobility and subordination were also potentially affective and vital for black audiences. He drew on his macrocritique of the "white guys" who ran the industry and his microexperiences of race baiting on set as resources to fuel this performative edginess. In interview, Poitier described himself as "intense, dignified and angry" and explained how he came to "employ [these emotions] in my work."[123] In the reflexive credibility of Poitier's role as Tibbs, he seems to self-consciously register the "rather grim bind" of the mainstream black performer, as his friend James Baldwin noted: "He knows, on the one hand, that if the reality of the black man's life were on that screen, it would destroy the fantasy totally. And on the other hand, he really has no right *not* to appear, not only because he must work, but also for all those people who need to see him."[124]

Poitier's iconicity in this role staked out a model for post–civil rights black cultural industries success, electrified not just by racial mobility but also by racism, both of which were warranted by workplace experiences. This combination of the charismatic individual overcoming yet remaining mired in racist power relations would lend extraordinary credibility and marketability to postracial black screen stars thereafter. But making the "inhumanly unrealistic" believable came with far-reaching political costs. In his roles, Poitier may have been true to his own rags-to-riches experience in the cultural industries. However, his positive-impression-yielding screen image simultaneously obfuscated pervasive and entrenched racial power dynamics. Poitier's brief superstardom in part served to shore up white sincere fictions at a critical moment that vastly overestimated actual black mobility both in the film industry and in America generally, leading to unwarranted stirrings of white racial resentment. In the face of flak at a moment of black-power-informed politicization, Poitier's trade-off was soon deemed unacceptable. Blacks' strong objections to his screen image would force a long cinematic hiatus across the 1970s in the emergence of this seminal "postracial" black archetype and forced a hurt Poitier to divest of this iconic image and double down on his pursuit of developing a viable mainstream black-film-producing unit (explored later in this book).

■ ■ ■

Hollywood continued to be highly exclusionary in its division of labor in the period of heightened antiracist mobilization immediately following the passing of the Civil Rights Act in 1964. Many in the industry continued to normalize this workplace exclusion by reproducing sincere fictions about the benign white self. Some in Hollywood, however, were attuned to the antiracist project and worked to trouble the practices and discourses that legitimated white opportunity hoarding. They included the cinematographer, script writer, and black star of *In the Heat of the Night*. Poitier's Tibbs, though gratifying in ways that were ideologically containing, was a complex portrayal that was meaningful to black people in ways that exceeded racial false consciousness. The film's central employment-justice theme was introduced in good faith, drawing on the wider debate in the mid- to late 1960s about the importance of jobs in bringing about racial equality. However, the way it was developed narratively ended up being troublingly retreatist. *In the Heat of the Night*, though admired by many at its time of release, presented a highly romanticized view of white northern employers, which by extension included the film industry. This romanticization was projected back to the industry's own workers and, through its acclaim, projected outward as public relations about the film business to wider publics. As much as any film, *In the Heat of the Night*, praised by the pro-business head of the MPAA, Jack Valenti, as "one of the best films of our times,"[125] was anti-interventionist, serving to perpetuate the white-liberal retreat from race. Hollywood was thus an early fomenter of what would come to be called postracial discourses that took hold as the post–civil rights period progressed, lionizing individual African Americans at the expense of the group.

As a result of such sincere-fiction film narratives, which worked to cement Hollywood's vestigial March on Washington public-relations image, the industry was able to drag its feet, continuing with its general practices of white cronyism in funding, production, and hiring decisions. However, the social turmoil and collectivist politics that engulfed America in the late 1960s traveled into film culture and commerce, and Hollywood's liberal fictions and entreaties to let "the screen speak for itself" were unable to suppress the growing calls for racial and politicoaesthetic change.

2

RACIALIZING THE HOLLYWOOD RENAISSANCE

Black and White Symbol Creators in a Time of Crisis

By the Oscars in April 1968, the "best picture" *In the Heat of the Night* probably no longer felt, even to its many mainstream admirers, like the pounding pulse of truth. The assassination of Martin Luther King Jr., the social unrest and urban rebellions, the rise of black nationalism, the attempts to implement civil rights laws, and the stirring white backlash gave race politics enormous salience in America. The Kerner Commission report issued that same year called not only for more jobs and resources for urban communities but also for better representations in the media, which, it argued, "report and write from the standpoint of a white man's world."[1] Though the report referred above all to television and the press, which briefly became somewhat more receptive to black-determined perspectives, the critique was also patently relevant to cinema.[2] Some in the film and television industry started to take note. African American actor turned organizer Cliff Frazier describes 1968, the year he became head of the Community Film Workshop Council with $50,000 financial support from the American Film Institute, as "a time when people felt guilty. Dr. King had been killed. You've got cities burning. People were saying, 'Look, we need to do something.'"[3] The impetus for action in cinema was spurred in part by a desire for constructive racial change. But it was also spurred by an awareness of the marketability of racial themes, particularly following Poitier's success and a much-discussed *Variety* cover story in late 1967 that declared, only somewhat hyperbolically, "One-third film public: Negro."[4] As scholars such as Ed Guerrero and Jesse Rhines have suggested, commercial self-interest fueled a turn to black-themed films in a moment when, as *Newsweek* quipped, the film industry was becoming aware of "the financial significance of social significance."[5]

The new interest in race-themed content came at a time of dramatic film-industry reconfiguration. Under the leadership of Jack Valenti, appointed in 1966, the MPAA had rapidly moved to suspend the regulative industry guidelines on content known as the Production Code, finally replacing it in 1968 with the new ratings system. This change opened the way for more controversial themes and taboo-breaking films. Responding to falling audience numbers and profitability, the studios underwent corporate restructurings that gained pace in the mid- to late 1960s. These changes installed younger studio leaders, who shifted away from traditional product lines by employing a new generation of filmmakers to attract the increasingly youthful cinema-going market. Industry commentators declared a "Hollywood renaissance," during which, in the words of the *Time* writer Stefan Kanfer, a more "intellectually demanding, emotionally fulfilling kind of film" was possible.[6] Although the renaissance decade that spanned roughly from 1967 to 1977 has been extensively explored by film scholars and stands as "American cinema's most celebrated era," as Peter Krämer and Yannis Tzioumakis put it in their book title,[7] the racial dimensions of the story are seldom considered. The "black is box office" trend, often loosely dubbed "the blaxploitation era," is instead treated separately. Yet the rapidly changing industrial and aesthetic environment in mainstream cinema of the late 1960s presented exciting pull factors for politicized black symbol creators long barred from and pessimistic about meaningful work in film. Cross-platform star Harry Belafonte captured the shift from exclusion and self-exile to a new sense of opportunity in the transitional decade, asserting in 1969, "In the past ten years I committed myself wholeheartedly, passionately, to the civil rights movement. Hollywood only reflected the illness of society. Now there have been changes. The mass media has [*sic*] begun to look at things differently."[8]

The story of the period from 1968 to 1970 developed in this chapter focuses on the activities of selected black and white filmmakers who were beginning to look at things differently. I explore many of the most significant black-oriented projects of these tumultuous years. The chapter begins by continuing the discussion of white self-fictions, focusing on Norman Jewison's failed project *The Confessions of Nat Turner*. It shows how the possessive investment in whiteness in this planned production rebuffed the challenge by black and left protestors, with catastrophic consequences for the project. This black left rejection of liberal retreatism sets the context for the rest of the chapter, which turns to the belated arrival of black directors in Hollywood: Gordon Parks Sr. with *The Learning Tree* (1969), Ossie Davis with *Cotton Comes to Harlem* (1970), Melvin Van Peebles with *The Watermelon Man* (1970), producer Harry Belafonte with *The Angel Levine* (Jan Kadar, 1970), and script writer Bill Gunn (who had previously directed *Stop* for Warner Bros. in 1970, which was never released) with *The Landlord* (Hal Ashby, 1970). I explore these films' production cultures to explain and assess the emergence of black filmmaking in major-studio-distributed pictures, revealing practices of interracial collaboration and mentoring, exceptions to a continuing supertrend of white opportunity hoarding. By presenting production histories and then connecting them to thematic priorities in the resulting films, I continue to draw out critical intersections behind and in front of the camera.

The salience of black culture around the end of the 1960s and the belated realization by white filmmakers and executives of the need for black talent as a source of marketing legitimacy, thematic value, and formal innovation generated some new leverage for African Americans. Those who stepped into the breach were remarkably politicized symbol creators, many with years of experience in black and left mobilizations and with a powerful sense that popular culture could be an instrument of political change. As Ossie Davis remarked, "Like Paul Robeson, and Sterling Brown, and Langston Hughes, and Alain Locke, and Richard Wright, and Marian Anderson—I wanted to sing my service to my people."[9] With black and white allies, symbol creators such as Davis helped to shape film-renaissance energies in ways that have been underacknowledged in orthodox accounts of this filmic golden age.

The Unmaking of *The Confessions of Nat Turner*

With surging new black consciousness, African Americans wanted narratives about their underrepresented history and experiences. As African American filmmaker Charles Hobson put it, "Black people have been in this country and visible to all for over 300 years, but the story of our history, until recently, was always a national secret, and much of the story remains untold."[10] Of course, the history of slavery and emancipation had also been spectacularly *mis*told within cinema ever since *Birth of a Nation*, but by the late 1960s the medium was beginning to introduce a few less-demeaning black characters in historical features. These features included Herbert Biberman's *Slaves* (1969) and the comedy-Western *The Scalphunters* (Sydney Pollack, 1968), costarring Ossie Davis, whose protagonist turns from slave to frontiersman, thus presenting "a different kind of slave than those our children, black and white, have been exposed to historically," as Davis remarked.[11] Resonating with the nationalist tenor of the late 1960s, the slave Nat Turner, who had led the rebellion in Southampton, Virginia, in 1831, seemed a perfect subject to expand this revisionist project in cinema. In early 1968, Twentieth Century-Fox announced a new project, *The Confessions of Nat Turner*, to be a high-end feature about the most prominent slave rebel in African American history. It was an adaptation of white author William Styron's best-selling novel published the previous year, which had enjoyed huge mainstream acclaim and won the Pulitzer Prize for fiction, and Styron was taken on as a paid adviser.[12]

However, the announcement of this project angered many in black and left circles, based as it was on a source novel that had "provoked the most bitter, interesting and far-reaching literary controversy in recent memory," as the *New York Times* reviewer Eliot Fremont-Smith summarized.[13] Told from the first-person perspective of Nat Turner, Styron's novel portrays the slave leader as having been treated relatively well by his slave masters, who teach him to read, as sexually obsessed with a white woman, and as deeply ambivalent about the violent revolt that he spearheads. In 1968, Black Arts Movement writer John Henrik Clarke released a collection titled *William Styron's "Nat Turner": Ten Black Writers Respond*, which mounted forceful critiques of the novel.[14] Even Fremont-Smith, whose review of the novel had been highly laudatory, allowed: "The real Nat Turner was taught to read by his parents and later had a wife—while Mr. Styron's Turner is coached by white masters and depicted as an unmarried celibate haunted by masturbatory fantasies of the white girl he later kills."[15] The black writers pointed out that the novel was, as Styron himself admitted, a critique of rising black nationalism in the present, crystallizing currents of incipient white-liberal resentment and retreat. Styron cast the slave-rebellion leader as an unreasonable and unhinged black agitator and later claimed in a tirade in 1968 that "any intelligent person is going to be appalled" by Nat Turner, who is "not very heroic looking at all. He looks like a nut . . . like some crazed Harlem preacher."[16] As the political scientist Michael Brown and his coauthors detail in their classic study of the post–civil rights period, *Whitewashing Race*, whites would come to attribute the failure to create an antiracist society not to white intransigence but instead to unreasonable black separatism. Echoing the sincere-fictions framework, whites lambasted "racial agitators" who exploited their blackness to make undue demands,[17] and Styron's discrediting of Nat Turner's black nationalism mobilized such whitewashing racist tropes.

Styron's antiblack critique seems to have been one of the attractions of the Nat Turner project for liberal-retreatist Jewison, who remarked that he wanted to "apply the feeling I got from the book to the problems of today."[18] Jewison was aware of the growing backlash by the time he signed on as director of the project in early 1968 because the first major dissent from the mainstream approval of the novel, including Marxist historian Herbert Aptheker's review in *The Nation*, had come in the fall of 1967.[19] Because the movie's prestige was predicated largely on the stature of its source book, Jewison had in signing up shown that he bought heavily into Styron stocks. Jewison's enduring investment in this novel is evident in his memoir, where he would much later describe it as "the most important American novel of my lifetime."[20]

In March 1968, black film workers and activists responded to the planned film by forming the Association to End Defamation of Black People, later shortened to Black Anti-Defamation Association (BADA), headed by black freelance writer Louise Meriwether. Although BADA welcomed a film project about Nat Turner, it insisted on its being distanced from Styron's charged depiction of black masculinity, sexuality, and rebellion and his romanticized depiction of slave owners. In a letter to Jewison and the film's producer, David Wolper (and copied to Jack Valenti), BADA demanded that changes be made to the script and that "no picture bear the title of William Styron's book lest it lend validity to his falsification of history."[21] A press release from BADA included quotations from Kwame Ture, H. Rap Brown, John Oliver Killens, and Amiri Baraka and stated: "The tragedy is that most Americans—black and white—have not been exposed to the true history of Nat Turner and will accept Styron's version as the truth. We need tireless hands to pass out brochures and collect signatures. We need money to carry on this fight. JOIN US NOW."[22] Ossie Davis emerged as the group's leading spokesperson. In a BADA advertisement in the *Hollywood Reporter* later that spring, he stated emphatically: "Styron's implication about black men and black rebellion is that what agitates the black man is not a search for freedom but a search for white women. To magnify this inflammatory lie on a mass scale—as only a motion picture can magnify it—is the height of social irresponsibility."[23] Davis's comment exposed the stakes in Styron's vision of Nat Turner and why it would have been so damaging had it been brought to cinema screens, perpetuating sexualized racist cinematic stereotypes that had been circulating at least since *Birth of a Nation* was released in 1915.

The filmmakers swiftly responded. In a *Variety* article titled "Wolper and Jewison Brush 'Turner' Beef," Jewison asserted: "I can only say that whatever goes into the film is to be determined by me." Several weeks later, just back from Martin Luther King Jr.'s funeral and under mounting pressure from BADA, Jewison still had not relented: "I'll make the film my way—and nobody is going to tell me how to do it."[24] Even with the wave of white-liberal contrition that followed King's assassination, which had led to widespread urban revolt, Jewison did not regard any African American input as desirable in the making of a story that was supposedly about the struggle for black self-determination. His decision to direct *Confessions* and his statements seem to be informed by the idea that he (along with Styron and Wolper) was better positioned to handle black representational politics than were African Americans. Styron furthered this sense of white ethnocentrism in the telling of black history, later reflecting on the controversy surrounding the film adaptation: "I don't want to seem self-assured, but I wouldn't change much."[25] Such positions resonate with the sincere fiction, discussed in chapter 1, that whites are more insightful about racial amelioration than blacks. This powerful racist fiction helped justify many liberals' retreat from race just as blacks were finding new ways to challenge their cultural-historical confinement. Jewison captures this retreatism in his autobiography, invoking *In the Heat of the Night* and asking rhetorically of the BADA activists: "Didn't they know where I stood on the issue of racism in America?"[26]

As John Downing and Charles Husband suggest dryly in their commanding book on race and media, "Progressive liberals within the majority-ethnic populations may feel confused and angry when what they see as their tolerant niceness is reflected back as tokenistic, paternalistic and self-interested. This defensive response leads to renewed attempts to reassert the 'limits of tolerance' as natural and reasonable and necessary for the continued cohesion of the nation state."[27] Styron starkly captures this white "reasonableness," later dismissing the complaints about the novel and film project as "almost all . . . invalid, irrational, and hysterical, based on bigotry and prejudice,"[28] thus continuing to reduce the eloquent and far-reaching black protests to dysfunctional and unwarranted racial agitation.

Dismissing BADA's concerns, Wolper and Jewison first approached leading white screenwriters (including Styron) to adapt the novel.[29] The pronounced disjunction between the white production team and the black content was seemingly not evident to Jewison even in the face of sustained critique. Initial activity on *Confessions* occurred inside the insular space of a white production team, fueled by the unalloyed self-confidence that they could by themselves understand and represent these issues. BADA was intent on disrupting this taken-for-granted sense of white authority. "Relatively few whites think reflectively about their whiteness except when it is forced on them by encounters with or challenges from black Americans," explain the sociologists Joe Feagin, Hernan Vera, and Pinar Batur.[30] So it was with Jewison and Wolper, and it soon became evident that the filmmakers' lack of self-reflection resulted in a grave tactical error. Once the filmmakers finally understood the strength of the challenge to their project, they were forced to agree to changes to both script and title, which was shortened to *Nat Turner*. This was a significant compromise because distancing the film from the novel undermined the project's key presold attraction.[31] In February 1969, the month that Wolper agreed to the picture's name change (suggestive of a distancing from the novel's backlash themes), Jewison left the production, citing scheduling conflicts. The film continued into preproduction, but under the pressure of mounting costs, bad publicity, and film-industry slump the project lost momentum. In 1970 came the announcement by Fox that the film had been shelved indefinitely, losing the studio a great deal of money. Buying the rights to the film from Wolper alone had cost $600,000.

Jewison and Styron emerge differently from Wolper in this case. In his autobiography published in 2005, Jewison commented that not getting "the opportunity to make this film" was "the biggest disappointment of [his] career." Styron continued to maintain that his version of history was authoritative: "Even when we speak the truth about history, we are branded as racists. The whole thing soured me in being a friend of black people."[32] His white novelistic framing of history was, quite simply, "the truth." In contrast, Wolper's public statements during the racial controversy had always been more thoughtful, and he seemed better able to take BADA's concerns on board. Of course, as the producer, he had very different financial stakes than did Jewison in reaching resolution. Nonetheless, on finally agreeing to change the film's title and aspects of the plot, Wolper was relatively measured and flexible, stating, "If we were going to do the definitive story of Turner it was acceptable to us to use other source material available, the story being as important as it is to the blacks, we don't want it to be harmful to that community."[33] This was an expression of concern about the potential damage of this Hollywood film for black viewers, not to mention its damaging reproduction of racist stereotypes for white viewers. Not wanting to do representational harm, Wolper, perhaps learning from the *Confessions* debacle, chose his source material somewhat more carefully when he went on to make what turned out to be a runaway television blockbuster in the 1970s, *Roots*, based on a novel by the African American writer Alex Haley. We must gauge the degree of racial self-reflection of whites such as Jewison, Styron, and Wolper because such reflexivity about the workplace is one of the first steps, as critical race scholars insist, toward meaningful change in employment attitudes and practices.[34]

Scholars have debated the reasons for the cancellation of *Nat Turner*. The historian Scot French offers a meticulously researched account of BADA's campaign, ultimately answering the question in the subtitle of his article— "Should black power take the rap for killing *Nat Turner*, the movie?"—in the negative.[35] He argues instead that the industry's economic troubles and Fox's losses of 1969 were the main reason for the film's cancellation. Disputing French's conclusion, however, the film scholar Christopher Sieving puts most of the responsibility for the cancellation onto BADA: "French's downplaying of black activism as a cause for *Nat Turner*'s premature death is curious, especially in light of the fact that the bulk of his essay is devoted to an explication of the efforts of those groups."[36] Sieving argues that the BADA campaign generated bad publicity, increased preproduction costs, and brought about the enforced distancing of film from book that so damaged the project's established selling feature for white audiences. He therefore concludes persuasively that the black protests were the principal reason for the abandonment of the project. However, his argument is premised on the idea that the demise of this Jewison-helmed project was damaging to black progress in Hollywood. He concludes: "The heaviest irony of the *Nat Turner* episode may be that organized black protest effectively ended any serious commitment by the majors to 'A' pictures about African American themes and stories, and in turn this resistance helped pave the way for the much-derided blaxploitation era."[37] However, I suggest by contrast that the highly effective BADA campaign must be understood not as an unintended and ironic defeat but instead as an important victory, for two main reasons.

First, because Hollywood was interested in broadening its black audience by greenlighting black-themed films and needed good community relations to do so, the protests targeting this project surely helped "pave the way" for the late entry of a few black filmmakers into Hollywood. The controversy contains evidence of how pressure exerted by activists led to new behind-the-camera participation by blacks: after an initial quest for a white scriptwriter, Wolper, under pressure from BADA, had then signed a black one—playwright and television/film writer Louis Peterson (whose drama *Take a Giant Step* was one of the first African American–scripted dramatic plays on Broadway in the early 1950s, which had been adapted into a film coscripted by Peterson). A more far-reaching example of how the protest was connected to new black opportunities surrounds the BADA campaign's champion, Ossie Davis. At the same moment that Jewison walked away from *Nat Turner* in the spring of 1969, Davis was asked to take over the writing and then directing of another controversial black-themed film project, *Cotton Comes to Harlem*. Protests that helped dislodge the hegemonic authority of white filmmakers and producers should be heralded because they led to the hiring of blacks into positions of some creative control. This is not an essentialist argument: it is not to say that white people should not make black-themed films, and, indeed, BADA resisted making this kind of essentialist claim. As Ossie Davis remarked later, "There is from time to time a big brouhaha—sometimes it gets quite excitable—over whether or not a *white* director can really ever make a film truly representative of *black* lifestyle and *black* culture. This question, in my opinion, is more about jobs—and ultimately about power—than it is about race."[38] This crystallizes Davis's political position, as Judith Smith explores in *Visions of Belonging* when she describes him as a black-nationalist-informed "principled interracialist."[39] His concern was with the racist Hollywood power structure that did not sufficiently recognize and hire black and minority ethnic actors, writers, and directors. The *Confessions of Nat Turner* storm meant that by the end of the 1960s producers putting together packages on black-themed film projects for major-studio distribution faced pressure to bring in some meaningful black creative input—both to develop and effectively to market their projects.

The second related reason why the BADA protest should be seen as a victory concerns the film's prospective race-representational politics. Without the (probably fatal) changes BADA sought, what kind of ideological work would the film version of *Confessions of Nat Turner* have performed? The filmmakers' pre-BADA intentions were for an adaptation fairly faithful to the novel, and as the protestors convincingly argued, Styron's narrative serviced white outlooks and expectations in ways that were inimical to black cultural-political priorities and sensibilities. Far from being about the black freedom struggle, this narrative was about the white limits of tolerance rebuking the black-power movement. If the film adaptation were to include any inkling of a Turner "haunted by masturbatory fantasies of the white girl he later kills," to repeat Fremont-Smith's description, the film would surely have delegitimized the slave leader's struggle for freedom. The essential fight for black self-determination is underestimated by the white cultural producers, from Styron's portrayal of Turner's insurrectionary motivations to Jewison's failure to grasp the legitimacy of BADA's concerns.

The demise of this project, I suggest, was an antiracist achievement against white job hoarding and racist liberal-retreatist fictions. It was the disjuncture between the proud black readings of Nat Turner as an emancipatory leader in the struggle for self-determination and the white-determined production context that presented the protestors with powerful leverage points. The case I discuss next is a very different antiracist victory: rather than being attained through protest based on production/text dislocation, it was attained through production/text complementarity, leading to the first studio-made film of the sound era to be directed by an African American.

The Learning Tree

In 1967, when veteran mogul Jack Warner sold his share of ailing Warner Bros. to the television packager Seven Arts Productions for just $183,942,000, it was indicative of the period's industrial flux.[40] Seven Arts cofounder Elliot Hyman became the new CEO of Warner Bros.–Seven Arts and made his son, film producer Kenneth Hyman, the studio's new head of production.

Mergers and takeovers in the film business of the 1960s shook up the old studio management, bringing in heads who were less socialized in the industry's corporate culture and often more open to new talent and fresh themes. Kenneth immediately stated his intention to sign up as many young talented filmmakers "as we can get hold of," attracting them with the promise of greater artistic control. He later described his stint at Warner–Seven Arts as "taking chances with new directors and new stories."[41] Hyman had already displayed racial open-mindedness in casting decisions at his previous job at Seven Arts, where he produced *The Hill* (1965) for progressive filmmaker Sidney Lumet, which featured Ossie Davis. Moreover, in Hyman's film *The Dirty Dozen* (Robert Aldrich, 1967), there was a high-profile role for football star Jim Brown that heralded the emergence of the black action heroes of the early 1970s. Brown was well cast as one of the convicts who take on the Nazis in this ensemble film, which was the sixth-highest earner of 1967. It was a launch-pad role for Brown, defiant and brave (though he ends up as the "noble Negro" through his fatal sacrifice for his country at the end of the film), which Bosley Crowther described in the *New York Times* as the film's "stand out" performance. Brown gets to reflexively showcase his football skills in the climactic scene, remarking at the time, "I strongly identified with my part."[42] Once Hyman became head of production at Warner–Seven Arts, in addition to making Francis Ford Coppola's first feature (*You're a Big Boy Now*, 1966) and working with bête noir of the business, Sam Peckinpah, he signed the first African American studio director.

Hyman had been approached by filmmaker John Cassavetes, who had acted in *Dirty Dozen*, with the idea of *Life* photographer Gordon Parks directing a screen version of Parks's memoir *The Learning Tree* (1963).[43] Cassavetes, who had become friends with Parks after a photo shoot, was a preeminent independent auteur of the 1960s following his celebrated art-house debut *Shadows* (1959), which dealt critically with questions of white identity and passing. Set in a bohemian New York jazz scene, the film challenged fixed racial boundaries. Parks was an award-winning photojournalist who came to prominence in the 1940s, working for the Office of War Information and the Farm Security Administration, and he went on to develop a towering reputation for images of poverty, work, civil rights, and black urban America. But he had little filmmaking experience, having made just one well-received independently distributed documentary, *Flavio*, in 1965. Nonetheless, with Hyman taking chances on new directors, Parks was given real decision-making power on *Learning Tree*. He was signed on not just as director but also as screen adapter, score composer, and coproducer, and he got to choose his director of photography, opting for Burnett Guffey, who was fresh from his *Bonnie and Clyde* (Arthur Penn, 1967) Oscar-winning success. As the *Hollywood Reporter* wrote at the time, "No other Negro in the industry has been given such autonomy."[44] Hyman was not simply being racially magnanimous in this landmark signing. As one black film-industry worker commented, "[Parks] comes in with a package to Warners, a best-selling book, a score and lots of publicity behind him as a *Life* photographer. They couldn't turn that down if it were handed to them by a two-headed, one-legged Martian."[45] Although the worker's cynicism is understandable, this signing was more than simply an act of commercial opportunism and refreshingly different from Jewison's trenchant white production relations.

Much of the racial significance of Parks's signing rested on the degree to which he would make efforts to extend his own opportunity to others. Like many black symbol creators, Parks had had to struggle to be recognized as an artist, and rather than serve as a token "success," he wanted to challenge black exclusion more broadly. Logistically, training up and getting union cards for black technicians and installing them as working members in the film business was not an easy task, as described in chapter 1. Yet Parks did manage to hire black technicians and trainees for *Learning Tree*, eventually securing a dozen (on what was nonetheless, according to Parks, a "predominantly white crew"[46]). Two of them were nonunion members who, through work on the film, obtained union cards. Parks's success in signing minority technicians and apprentices casts doubt on Hollywood management's assertions that the main problem in employment diversification was a lack of supply.

If the film's production relations pushed racial boundaries, so did some of its themes. The rites-of-passage narrative about black teenager Newt Winger (Kyle Johnson), set in rural Kansas in the 1920s, offers a rich account of black life and the destructiveness of racism. The film's resolution revolves around a moral dilemma: Should Winger intervene in the wrongful arrest of a white man for a murder Winger has witnessed? Winger's painfully decided intervention, telling the authorities that the killer was actually a black man, who subsequently dies, is a demonstration of complex ethical negotiation. However, it is also open to being read as a somewhat color-blind ending in its overcoming of "surface" racial solidarity in order to tell the truth, and the film's setting in the 1920s presents a somewhat reassuring temporal distance from the film's serious presentation of racism. The universalist themes were certainly emphasized in some of the mainstream press responses. According to the *Hollywood Reporter*, the film, about "one proud young black man's growing up in the historically free state of Kansas in 1925, is an indelibly American film, unashamed in its honest emotion and sentiment, remarkable in its morality, tolerance and idealism, enriched by understanding of those characteristics which bind and separate men."[47]

A sense of racial conciliation, alongside the pain of racism, in the narrative and in its mainstream reception is perhaps furthered in some of Parks's own early interview comments. As Parks exhilaratingly entered Hollywood, he lent weight to the notion of Hollywood as a racially meritocratic labor market: "[Hyman] gave me the chance because he believes I can do it, and not because I'm a Negro. It's been that way all my life. White men have made the breaks for me, and I've made sure that I was prepared for them."[48] Here, the acclaimed Parks perhaps understandably stresses that his Hollywood hiring had to do with talent rather than with tokenism. But such statements risked inadvertently bolstering the sincere fiction that the industry was already benignly giving talented African Americans the chance.

In fact, preferential policies were desperately needed because so few whites were willing at the time and thereafter to "make the breaks." Indeed, once Parks had been in the industry for a little while, his tone shifted, challenging the industry's excuse that it couldn't find black talent. "It's rotten in the rest of the industry. They should go out and get more black people. The fact that I was told I would never find qualified black kids—and then went out and got 12 of them—proves that they can do it if they want to."[49] The *Learning Tree* project, which broke even ($3.15 million returning to the industry in rentals after $1.9 million spent on production costs plus expenditure on marketing), emerged out of unusual interracial exposure, friendship, and collaboration among members of the creative elite.[50] Although many whites, according to opinion polling cited in chapter 1, were by the late 1960s willing to reject racial employment discrimination in principle, fewer were interested in equality in practice. Cassavetes and Hyman were among those in Hollywood whose production-culture parameters extended somewhat beyond the white bubble and its concomitant fictions. There were others. Ralph Nelson, for instance, director of *Tick . . . Tick . . . Tick* (1970), starring Jim Brown, piloted a program with MGM to hire a minority assistant director trainee. Also Poitier's director in *Lilies of the Field*, Nelson was a left progressive who had first developed his career on Broadway (he had performed in Irving Berlin's show "This Is the Army" during World War II, an all-soldier revue performed by one of the first desegregated army units).[51]

Minority-training initiatives and race-conscious hiring practices by individual white filmmakers who had already-established interracial networks were essential to interrupting the culture of cronyism in Hollywood. As Downing and Husband explain, "Mentoring practices and cronyism overlap in significant ways, in that mentors also tend to choose people of the same ethnic group to help. The contribution of those who do not mentor on this basis is critically important for the diversity of the industry."[52] Cassavetes, Parks, and Hyman's setting up of the package that led to Parks being in a position to mentor and hire other black workers captures on a microlevel a model for bringing about some film diversification. In the face of the unraveling of *Confessions* and the making of *Learning Tree*, several other black-oriented films started production, employing minority film workers both above and below the line.

Race-Themed Productions in the Hollywood Renaissance Years

Surprise superhits such as *Who's Afraid of Virginia Woolf?* (Mike Nichols, 1966), *Bonnie and Clyde*, and the most successful film of 1967, *The Graduate* (Mike Nichols), which grossed $105 million, came to exert a strong influence on film-industry production patterns at the end of the 1960s.[53] New, more socially and aesthetically challenging features—results of a suspended Production Code and made by new-generation directors—entered mainstream filmmaking, creating space for, among other things, stories that spoke to racial change. White filmmakers increasingly realized, especially in light of the high-profile *Confessions of Nat Turner* debacle, that they needed creative input from black symbol creators to help develop and validate their films. Some industry whites were far more racially self-aware and open in their practices than other self-described liberals, who were both retreating from and trying to capitalize on the currency of antiracist themes.

Cotton Comes to Harlem, the second studio picture in the sound era to be directed by an African American and the first to turn a significant profit, was based on the comedy-laced crime novel by Chester Himes. Himes was an important political writer of the left in the 1940s who had turned away from overt protest literature and won critical acclaim and a new audience— mainly in Europe, where he had relocated—for his detective fiction starting in the 1950s. The literary scholar William Turner, who has ably traced this shift, describes Himes's acclaimed yet exploitation-laced detective fiction as "pulping the Black Atlantic."[54] As part of the burgeoning interest in black-themed material, producer Sam Goldwyn Jr. bought the film rights to Himes's crime novels featuring black detectives Gravedigger Jones and Coffin Ed Johnson. The producer was the son of veteran studio head Samuel Goldwyn, who had produced the throwback black-cast film *Porgy and Bess.* In the context of the suspended code and changing mores, next-generation Goldwyn Jr. saw commercial possibilities in Himes's work, which might previously have been too outré for mainstream cinema, as *Variety* put it: "Although expatriate writer Himes has been writing about his two Harlem detectives for a long time, the background and plots of their exploits have evidently been a bit too ethnic and too strong of language to suggest film treatment."[55] Himes's agent sold the film rights for all the detective novels in the series to Goldwyn Jr. for only $25,000, with no gross participation, of which sum, after agent fees, Himes ended up with $18,000—his agent later apologized about the poor deal negotiated.[56] Having optioned the novels for so little, Goldwyn set about putting a multifilm package together, signing a deal with United Artists in March 1968.

According to Goldwyn, white-liberal discomfort with the *Cotton* project was evident from the beginning: "My lawyer, who was very active in the American Civil Liberties Union, didn't want to handle the contract on it, because he thought I was getting into something which was putting black people down."[57] In an effort to ward off bad press and to achieve racial credibility for the controversial content, Goldwyn turned first to black writers to develop the screenplay, working briefly with Himes as well as with Amiri Baraka. These script treatments were, however, not accepted by Goldwyn, nor was the version produced next by white screenwriter Arnold Perl. Perl had a track record of writing nonstereotypical black material for radio and television, including for the television series *East Side/West Side* (1963–1964), costarring Cicely Tyson. But, according to Goldwyn, "the tone was wrong" in Perl's script treatment. On Perl's advice, Goldwyn asked Ossie Davis, who was in line for the part of Coffin Ed, to further develop the script. Goldwyn "kept asking me if this or that in the script was right," explained Davis, "and I would suggest this or that change."[58] Under mounting pressure from both black and white quarters about the film's content, and after working closely with the actor on what became a major rewrite, Goldwyn asked Davis to direct. An experienced playwright, stage director, and film actor, Davis already had many of the skills required to move into feature-film helming as well as extraordinary black political authority, having emceed the March on Washington and eulogized Malcolm X at his memorial service in Harlem in 1965. Moreover, the potential protection offered to Goldwyn's film by hiring the man who was then taking a stand on the *Confessions of Nat Turner* project was considerable. Thanks to the actions of industry activists such as BADA and the wider climate of racial upheaval, business-savvy producers such as Goldwyn Jr. had a social and commercial imperative to create opportunities for previously excluded black film creatives.

The entry of African Americans into the exclusively white domain of film often emerged out of cross-racial artistic collaborations developed in the cultural fields of photography, music, and especially theater under the shadow of the McCarthy hearings. Arnold Perl and Ossie Davis had met when they were part of a group of blacklisted artists who mounted the production of the classic play *The World of Sholom Aleichem* (1953), penned by Perl and stage-managed by Davis. Their friendship from that time led to Perl suggesting to Goldwyn that Davis rewrite the *Cotton* script. Following multiple anti-Communist investigations, from the House Un-American Activities Committee sessions to the Red Channels report in *Counterattack* magazine, both of these artists were "named" and thus struggling to earn a living. The play, which also featured Davis's blacklisted wife, Ruby Dee, had been, according to Davis, "one of Broadway's answers to the Hollywood blacklist."[59] *Cotton* thus continued an important interracial collaboration, with deep roots, through Davis and Perl, that stretched back to the cultural-front left activism of New York in the 1940s, organized around labor rights, antifascism, and black civil rights.[60] Davis had developed the skills of organizer, protester, pamphleteer, and fund-raiser when in 1951 he became a labor representative in the Actors Equity Association in New York theater. The association was, according to Davis, "a sort of command center in the sometimes vicious and bloody fight against McCarthyism."[61] There, he honed the political skills that made him a formidable adversary for the *Confessions of Nat Turner* filmmakers.

It is thus remarkable that this key member of the "U.S. Third World Left" became the second black film director for a major studio in such a risk-averse mass-cultural industry. By the late 1960s, with his wife Davis had worked indefatigably for civil rights, workers' rights, black liberation, and anti-imperialism—he was someone, in Sidney Poitier's words, whose "commitment has been etched in damn near every aspect of Black consciousness."[62] Stepping into the role of director, Davis saw that there were no minority workers or trainees on set. According to Cliff Frazier, once the film started production in Harlem, Davis told Goldwyn: "I will not shoot another foot of film until we get some black recruits." They quickly found eight minority trainees, using Frazier's New York–based Community Film Workshop, several of whom ended up with union cards, and the resulting film went on to gross around $6.5 million.[63]

FIGURE 2.1 Godfrey Cambridge (Grave Digger Jones), Raymond St. Jacques (Coffin Ed Johnson), and first-time director Ossie Davis on the set of *Cotton Comes to Harlem* (1970).

Source: Courtesy of the Academy of Motion Picture Arts and Sciences.

Just after Davis agreed to direct *Cotton*, in late spring of 1969 a third African American was signed on as a major-studio director: Melvin Van Peebles struck a three-picture deal with Columbia. Van Peebles was the first African American to be signed as a promising young film auteur in the mold of new-generation Hollywood Renaissance white directors. The major-studio interest was based on Van Peebles's independent success, having written and directed an acclaimed indie feature in France, *La Permission* (distributed in the United States as *The Story of a Three-Day Pass*) in 1968, about an affair between a black American soldier and a white French woman. Unable to make headway with his film career in the United States, Van Peebles had moved to France and begun to build an image of hip black Atlanticism. Once he had established himself in Europe, he used his French profile to market himself to a previously uninterested American film scene at a time when European auteurism and the French film wave became very influential. According to Van Peebles, signed up as a French delegate at the San Francisco Film Festival when *La Permission* won the Critic's Choice Award, "Nobody knew I was American, let alone a black American."[64] His first American feature for Columbia was the rollicking, topical comedy-drama *Watermelon Man*, about a racist white insurance man (Godfrey Cambridge) who early in the film suddenly turns black. Van Peebles, like Parks and Davis, negotiated a significant degree of control on this project, taking on the role of score composer and negotiating important changes to the film's narrative.

Whereas Van Peebles came to the U.S. film industry as a "European" director, Harry Belafonte had much more in common with his friends Ossie Davis and Ruby Dee, coming from the New York–based worlds of acting, theater, and protest as well as from the world of music. *The Angel Levine* was Belafonte's project: made and funded in part by his production company HarBel for United Artists and starring Belafonte. He used his leverage as a top creative and invested his own money to wrest control of the project. With input from the Jewish writer Ronald Ribman, the acclaimed black playwright, actor, and novelist Bill Gunn scripted *Angel Levine*, a low-key drama based on a Bernard Malamud short story about the meeting of an old Jewish tailor (Zero Mostel) and a young black Jewish hustler (Belafonte) in New York. Down on his luck, the tailor asks God for help and is sent the angel, Alexander Levine (Belafonte), who is seeking redemption. *Angel Levine* was also the first U.S.-made film of Hungarian director Jan Kadar, who had won the Best Foreign Language Film Oscar for his previous release.

In Kadar, Belafonte had sought out a director who, like Van Peebles, was part of the wave of European directors who came to make films for the studios during the Hollywood Renaissance. It was this new politicoaesthetic openness in mainstream filmmaking that lured Belafonte back to filmmaking after a self-imposed absence of eleven years, following his disappointing experiences of Hollywood's race-representational constraints in the features he had starred in during the 1950s.[65]

Belafonte teamed with experienced producer Chiz Schultz, with whom he had first worked on the acclaimed television special *Belafonte: New York 19* in 1960. Schultz, a white producer with a commitment to racial justice in film and television, became vice president and executive producer of Belafonte Enterprises, and the two men made several television shows together. *Angel Levine* was their first film feature. Its star, Zero Mostel, was the award-winning lead character of *The World of Sholom Aleichem*—another creative who, blacklisted under McCarthy, had a hard-won sense of outrage at employment exclusion and a political commitment to cross-racial solidarity extending back to the cultural front. A couple of months before Ossie Davis and Cliff Frazier found their black recruits for *Cotton*, producers Belafonte and Schultz had set about diversifying the crew for *Angel Levine*. "When I started to hire for the film, I saw the absence of black people," recalls Belafonte, which led him to "seek all the black and Puerto Rican technicians who were available." Realizing that there was a problem with pipelines into the industry and the need for job training, the producers submitted a proposal for a minority apprentice program to the Ford Foundation. They received a grant of $25,000, which they used to employ fourteen interns (two Puerto Rican and twelve black) to assist on the production.[66] The money paid a basic wage to the apprentices, who shadowed workers in the areas of assistant director, sound engineer, script prompting, casting, publicity, wardrobe, and production. The apprentice program was overseen by the film's associate producer, Hal De Windt, who had been a director at the famed Negro Ensemble Company and would go on to be a leader of expanding opportunities for minorities in the arts. Thus, the Harlem-made *Angel Levine* strove to be a model of film-industry diversification.

The *Landlord* project came from a source novel authored by the African American writer Kristin Hunter, the rights for which were bought by Norman Jewison.[67] The novel was a racial satire about a white upper-class landlord who buys and renovates an apartment building in a black working-class neighborhood in Brooklyn, New York. As with *In the Heat of the Night*, Jewison intended a package that included him as director, Hal Ashby as editor, and Walter Mirisch as producer for United Artists. And as with *Confessions of Nat Turner*, Jewison initially turned to a white author to develop the race-themed content, signing newcomer Erich Segal, a young scholar from Yale University (who would soon go on to write the novel and script for *Love Story*, the biggest hit of 1970, directed by Arthur Hiller). Christopher Sieving has explored in illuming detail the development of the *Landlord* project, recounting how Segal, in a letter to Jewison in January 1967, first tried to persuade the director to hire him as the writer, encouraging him "not to worry about achieving 'authenticity' in the depiction of the black ghetto: 'I mean its [*sic*] gotta seem right, but I doubt if you need a technical consultant from Elijah Mohammed [*sic*]'"[68] Where Arnold Perl, struggling with the black-themed adaptation of *Cotton Comes to Harlem*, had the racial insight and network base to recommend writing input from Ossie Davis, Segal had and sought no such resources. In early 1968, just as the *Confessions* storm heated up, Jewison rejected Segal's script and, on the recommendation of Chiz Schultz, turned to Bill Gunn, who had just coscripted *Angel Levine*.

However, Gunn's and Jewison's visions of the project were at loggerheads. Once Gunn, with his Black Arts sensibilities, started to work on his script, Jewison—who wanted a much warmer and less-experimental race comedy (hence his initial hiring of Segal)—began to drift away from the project. He eventually handed over directing to Hal Ashby, who had never directed before, and turned to producing the film instead. From there on, through production and postproduction, Jewison and Ashby clashed over the film's content. Jewison increasingly relinquished control, pursuing other projects, leaving "Ashby to his own devices on the East Coast," in Sieving's words.[69] Ashby and Bill Gunn worked closely together to complete the project and, with Jewison's agreement, sought to hire black technicians, appointing Hal De Windt as assistant producer off the back of his successful *Angel Levine* training program.

Political wrangles between creative partners Jewison and Ashby over racial content and personnel on *Landlord* led them, after producing a string of acclaimed hit features, to never collaborate on another film. When Jewison left the United States in 1970, having failed to get *Confessions* made and having been creatively sidelined on *Landlord*, he cited the assassinations of Martin Luther King Jr. and Robert Kennedy as reasons for leaving. But the

FIGURE 2.2 Beau Bridges (Elgar Enders) and first-time director Hal Ashby with schoolchildren during production of *The Landlord* (1970).
Source: Courtesy of the Academy of Motion Picture Arts and Sciences.

picture is likely more complex than that: the director, like his hero William Styron, was out of tune with the far-reaching black and left politicization where the creative vortex of the period lay. Haskell Wexler later remarked: "I saw what a force Hal was, making Norman's creativity blossom. They were a good combo, and I don't think Norman's made as good pictures since he and Hal were partners."[70] In Europe, Jewison made hits such as *Fiddler on the Roof* (1971) and *Jesus Christ Superstar* (1973), both musicals with white ethnic revival themes. Meanwhile, Ashby remained in the United States, grappling with challenging racial subject matter in productive liaison with black symbol creators. In several letters to Jewison from 1970, after *Landlord*'s release, Ashby described how he was working with another black writer, Cecil Brown, on the screen adaptation of Brown's novel *The Life and Loves of Mr. Jiveass Nigger* (1969): "Did you remember that Cecil is one of the ten black writers who did the anti 'Nat Turner' thing . . . ?"[71] Presumably

Jewison did recall. Ashby commented on mentoring Brown in script development: "We got Cecil into LA for a few days, so I could work with him. . . . We did some long long hours on it page by page, so we should still have a first draft by the end of the month."[72] Ashby was mentoring an established black author in the art of script writing, an area in which African Americans had with very rare exceptions been racially excluded. Writing back to Ashby from the Yugoslavian set of *Fiddler on the Roof,* Jewison stated about the *Jive-ass* project: "If you have any doubts about the validity of what the film can say, what it can be, or if it should even be made, then you shouldn't become involved."[73]

Altogether, the new black filmmakers—Parks, Davis, Van Peebles, Belafonte, and Gunn—and their collaborations with white filmmakers stand as an undertold part of the well-mapped generational and aesthetic overhaul of the early Hollywood Renaissance years. Like the new-generation white directors, almost none of whom had come up through the Hollywood studio system, the black filmmakers had first established themselves in the somewhat less-exclusionary fields of television, theater, photography, music, book publishing, and acting. Gordon Parks Sr., like Stanley Kubrick, had been a famed *Life* photographer before moving into motion-picture directing. Ossie Davis, Bill Gunn, and many of the fine black actors who finally got offers of meaningful film roles in the late 1960s and early 1970s, including Diana Sands, Roscoe Lee Browne, Pearl Bailey, Brock Peters, James Earl Jones, and Yaphet Kotto, had well-established careers in theater, as did cross-platform star Harry Belafonte. New York of the late 1960s, where many of these films were made, was a flourishing new setting for film production, tapping into Broadway and off-Broadway black and white actors, writers, and directors. Those who didn't come from different media arose instead from European filmmaking scenes, notably Melvin Van Peebles and Jan Kadar. Many of the most successful Hollywood Renaissance directors were from the interwar generation, and so were Van Peebles (b. 1932), Bill Gunn (b. 1937), and Belafonte (b. 1927).[74] Notably, however, some of the "new" black directors were part of the generation born in the 1910s (including Ossie Davis [b. 1917] and Gordon Parks Sr. [b. 1912]), whose entry into commercial filmmaking was delayed by the industry's racial exclusionism. They made a ready talent pool once a few opportunities were finally generated in the industry in the wake of the antiracist movement. This entry of blacks into filmmaking was in part a product of broader generational changes and film-business restructurings, which, combined with racial politics, created conditions of possibility. And like Parks on *Learning Tree*, they refused the position of token black filmmaker on these pictures but instead worked diligently to bring their representational values to bear not just on staffing but also on the film texts.

Textual Negotiations

The films that resulted from these efforts, *Cotton, Watermelon Man, Angel Levine*, and *Landlord*, contributed to the racializing of the film renaissance years, this period of unusually intellectually demanding and taboo-breaking movie fare. Four dimensions of these films drew on and dramatized film renaissance priorities and black cultural repertories in deeply politicized times: they worked within and against classical Hollywood narrative and thematic parameters; they offered a new cinematic staging of African American humor; they mapped urban geographies in a time of crisis; and, finally and most reflexively, they portrayed urgent racial workplace and wealth-distribution themes. These films worked variously to develop aesthetic value and social meaning through these dimensions, dramatizing issues of race, culture, power, and oppression that were energized by and contested through the films' own socially situated production relations.

First, many filmmakers dealing with race themes at the time called for more pessimistic and ambivalent treatments and a move away from the conventional happy-ending resolutions epitomized in classical Hollywood cinema. The trend of unresolved endings, which extended more broadly in the renaissance years, was compounded in racial dramas. Sterling Silliphant— whose next screenplay after *In the Heat of the Night* was the much darker race drama *The Liberation of LB Jones* (William Wyler, 1970)—captured the sentiment of many film-industry progressives: "If we give happy endings to racially oriented films, we tend to mislead the vast white middle class, which has limited daily contact with black people, and we certainly frustrate minority persons and the underprivileged[,] who know damn well they are a long, long way from all that honey and light we tend to show."[75] Such a belief that more-discomforting narratives were needed at a time of riots, state repression, and political assassination fed into many of the race-themed pictures under discussion, which Christopher Sieving ably describes as "racial impasse films."[76] On *Landlord*, Gunn and Ashby were drawn to satirical and sad narrative imperatives. The film ends with black tenant Fanny Copee (Diana Sands), having had an affair and conceiving a baby with the white upper-class landlord Elgar Enders (Beau Bridges), coming to the decision that she can't take care of the baby because she is already married to and loves Mr. Copee (Louis Gossett Jr.). Fanny ultimately persuades the reluctant Elgar to take the baby after she pointedly explains to him, "I want him to be adopted white so he can grow up casual. Like his daddy." A memorable line about white racism from Gunn's script captures the film's identificatory edginess: "You whites scream about miscegenation and you done watered down every race you ever hated!" *Angel Levine* is also dark and more tragic. The two anti-heroic characters, the old tailor and the young numbers runner, who by chance are coreligionists, do not recognize a common humanity in each other until it is too late. The Jewish tailor can't recognize the black man as inside his community; it is the tailor's ailing wife who does recognize the kinship before she dies. For Belafonte's angel on probation, the failure of recognition leads to annihilation.

Such downbeat endings, which proved difficult to market to a wide audience, were not unusual in race dramas. In 1970, another impasse film was released, *The Great White Hope* (Martin Ritt), based on a hit Broadway play about boxer Jack Johnson and starring James Earl Jones. Its very poor financial performance (with rentals of less than $1 million off a budget of around $6 million), despite critical acclaim, was widely attributed to its bleak ending for the boxing great.[77] The early Hollywood Renaissance release *Uptight* (Jules Dassin, 1968), coscripted and costarring Ruby Dee and distributed by Paramount, which included electric scenes of actual rioting in the wake of King's assassination and a narrative of black political unraveling, also failed to recoup its costs.[78] Similarly, *Landlord*'s budget of $2.5 million (considerably more than the three other films under discussion) was not fully recouped at the box office. Although the impulse of many of these filmmakers was to make intellectually and narratively challenging films, their political commitments meant they also wanted to engage a popular audience, which led to conflicting priorities.

Indeed, the most affirming and conventional endings are to be found in the most commercially successful of the films: Van Peebles's *Watermelon Man* and Davis's *Cotton Comes to Harlem*. In the latter, the antiheroes

Coffin Ed (Raymond St. Jacques) and Gravedigger (Godfrey Cambridge) prevail at the film's resolution, consistent with the source novel. In addition, Davis introduced into the script a humorous, utopian ending for the poor, Old South protagonist Uncle Budd (in the film debut of famed black comic Redd Foxx), who ends up with the much sought-after cotton bale of the title. Van Peebles negotiated important changes to *Watermelon Man*, delivering a black-power narrative resolution: after the white insurance man turns black, he first reacts against his predicament before coming to embrace it. The film historian Thomas Cripps describes how Van Peebles "fought both Columbia and his writer, Herman Raucher, into tolerating political changes," which see the erstwhile white advertiser fully affirming his new identity, becoming a black nationalist, and opening a successful community business at the film's point of utopian closure.[79] Strikingly, once Van Peebles became the film's director, he negotiated with the studio a shift from blackface performance to whiteface. Although the insurance broker is white for only the first few scenes, the studio had looked for a white actor to play him. Inverting the history of blackface, Van Peebles insisted that the lead be African American, and actor-comedian Godfrey Cambridge was soon signed on, and he performs these early scenes whited up. This move at once counternarrativizes racial categories and employs an African American rather than a white actor as the film's hero.[80] The casting and script changes on both *Cotton* and *Watermelon Man* were testament to the populist black-nationalist sensibilities and strategies of Davis and Van Peebles, who were at pains to reach out to black audience members with politicized, entertaining fare and pointed the way for things to come.

These filmmakers' attempt to find the best mode to simultaneously educate and entertain introduces the second textual feature I foreground: humor. *Cotton Comes to Harlem*, *Watermelon Man*, and *Landlord* are comedies, and *Angel Levine* is a drama strongly laced with Jewish humor emanating from its comic star Zero Mostel. The 1960s marked an exciting moment when black comedians, who had worked for decades on the African American theater circuit, came to be screened on television and in film in unprecedented ways. Once again, though, it tended to be the entry of black people into producing roles that opened the way for this black comic showcasing. Belafonte had produced an hour-long variety special in 1967 for ABC, *A Time for Laughter: A Look at Negro Humor in America*, which helped to introduce mainstream television audiences to black talent, including long-standing comic entertainers such as Redd Foxx, Moms Mabley, George Kirby, and Pig-meat Markham as well as up-and-coming comedians such as Dick Gregory, Godfrey Cambridge, and Richard Pryor. The special also opened space in which "respectable" stars such as Sidney Poitier and Diahann Carroll could change register and communicate black-scripted and self-improvised humor. It showcased a range of black comic subjectivities while also satirizing white racial assumptions and practices to a broad audience. Belafonte explained the political significance of unleashing these comic talents onto primetime: in the past, "negro comics on television . . . knew white audiences wanted to laugh *at them*, not *with* them, and so they obliged, laughing all the way to the bank. I wanted the jokes and routines Negroes told one another, the humor they shared away from white folk, the humor that came directly from the severity of their lives: poverty, joblessness, prejudice. And I wanted white audiences, as well as black, to hear it."[81]

With *Cotton Comes to Harlem*, Ossie Davis transposed this agenda onto movie screens. He drew on some of the same black comics (Foxx and Cambridge) to stage subcultural humor, which was compounded by the racial absurdity of Himes's source novel. The black novelist Ishmael Reed later wrote to Himes: "Whole family saw *Cotton Comes to Harlem* on the TV the other night. . . . It was the best of the black films and they captured your humour, style."[82] Davis's investment in humor was rooted in the folklore of his southern upbringing, which he fed into the highly regarded script of his racial farce *Purlie Victorious*. This play had been made into the film *Gone Are the Days* (Nicholas Webster, 1963), starring Davis, Dee, and Cambridge. As with Belafonte's television show *Time for Laughter*, the screening of black vernacular humor discomfited some black and many white viewers.[83] The *New York Times* film critic Vincent Canby panned *Cotton Comes to Harlem* before watching it again in an urban theater several weeks later and publishing a second revisionist review in which he claimed that it displays "an exuberant irreverence toward just about everything—including narrative sense, stereotyped racial sensibilities (white as well as black), and virtue." He noted the chaotic extended car chase that opens the film, which presents a string of Harlem vignettes, which "you probably never saw in a nice, liberal, 1960s movie made with good taste."[84] This was the response from whites that Davis intended. He recalls in his memoir that producer Sam Goldwyn Jr. had urged him to ramp up the racialization.[85] In response, Davis introduced into the script the film's reflexive refrain: "Is it black enough for you?" This rhetorical question speaks ambivalently to burdens of representation in production relations: it provocatively addresses critical reception by blacks and expectations about black film culture among industry whites. The resultant film, created by Davis via Goldwyn and Himes, was a self-conscious, overdetermined expression of black resistance, black style, and black humor.

A common target for the humor across the four films was racial bigotry, critiquing the period's mainstream racial discourses and white tolerance of racial injustice. There had been a strong emphasis on serious, sometimes ponderous treatments of "the race problem" in the mainstream media, exemplified not only by earnest problem pictures but also, especially in the aftermath of the assassinations and riots, with the slew of race-themed current-affairs specials aired on network television.[86] Van Peebles's response was to start his three-picture Columbia deal with the broad comedy *Watermelon Man*. He and scripter Herman Raucher aimed to send up the liberal retreatism of those whites who espoused tolerance in principle but not in practice. When the insurance broker, who lives in a white suburb, wakes up black, he immediately starts to receive anonymous phone calls from locals telling him to "move out, nigger." Similarly, the racial farce that Bill Gunn and Hal Ashby were aiming for on *Landlord* targeted both blacks and especially whites. *Landlord* lampoons white sincere fictions espoused by liberals who live in affluent white neighborhoods, whose self-serving racial perceptions are informed by pop-cultural fictions. Gunn's early extensive script treatment had the landlord's mother "seated on a lounge chair . . . reading a copy of *The Confessions of Nat Turner*," but that scene was soon cut—unsurprisingly given that Jewison was the film's producer.[87] The comedy across the four films emanated from an overlaid combination of black, Jewish, new-wave, and class-conscious New York cultural formations.

Indeed, New York City brings us to the third shared thematic feature: the new cinematic mapping of black urban geographies. These films were some of the first major-studio-distributed features to depict on-location black urban communities, which fed powerfully into their racial credibility. From Poitier's liberal-reformist heroes operating in a mainly white and often middle-class world, there was an abrupt shift to race-oriented films set and shot in working-class, predominantly black milieus.[88] Many of the actors and filmmakers lived in New York, where these films were set, enhancing the films' place-based locatedness. Harry Belafonte was born and later lived in

Harlem, where *Angel Levine* was set, and he used the area's facilities at Film-ways Studios to make the film. Its Harlem geography, shot by Kadar, was nonetheless sometimes confused. Much more closely attuned to the actual cityscape of Harlem was Ossie Davis, who described his sense of responsi-bility and excitement when he took on the role of directing a film that had this hallowed black locale in its title: "I know Harlem. . . . I was very much aware of the significance of being the first black man to direct a Hollywood studio movie in Harlem."[89] Davis lovingly shot such iconic sites as Small's Paradise, the Spanish American barbershop, Frank's Restaurant, the inter-section of 125th Street and Seventh Avenue, and extended scenes of the Apollo Theater. The theater features so prominently because, as Davis explains, it "was a solid, irrefutable display of Negro expertise, authority, and power [that] doesn't give a damn about white folks."[90] This second stu-dio film directed by an African American thus became a showcase not just of previously underdocumented black comic talent but also of black place-based performative capital. Shooting on location added to both films' cultural-political importance and value, enhanced by the close connection between symbol creator and community.[91]

Landlord was a foundational film in this opening of the black urban cin-emascape. Hal Ashby had hired New Yorker Gordon Willis as cinematog-rapher, who filmed the heavily foregrounded, sumptuous shots of rundown tenement buildings in Park Slope, Brooklyn. This was Willis's first major film, on which he formulated his vision of New York using overblown light-ing to brighten and flatten the landlord's upper-class white family in the perniciously affluent Hamptons, contrasted with what became his trade-mark use of sepia-toned shots of New York City and its interiors. Willis's use of contrastive lighting, in particular dark-brown shadows, was to gen-erate his industry moniker "the prince of darkness" when he went on to work as the celebrated director of photography for Francis Ford Coppola's films *The Godfather* (1972) and *The Godfather: Part II* (1974) as well as Woody Allen's *Annie Hall* (1977) and *Manhattan* (1979). The distinctive lighting style of these later classic cinematic representations of New York of the 1970s was first developed to convey both racial realism and satire on *Landlord*. Wil-lis's camera operator on the film, Michael Chapman, would also go on to create some of the most famous cinematic images of New York: he, too, worked on *The Godfather* before becoming director of photography on Mar-tin Scorsese's *Taxi Driver* (1976), set on the streets of New York City, as well as Scorsese's Bronx-set *Raging Bull* (1980). The satirical, interracial vision of *Landlord* (which drew together Black Arts Movement and Hollywood Renaissance energies) essentially helped to shape not only the uptown urban imagery of black ghetto action films thereafter but also New York's white ethnic renaissance in films of the 1970s.

Although all three textual areas discussed so far foreground ways in which cross-racial production processes fed into textual priorities, the final area takes us directly to reflexive themes of labor and wealth distribution in these films. Employment is generally portrayed in precarious terms. The black cops Gravedigger and Coffin Ed in *Cotton Comes to Harlem* are morally and economically tenuous in comparison to the classical, white-conceived black detective Virgil Tibbs, whose expert training helps to restore order in Sparta. Himes's iconic heroes in both novel and film are by contrast hard-pressed workers, unable to establish anything but a makeshift, transient order in the chaotic and chronically underfunded world they police. *Angel Levine* is about the coming together of a demoralized young hustler, excluded by race and class from meaningful life chances, and an old immigrant tailor who had forged a meager life for himself and family only to watch it fall apart. Where the humiliations of poverty and a lack of legitimate opportunities steer the hustler to an early and meaningless death when he is hit by a car while stealing a fur coat, the tailor grapples with depression, chronic pain, family loss, and an unsuccessful application for welfare. Both *Angel Levine* and *Cotton* (in the character of "back to Africa" con artist Deke O'Malley) show hustling to be a negative, dead-end, pernicious, ultimately tragic pursuit, which is expressive of the false promises of capitalism. This theme speaks to the politically conscious input of black symbol creators Himes, Davis, and Belafonte. However, the early 1970s would see such hustling characters transmogrified into the enterprising ghetto heroes and dynamic, stylish wealth generators who would prove so attractive to post–civil rights youth audiences (see chapter 4).

Reflexive work themes were also at the heart of *Angel Levine*. Belafonte had decided the "making of *Angel Levine* would be, in itself, an exercise in race relations (and since HarBel Productions was financing it, I could make that decision)."[92] A fuller account of the film's labor relations is reserved for the next chapter, but the experience of introducing the black and Puerto Rican trainees into an otherwise white crew proved challenging, and this challenge is mirrored in the film's thematic concerns. The subject matter, according to Belafonte, "really dealt with communication, dealt with people who are totally alien to one another finding some basis on which to identify with one another, because their destinies were inextricably bound."[93] As the film historian Judith Smith has explored, Belafonte was working within a long-lived framing from the left about a special relationship between blacks and Jews that emerged from their shared experiences of racialized oppression, a relationship that was facing strong challenge from both sides and acutely focused on tensions around fair employment (see chapter 5).[94]

Landlord also drew attention to the breakdown in interracial communication, implicitly engaging black cinema's workplace exclusions as a thematic priority. In the film, Mrs. Copee explains that her early promise as a beauty queen had ultimately amounted only to a home-based, one-room beauty-and-hairdressing outfit in the tenement building. She had been "Miss Sepia, 1957. That's like Miss America, 'cept in color." Then she quietly states in close-up: "I don't know what happened." The movingly understated scene intimates the dearth of decent film roles Diana Sands had been offered since her highly acclaimed performance in the film version of Lorraine Hansberry's novel *A Raisin in the Sun* (Daniel Petrie, 1961). The celebrated vaudeville star Pearl Bailey, who plays the charismatic tenement mother Marge, hadn't had a substantial screen role for a decade. *Landlord* was filmed in the year when Diana Sands gave testimony at the New York State Division of Human Rights hearing about the lack of equal opportunity in motion pictures.[95] As Van Peebles commented in the early 1970s, "She was supportive of all black people trying to work in this industry."[96] The introspection of beautiful Mrs. Copee's wistful scene seems to capture the disappointed hopes in the face of racial, gendered, and class-based employment exclusions in the film industry as well as in beauty culture. The way this scene is written seems to acknowledge that good film roles for blacks were few and far between and emphasizes the pain of living with those exclusions.

Along with workplace circuitry between production and text, wealth distribution is a central reflexive theme. The novel *Cotton Comes to Harlem* revolves around a quest for the valuable missing cotton bale, invoking as it does a history of white accumulation built on stolen black labor. The search for the elusive bale, a much needed economic resource for the impoverished protagonists, remains central in the film adaptation. But in developing the script, Davis inserted an ending in which Uncle Budd, the Deep South character who is the only one to understand the true value of cotton, obtains and sells the precious commodity. This outcome stands in antithesis to the "pastoral" plantation long shots of nameless and resourceless cotton pickers Jewison insisted on for *In the Heat of the Night*. With the proceeds from the cotton, Budd buys a cotton plantation in Africa, a utopian comic resolution that converts historic peonage into start-up capital, leading to the promise of black wealth creation on the continent. Continuing this foregrounding of a liberated Africa as part of worldwide black culture, Davis turned for his next directorial signing to the film adaptation of playwright Wole Soyinka's work *Kongi's Harvest* (1970), the first of two Davis films shot in Nigeria in the 1970s.

In Van Peebles's *Watermelon Man*, following the racial transformation of the insurance broker, his white boss wants to exploit the metamorphosis by sending the hero into the ghetto to sell insurance and expand the company's share of the black market. This decision speaks to and satirizes the large white-owned companies that were at that time making aggressive bids to expand their share of African American markets, which included moving into black areas. As the historian Robert Weems traces in *Desegregating the Dollar*, this process was deleterious for the smaller black-owned insurance businesses that had previously serviced their own communities.[97] Corporations now needed black agents, such as the Watermelon Man, to win African American consumers' support. The film, however, having first dramatized the avaricious attempts by white businesses to target the "Negro market," then flips the racial script. When the hero embraces his blackness, he decides to set up his own successful community-based insurance company.

If this narrative recognized and resisted general trends in post–civil rights corporate America, it also reflexively spoke to the dynamics of production and marketing in cinema. Some of the major film studios started using black public-relations outfits in the mid-1960s to niche-market their product and better capture African American film consumers for both race-themed and non-race-themed productions. Indeed, Columbia, which released *Watermelon Man*, was the forerunner in employing local black marketing firms to sell to African American audiences—mirroring the hero's activity in black locales on behalf of the white company.[98] The hero becomes a kind of stand-in for black marketing expert D. Parke Gibson, who advised Columbia Pictures and many other corporations.[99] Van Peebles's insistence on changing Raucher's original screenplay to introduce an ending featuring independent black wealth creation echoes Ossie Davis's script intervention on

Cotton with Uncle Budd. In both, there is a utopian dream of abundant black wealth generation replacing exploited black labor, offering a counternarrative to the de facto general racialized business trends. Van Peebles's self-determination speaks to his next move, which was to leave Columbia without completing the three-picture deal in order to make his own independent hit, *Sweet Sweetback's Baadasssss Song* (1971), outside the studio system, which he both wrote and coproduced (see chapter 4).

Material relations between races are also at the heart of *Landlord*, captured in the film's title: it concerns the relationship between black tenants and the white rentier class. The film raises salient themes having to do with residential segregation and dispossession, racialized wealth inequalities, and discourses of urban social deterioration that were particularly charged in New York at that time.[100] Both rentiers and residents are satirized in the film. Although the film ends by abandoning the gentrifying landlord's superficial illusions of racial amity, the resolution also revolves around wealth redistribution. After initially renovating the rundown tenement building with a view to evicting the black tenants, the landlord ultimately gifts the Park Slope house to Fanny Copee and its black occupants. Made at a moment of peak white flight and dawning gentrification, the film ends with this important act of racial redistribution. It shows that the landlord recognizes and accepts his responsibility to the child that he and Mrs. Copee have conceived, while the film also acknowledges the broader context of informal and red-lining housing discrimination, which had led to disastrous black property and wealth disadvantage. The landlord comes to the realization that "he is just a clueless white tourist in the black experience, and doesn't belong," as the film critic John Patterson puts it.[101] In contrast to Jewison and Styron's white-knows-best ethnocentrism in the *Confessions* project, what emerges from the production and text on *Landlord*, channeled through the white protagonist, is a self-awareness of the damage performed by white liberalism.

Such housing discrimination was affecting not just working-class blacks such as the Copees but also the growing black middle class and even extended to cross-over black stars. Substantiating *Watermelon Man*'s "move out, nigger" critique, Harry Belafonte recalls trying to rent an apartment in well-heeled neighborhoods of Manhattan a few years earlier and repeatedly being rejected by racist landlords.[102] Jim Brown, a year after starring in the hit film *Dirty Dozen* and the year *Landlord* was made, describes being denied in his attempts to buy an apartment in Cleveland near his training ground: "You've earned the money to buy yourself a better home in a better residential area, and you haven't even signed the papers before the word gets out and white people start running before they'd live near you. The poor, ignorant type? No! Your better-class white people. The people who in another setting would smile to see their kids rushing you for autographs."[103] Brown's "better-class white people" are the kind lampooned in *The Landlord*, as when Elgar's upper-class mother (Lee Grant) comments in response to accusations by her son that she is racist, "Didn't we all go together to see *Guess Who's Coming to Dinner?*"—curiously reminiscent of Jewison's comment "Didn't they know where I stood on race?" Indeed, all four films thematically challenge powerful limits-of-tolerance justifications of glaring and continued racial inequalities in housing, employment, business, and wealth.

■ ■ ■

The period 1968–1970 was one of high levels of institutional and aesthetic autonomy within the U.S. film industry, and this autonomy was strikingly evident in film projects concerned with race. This chapter has described the push-and-pull factors that brought about the belated arrival of black filmmakers into the industry at this moment of possibility and the whites who either thwarted or aided their journey. Some of the white makers of race-themed films continued to compartmentalize production from text in ways that suggested a kind of backlash to anything that implied a more vigorous racial equality. Other white symbol creators did see the complex interconnections between racial working environments and filmic outcomes that were clearly evident to black filmmakers. Together, key white and black filmmakers of this period produced challenging, comic, credibly located films that formally and thematically lampooned retreatist-liberal sensibilities, particularly in the areas of work and wealth. The new black filmmakers in this story, even though they may have been neophytes in filmmaking, were steeped in a civil rights and collectivist consciousness that linked race and labor mobilizations. This experience furnished them with a sophisticated sense of cinema's power relations, which they brought to the films and their making.

However, the fledgling cross-racial and often leftist filmmaking alliances considered in this chapter remained far removed from the film industry's big management and big labor. At the same time as these individual race-oriented film packages were being developed, bringing a few minority workers and trainees onto sets, the federal government, following the Civil Rights Act, briefly mounted a top-down challenge to the structural racism in motion pictures. It targeted employment at the studios and in the technical and craft unions, over which the filmmakers described in this chapter had no control, despite their best efforts. And so the industry-wide battle for inclusion spread to film management and unions.

3

CHALLENGING JIM CROW CREWS

Federal Activism and Industry Reaction

The arrival of a few black filmmakers in Hollywood at the end of the 1960s, described in chapter 2, was a racial landmark in American cinema, serving to interrupt some white sincere fictions in production processes and film narratives. However, the black people who made these inroads and the white people who supported them were as far from rank-and-file film workers as they were from management executives. They all were, in different ways, part of the black and interracial creative elite—an esteemed pool of symbol creators whom the film industry could readily draw on when it belatedly saw the financial and political potential in black-themed productions. Although these individuals made able efforts to bring in other minority practitioners on particular film packages, their arrival in Hollywood, on its own, could do little to change the racial division of labor at the studios or in the industry's craft unions and talent guilds. To challenge motion picture's pro-white institutional arrangements would take top-down government action. This chapter thus turns to how the federal government, spurred by the black movement and armed with the Civil Rights Act, mounted an extraordinary challenge to discriminatory practices in the film industry's creative and labor classes.

At the heart of this chapter is the dramatic and curiously neglected showdown that occurred when minorities and their federal allies targeted film-industry management and big labor from 1969 to 1972, the early years of affirmative action. As we shall see, the EEOC forced the industry into embarrassing and public self-reckoning on its hiring record. But in doing so, it set off powerful counterdiscourses and counteractions. In a move already foregrounded in this book—and much repeated thereafter—management touted the success of a black film star, Sidney Poitier, and a studio director, Gordon Parks, as evidence of the new era of racial meritocracy. By lionizing these individuals, the industry would suggest that interventionist measures were unnecessary.

The import of this story travels beyond the film sector to the nation as a whole. The industry, led by the MPAA and its corporate head, Jack Valenti, came to intervene in national race politics, lobbying effectively against antiracist reform efforts while ably propagating "neoconservative" discourses to face down state intervention (except in the area of government subsidies for film companies). This struggle was influenced by two trends that militated against a successful outcome for black film workers. The first was the financial crisis in the industry. Having suffered declining ticket sales, profitability, and job prospects across the 1960s, the industry went into full-on recession just at the moment when the antiracist project mounted its concerted challenge against discrimination, making white resistance to diversification only more intense. As Sidney Poitier remarked, "Things were starting to get better and then the bottom fell out of the industry."[1] The second, more far-reaching contextual development was the growing anti-affirmative-action and anti-black-power discourses in mainstream political culture. Although some white film executives, technicians, and union locals supported affirmative-action targets, most did not. Indeed, the backlash in Hollywood management, which pitted labor against minorities in a story of aggressive corporate maneuvering, and among some in the craft unions explored in this chapter came notably early in the gestation of these anti-affirmative-action discourses and policies. This pivotal industry played not just a reflective role but also a significant formative role in the national turn against racial justice.

The EEOC Goes to Hollywood

When the Civil Rights Act of 1964 came into effect in the summer of 1965, backed by the increasingly assertive freedom movement, it paved the way for action. Title VII was the historic section of the Civil Rights Act legislation that outlawed employment discrimination on the basis of an "individual's race, color, religion, sex, or national origin" and created the EEOC to enforce the new law.[2] This legislation created an unprecedented resource for those with grievances to seek justice. But antiracist activists knew that Title VII was deeply contested and "not self-enforcing," as Herbert Hill, the NAACP's labor secretary, wrote to branch presidents in 1965.[3] It would take great efforts to turn these formal rights into concrete outcomes. As the historian Nancy MacLean writes, "No one really knew the full magnitude of the task ahead or the practical steps needed to end racial exclusion. People had the text of the law, but few guideposts for implementing it."[4] Workers in particular employment sectors, aided by the labor departments of the NAACP and the Urban League, quickly started working out steps to begin challenging whites-only workplaces. An important early step following the passage of the legislation in 1964 was to ask companies to start producing statistics of minority employment rates, and so some of the major film studios began submitting numbers of African Americans on the payroll in 1965 (other racial groups were added to this payroll audit in 1968, when data would also first be produced by films' craft unions).[5] The figures were patchy and submitted to the AMPTP on a voluntary basis, but the introduction of such audits was a necessary building block toward the goal of greater accountability and inclusion.

However, as chapter 1 detailed, the film industry didn't take the early audit results seriously as evidence that it needed to make change. The industry was therefore in for a shock when the government mounted its challenge in the late 1960s, taking action at both state and federal levels. First, the New York State Division of Human Rights scrutinized employment practices in the New York film sector in 1968. Following evidence from executives, actors, union heads, and technicians based in New York, the committee found that the industry was contravening equal opportunity under state law.[6] Then in March 1969 it was Hollywood's turn to be probed. The EEOC committee held three days of hearings in Los Angeles, targeting sectors with the greatest discrepancy between the number of minorities available in the workforce in the area and their representation in a given industry. We "tried to isolate some [industries] that were particularly venal, if you will, in their practices via those statistics," explained the EEOC head Clifford Alexander.[7] One day was devoted to the motion-picture business in Los Angeles, questioning the major studios' labor-relations executives and craft-union heads. Armed with a mountain of complaints filed by aspiring and actual minority film workers, the five-member EEOC committee focused on hiring and promotion practices. At the close of the Hollywood hearing, the EEOC's general counsel, Daniel Steiner, stated that the testimony had uncovered "gross underutilization" of minority workers in the film business and "recruiting systems that have as their foreseeable effect the employment only of whites." While exposing underrepresentation of all minority groups and women, the EEOC's heaviest focus was on African Americans, reflecting the particular salience of Title VII for black people. The unequal hiring system was "completely accepted by industry and the unions," Steiner's summary read. He concluded: "I think we have established on the record today clear evidence of a pattern or practice of discrimination in violation of Title VII of the Civil Rights Act of 1964."[8]

The hearing set off a four-month investigation into the Los Angeles film industry, the findings from which led the Justice Department to take the extraordinary step of preparing lawsuits under Title VII against practically the entire industry: the AMPTP; six of the seven major film studios represented by the MPAA (Warner Bros.–Seven Arts, Twentieth Century-Fox, Columbia, Walt Disney, Paramount, and Metro-Goldwyn-Mayer); the film industry's technical labor-union umbrella organization, the IATSE; and a considerable number of technical- and craft-union locals.[9] This was a high moment in the struggle for minority jobs in cinema. Had the Justice Department's case gone to trial, it would have been the first industry-wide trial of discrimination in America since the Civil Rights Act was passed.

The figures for minority employment at the major studios in the late 1960s revealed stark levels of exclusion, with behind-the-scenes utilization of blacks, Latinxs, and other minorities well below the average rates for industries in the Los Angeles area, as detailed in chapter 1. Questioned by the EEOC head Clifford Alexander at the hearing, labor-relations executive Arthur Schaefer from Warner Bros.–Seven Arts, the company that had just finished making *Learning Tree*, stated that of the eighty-one officials and managers at his company, one was African American. On further questioning, he admitted that this individual headed the janitorial department of a studio building—indicative of how the vast majority of minority employees at the studios worked in low-end service divisions as cleaners and messengers. In an unguarded moment that followed, Schaefer agreed that his studio's employment-opportunity program was "pretty dismal."[10] The executives' testimony exposed compelling evidence of the industry's attitudes and practices, which minority workers had long been lambasting. At some studios, such as notoriously conservative Walt Disney, there was no African American manager, official, or technician in the late 1960s. The exchange between Alexander and Disney personnel manager Kenneth Sieling ran: " 'How many officials and managers do you have at Walt Disney now?' . . . 'A total of 238.' 'Of that number how many are black?' 'We have no black employees.' " Asked about the 157 technicians, Sieling replied, "We reported 'no black.' "[11]

The partial exception to lily-white employment practices was Universal, the largest studio. It was the only one of the seven majors that had started not to refer all applicants to closed-shop union locals. It instead made some use of the new legislation that allowed studios, when unions failed to include any minorities in lists of potential applicants, to look beyond the locals for personnel. At Universal, fifteen African Americans were in permanent employment in white-collar jobs (many in clerical areas of the television divisions) by the end of 1968.[12] However, no studio, including Universal, had ever appointed any nonwhites into decision-making positions in their corporate corridors, the EEOC hearing revealed. To the knowledge of the studio representatives who gave evidence, summarized the *Hollywood Reporter* after the hearing, "there had never been any blacks or Mexican-Americans on any studio board of directors or in any policy-making position."[13]

The EEOC found that the film industry's craft unions were by and large no better than the studios because they were built on the "experience roster system," as explained in chapter 1. There were exceptions. They included the Los Angeles Costumers Local, which had 20 percent minority members in its nine-hundred-member workforce, with three Latinxs serving on its executive board. Costumers was an unusually capacious local, including skilled costume-house employees as well as laundry workers and some laborers and janitors, which explains in part its much higher minority representation.[14] But in most of the traditional and prestige crafts, white male opportunity hoarding was standard. As the industry journalist Vance King summarized, "There is no doubt that Hollywood contains father–son, uncle–nephew and other virtually hereditary rosters and prospective rosters of membership."[15] Indeed, the EEOC probe found that this nepotism was maintained not just through informal networks but also through formal union admissions procedures. The membership application forms for IATSE, the powerful union consortium that covered all the film-industry technical crafts, regularly included the question, "What type of vocation did your father and/or guardian pursue for a livelihood?"[16] This question held depressing echoes of the Jim Crow grandfather clauses (discriminatory practices that denied suffrage to black citizens based on the rights of their forebears). Put on the spot by the EEOC committee at the hearing, Josef Bernay, representing IATSE, attempted to explain the purpose of the application question and in doing so communicated gendered as well as racial possessive investments: "Maybe for background purposes as far as, let's say, persons who are engineers, and then maybe his son becomes one, or a person is an artist and the son takes the artistic trend, something similar to that, so maybe his background is more imbued with more knowledge so he is more apt to know about it."[17] Such hiring questions not only ran afoul of Title VII but also contravened the National Labor Relations Act of 1935.

Given the deep, state-sanctioned legacies of racism and exclusion, the persisting underrepresentation of blacks, Latinxs, Asian Americans, and Native Americans (and of all women) in this and other industries in the years immediately following the passage of the Civil Rights Act was hardly surprising. Building a minority presence within film's "communities of practice," as Downing and Husband call them,[18] was always going to take some time as procedures were implemented and personnel identified and trained. Union seniority arrangements and informal practices were means of channeling closely protected job openings to their own members and community, renewing the labor pool through the employment of kin and those in the kinship network. As the EEOC's Clifford Alexander explained, the genesis of this system "wasn't directly to keep Chicanos and blacks out; it was to include relatives and those in an in-group."[19] Alexander describes a process of white opportunity hoarding that points to the complexities and challenges of affirmative action, especially for an industry built on informal hiring patterns—even without the added impediment of white racism in practices and procedures.

In its probe of Hollywood labor, the EEOC focused on technical workforces rather than on the talent guilds. The latter included the Directors Guild of America, the Screen Writers Guild, and the Screen Actors Guild, whose workers contributed artistic skills to the industry. Unlike technical-craft workers, whose wages were set directly through collective bargaining, creatives were normally employed for each project under the terms of individual rather than collective contracts, often negotiated by their agents. This individualized employment structure and heavier emphasis on artistic skills made these areas harder to regulate, which helps explain why the EEOC didn't target them. The Writers Guild had set up a Negro writers' workshop in the mid-1960s, perhaps to ward off government intervention, but nevertheless remained overwhelmingly white (and remains so to this day).[20]

Things were also "pretty dismal" at the Directors Guild. Minority pipelines into directing were practically nonexistent, and access had been further blocked when in 1967 the guild introduced requirements that restricted the hiring of new assistant directors and unit production managers to those individuals with four years of college or equivalent. It thus became more difficult for nonelite novices, including minority ones, to gain access.[21] In the Screen Actors Guild, minorities had long been doing relatively better because, of course, they were the film workers who were on display in the products manufactured. With the rising salience of minority-themed films, there were some pull factors stoking labor demand. The divide between the struggle for jobs and the struggle for representation—used as a central analytic relationship in this book—overlaps in the case of screen performers. With industry pressure to diversify and to be seen to diversify, employing more minority actors was preferable to integrating behind-the-scenes workforces. Integration of the cast represented minority employment to appease the activists, less-stringent roster systems to negotiate, opportunities to project marketable minority themes, and more "screen speaks for itself" amplifications of color-blind industry rhetoric.[22] Nevertheless, the great majority of lead film roles were still given to white men, and whites were very overrepresented in the overall cast diversity of mainstream films.

Commentators at the time condemned the consequent "near-total freezeout" of new workers, especially nonwhite ones, in the craft unions and talent guilds.[23] By using their position to benefit family, friends, and acquaintances, craft unions and talent guilds tended to reproduce a racially homogenous workforce, which the studios had made very little attempt to contest. As the black commentator Charles Allen, who had been involved in minority training in the film industry, remarked tartly, "If labor unions provide Jim Crow crews, management has an option to insist on integrated ones—but doesn't."[24] As a consequence, the EEOC committee was equally emphatic in placing blame on labor and management. The committee reported that it had "heard no testimony that there is any intention to change the system" despite the flagrant discrimination in recruiting processes exposed by the hearing.[25] The committee had seen no evidence of the great efforts that industry whites claimed to be making on behalf of blacks. The hearing exposed these efforts as (perhaps sincere) fictions. Paying lip service to liberal principles, producing a few racially integrated films, and holding well-publicized meetings with the NAACP apparently sufficed.

What was shockingly revealed in the testimony of the studios' labor-relations managers and of IATSE representative Josef Bernay was that they seemed to have very little knowledge of affirmative-action procedures or even the broad implications of the Civil Rights Act. No company had a written affirmative-action policy even by 1969.[26] As *Variety* reported, "What really tripped up the studio execs was a repeated question about an 'affirmative action plan.' The studio reps, to a man, apparently figured the words were casually phrased. Actually," schooled the industry trade bible, "the expression 'affirmative action' is used in the 1964 law, and on-going programs in other industries utilize the standard nomenclature."[27] It was this combination of white inertia, ignorance, and intractability that explains why, following the hearing, the committee deemed the industry's "pattern or practice of discrimination" to be so egregious as to warrant recommendation that the Justice Department file suit. Hollywood seemed to see itself as outside of the law—with a separate corporate culture and community of practice shielded from both federal law and shifting norms.

Indeed, it was in comparison to other industries that Hollywood came off so badly. Of those industries isolated for the California hearings—aerospace, radio, television, and motion pictures—the latter was the only one, following the federal probe, whose practices were judged venal enough to be referred to the Justice Department. Aside from the arrival of a few feted African American symbol creators (detailed in chapters 1 and 2, mainly based on the East Coast), the film business had shown, even at the height of the antiracist movement, little intention of changing its exclusionary practices. The point to emphasize is that in 1969 the push for enforcement of Title VII was therefore absolutely necessary to change the existing employment pattern.

Management Responds

Following the EEOC hearing, the Justice Department investigators began gathering testimony in the late spring of 1969, poring over union books and studio hiring practices in preparation for a showdown with Hollywood's labor associations and big management—amassing, as one commentator described, "a five-foot shelf of signed affidavits from victims of discrimination."[28] Some whites in corporate Hollywood had been happy to help with fund-raising for the earlier civil rights movement when it had focused on the South, but as the film industry came to be directly targeted, when espoused principles needed to be turned into concrete practices, the terms of engagement shifted dramatically. As Clifford Frazier of the Community Film Workshop would put it emphatically in 1971, some executives "[take] strong public positions in favor of full integration, and contribute heavily to civil rights causes," but "they don't do a thing to cure the ills of their own industry."[29]

Now that the federal government had called them out, management and unions feared that the Justice Department's probe might result in one of the consent decrees that individual employers in other industries were facing around this time. If violated, decrees could hold executives guilty of contempt, leading to punitive court judgments.[30] Hollywood had always had a heightened awareness of its own image and was embarrassed as well as angered by the EEOC's widely publicized findings. The industry was "particularly vulnerable to federal investigators," the trade press pointed out, because "the possibility of national headlines is enormous."[31] However, although in the firing line, the film industry rapidly began to regroup. Indeed, in the wake of the EEOC's assault, both Hollywood management and Republican political leaders seemed to see opportunity. If the EEOC's attack on white privilege in Hollywood was indicative of the period's heightened progressive interventionism, the response from the industry crystalized the gathering forces of backlash.

The EEOC's public hearings in Los Angeles set off an immediate counterattack. After the film industry started its own lobbying effort, EEOC head Clifford Alexander, who had chaired the hearings, was summoned to appear before a Senate justice subcommittee just one week later. At this meeting, he was "subjected to a tongue-lashing," as one journalist described it, by the powerful Senate Republican minority leader Everett Dirksen.[32] The heated exchange between the two showcased the conflicting interpretations of Title VII—the momentous section of the Civil Rights Act that had outlawed employment bias and created the EEOC to enforce the new law. If workers believed they were being discriminated against by employers (governmental and nongovernmental) and labor unions, they could, thanks to Title VII, file a complaint with the federal government. However, this new legislation was deeply contested from its very inception. Indeed, it was Everett Dirksen, as Senate minority leader in 1964, who had extracted important concessions to curtail Title VII's power as the price of his support for the bill's passage. What became known as the "Dirksen amendments," which helped end the longest filibuster (534 hours) in U.S. Senate history, weakened the bill. These restraints deprived the EEOC of the power to issue the "cease-and-desist" orders that could have immediately halted illegal practices of discrimination.[33] Dirksen also won the inclusion of a ban on "preferential treatment" to remedy hiring and promotion imbalances. As Nancy MacLean explains, in the years after the bill's passage, "while seekers of inclusion focused on the spirit of the bill for which they had worked so hard for so many years, the restraints built into Title VII emboldened its critics."[34] The EEOC committee could set the terms of debate in "the spirit of the bill" at public hearings like the one in Hollywood but knew that its demands for compliance were not fully enforceable because of the revisions authored mainly by Dirksen. "We sort of gummed them to death if we could, but we had no enforcement powers," Alexander explained later.[35]

At the Senate subcommittee hearing in 1969, Dirksen stormed: "Stop some of this harassment of the business community . . . like your carnival hearing out there in Los Angeles . . . or I am going to the highest authority in this government to get somebody fired." Responding to Dirksen's emboldened pronouncements about the EEOC's "punitive harassment," Alexander stated that the "people who are being harassed [are] the blacks, Mexican-Americans, and other minorities, who are subjected to segregated housing facilities, hiring, and promotional policies."[36] The subcommittee's chair, Democrat senator Edward Kennedy, stepped in to support Alexander following Dirksen's tirade, telling the EEOC head, "Those who threaten your job because you do it well are going to have trouble getting rid of you."[37] However, a week later, on March 28, President Nixon announced that Alexander would be replaced. His position untenable, Alexander announced his resignation in April, more than two years before he was due to step down as the director of the EEOC. He was replaced by African American EEOC committee member William Brown, who in a press interview at the time described himself as a Republican "all my life."[38] The White House made, at best, a half-hearted attempt to deny the connection between Dirksen's tirade and Alexander's removal. But in a private letter in May 1969, Dirksen boasted about his victory, describing how at the Senate subcommittee hearing he had told Alexander "what an irrational, harassing approach was taken. The next day he resigned as Chairman." The short letter ends: "The President is fully aware of what I am doing and I regard my services to him as extremely helpful." In another private letter concerning "the Los Angeles vendetta and carnival EEOC put on," Dirksen described the federal agency as a "tribe."[39]

Getting rid of Alexander, a Johnson appointee who, as the civil rights historian Hugh Davis Graham states, was "uniformly regarded as exceptionally bright, energetic, and capable," was a victory for anti-affirmative-action Republicans.[40] With Alexander replaced by Brown, the rate at which the EEOC processed complaints dropped sharply. By 1971, the backlog of discrimination complaints stood at around nineteen thousand.[41] The EEOC did continue to achieve some victories, notably the forcing of American Telephone & Telegraph to make a settlement of $15 million to past victims of bias.[42] However, with Brown's appointment, the gathering legislative push to give the EEOC cease-and-desist powers suffered a major setback. In the summer of 1969, the newly promoted Brown, who had previously supported cease and desist, came round to the alternative court-enforcement approach strongly favored by Dirksen. Indeed, Brown actually drafted the court-enforcement counterbill. "I'm very happy that Senator Dirksen . . . is thinking the way I'm thinking," Brown stated, facing difficult questions about his U-turn.[43] The court-enforcement legislation, which involved handing responsibility for federal court action on behalf of complainants to the beleaguered EEOC—thus pushing it into protracted suits that were very difficult to bring to resolution—was, according to Clifford Alexander, "a cruel hoax."[44] The ultimate failure of the cease-and-desist discrimination legislation, strongly pursued by liberals in Congress, civil rights groups, and all the EEOC members except Brown, was a major blow.

Alexander was called to the Senate subcommittee hearing after film-industry complaints about the EEOC hearing "were relayed to" Dirksen, reported the Los Angeles Times staff writer Vincent Burke.[45] It is highly likely that the key "relayer" was Jack Valenti, the dynamic MPAA boss. Headquartered in Washington, D.C., the MPAA represented the business interests of the major studios that had come under attack by the EEOC. Valenti was its leading public-relations spokesperson and lobbyist—"a hard-nosed, charismatic lobbyist for the uninhibited distribution of Hollywood motion pictures stateside and abroad," as the film historian Kevin Sandler describes him.[46] Valenti had arrived at the MPAA direct from the White House, where he had worked for President Johnson coordinating speechwriting and lobbying Congress. Although Valenti retained his close symbolic association with Johnson in his new post, he brokered productive alliances with Republicans. Following Nixon's victory in 1968, he gave an interview to *Variety*: "Valenti Feels Easier in Approaching Republicans [Rather Than Democrats] on Film Trade's Behalf." Published in February 1969, just before the Hollywood hearing, this piece reported that "Valenti considers it fortunate that he counts several top Republicans among his personal friends." One of the two mentioned by name was Everett Dirksen.[47] Valenti would later recall that during his White House days he would "service [Dirksen's] account" with the president and "got to know him famously." "The day would hardly pass without at least one phone call from Dirksen," puffed Valenti.[48] The speed and strength of political reaction to the EEOC hearing in Hollywood was very likely facilitated by the film industry's D.C.-based top representative and his "friendship" with the pro-business Senate minority leader.

"Open Doors"

Whatever complaints Hollywood management quietly relayed to Republican politicians, the luncheon it held just afterward to honor Roy Wilkins, director of the NAACP, was all about publicity. The high-profile event, held in April 1969, was organized by Jack Valenti and attended by many industry executives, journalists, and stars—Roy Wilkins was, for instance, pictured with Julie Andrews in the press coverage.[49] In his opening remarks, Valenti characterized advances in African Americans' participation in the film business as "a curve reaching a new high in a road that is up." He used the example of *Learning Tree*, explored in chapter 2, to support this claim, making the false assertion that of the "47 people working before or behind the camera on the film, all but five [were] black."[50] In fact, as Arthur Schaefer of Warner Bros.–Seven Arts had reported at the EEOC hearing, the film had, in addition to its African American director, twelve black crew members and trainees in areas including assistant cameraman, men's wardrobe stylist, women's hair stylist, lamp operator, painter, transportation driver, publicist, and special photographer.[51] Thus, though the film did represent a landmark in the black struggle for film-industry integration—resulting from the concerted efforts of its black director and white producer—the crew was mainly white. This example indicates how although the first African American studio-made and distributed films discussed in chapter 2 might have disrupted commonsense white perceptions about blacks employability in motion pictures, they were also open to discursive reappropriation by corporate Hollywood at a moment of threatened breach.

The MPAA boss heaped on the flattery as he introduced Wilkins, whom he had known since his White House days: "When it comes to integrity, I know of no better example than Roy Wilkins," who was "one of the great men in this generation." The NAACP leader (a post he held from 1955 to 1977) made a thoughtful speech that included the comment on "educational role" of the entertainment industry in overcoming discrimination, criticizing its "slow pace" of racial progress. However, perhaps buoyed by Valenti's feel-good rhetoric, the moderate NAACP leader was also moved to make positive comments about Hollywood, which gave rise to the *Daily Variety* cover story "Roy Wilkins Praises Pic Biz: NAACP Leader Asserts Film-TV Industry 'Has Done a Very Satisfactory Job.' "[52] Reporting on the lunch, the *Hollywood Reporter* cover-story headline declared "Black Employment Pics, TV Up."[53] Wilkins's apparent public endorsement, even if qualified, represented a coup for industry management just as the Justice Department launched its probe, the headlines helping to repair some of the damage to Hollywood's image inflicted by the widely reported EEOC findings of the previous month.

It is worth noting that Roy Wilkins, writing in *Crisis*, was to condemn the removal of Alexander later that spring, perhaps chagrined by the pro-film-industry headlines he had played a role in generating. "A case of anti-Negro racial policy with a minimum amount of fuzziness has arisen in the Nixon Administration with the resignation of Clifford L. Alexander, Jr. . . . No matter how much gloss is applied, Negro citizens and their allies will remember that Republican Senate leader Everett M. Dirksen of Illinois publicly rebuked Alexander for allegedly 'harassing' businessmen to secure conformity with the 1964 Act outlawing discrimination in employment and threatened to get him fired," read his statement.[54] Despite his broadly centrist politics—notably, his public rejection of Martin Luther King Jr.'s anti–Vietnam War stance and his repudiation of black power—Wilkins maintained a critical stance toward Nixon's civil rights record.[55] Like Alexander, he strongly endorsed the equal-employment record of the Johnson administration, and Valenti's association with the former president no doubt worked to his advantage. As Wilkins reflected, "I met Valenti in Washington, we got to know each other and when he got the new job with the Motion Picture Association he said he would like to have me come out here."[56]

This was the second time Valenti had invited Wilkins to Hollywood. The first came a year earlier in the aftermath of Martin Luther King Jr.'s assassination—another critical moment to showcase the black leader. The film historian Stephen Vaughn describes the savvy Valenti's great facility for cultivating politicians: "His flamboyance and flair for dramatization and hyperbole, his enthusiasm and energy, and his willingness to flatter others effusively all went over well in Hollywood and in Washington, two places where fantasy and politics intermingle."[57] The EEOC committee had recognized that events such as the Wilkins lunch might serve more to legitimate than to trouble the status quo. Alexander had stated at the hearing that the EEOC "gives no points for dinners, Awards, meetings attended, etc."[58] He was only too aware that AMPTP officials, heads of major studios, and union business representatives could use these publicity events as public-relations opportunities, working to contain rather than to enact racial change. The industry's cultivation of Wilkins is indicative of the public co-optation of certain civil rights leaders during this period. After the lunch, Wilkins commented that Valenti had been "very kind and appreciative" but had "made no promises."[59] Thus, within a month or so of the EEOC's journey to Hollywood, one national affirmative-action leader had been removed from federal office and another had been publically positioned to condone the film industry's racial status quo—indicating motion pictures' political power and the virulence of its corporate lobbying and image management.

At the Wilkins lunch, Jack Valenti stated that, "generally speaking, the tendency among creative and executive people is to reach out for new talent and people, and it is most heartening and most important to me because the door is open to the black people without it being forced." After the lunch, Valenti repeated this key public-relations message: "We have the desire to open the door for new Negro talent rather than have someone force it open."[60] This metaphoric refrain was a clear counterproposal to the antidiscrimination initiatives under way: the "someone" trying to "force" matters was the EEOC, the Justice Department, and minorities—especially African Americans. Valenti's discursive sleight of hand is notable: the industry, so recently shown to be an exclusionary bastion of whiteness, was now apparently the moral champion of labor-market equality ("the door is open to the black people") in danger from the coercive threat of the courts. By suggesting that employment discrimination was not a problem, Valenti intimated that statist measures to facilitate racial redistribution of jobs were both unnecessary and illiberal.

Indeed, this was the signature discursive move of what would soon be called racial neoconservatism: the roles of victim and perpetrator—those opening doors or forcing them open—were reversed. Though the term *neoconservatism* did not emerge until several years after Valenti fashioned his anti-affirmative-action metaphor (and remains popularly associated with later conservative trends), it was in the late 1960s that neoconservatism's various discursive contours began to coalesce. As leading neocon proponent Irving Kristol later explained, "Neoconservatism emerged as an intellectual tendency in the late 1960s and 1970s," and the scholar Peter Steinfels concurs, explaining that neoconservatism was "in many ways a product of the sixties."[61] Neoconservatism was the most far-reaching strand of the liberal retreat from race, with influential advocates coming from the right of the Democrat Party (where Valenti publically positioned himself) and the left of the Republican Party. These advocates turned sharply away from the black freedom struggle after the civil rights victories in the mid-1960s that they had formerly supported. The key intellectuals who began propounding the neoconservative racial critique, along with Kristol, senior editor at Basic Books, were the scholar-politician Daniel Patrick Moynihan, the public intellectual Nathan Glazer, and the *Commentary* magazine editor Norman Podhoretz. Moynihan had worked for John Kennedy and Johnson before becoming a close Nixon adviser (a trajectory that mirrors Valenti's). He disseminated the new thinking in high-profile speeches and in a widely leaked memorandum from January 1969 called for a period of noninterventionist "benign neglect" of African America.[62]

As with any "racial project," according to Michael Omi and Howard Winant, neoconservatism was an explanation of racial dynamics that legitimated the organization of resources along particular racial lines.[63] The budding neoconservative interpretation of America as basically nondiscriminatory (with "open doors") legitimated the existing distribution of resources as a route to achieving equality, thus undermining calls for progressive racial redistribution. As Steinfels argues, such neoconservative discourses "vastly overestimate the degree to which meritocratic standards already operate in institutions."[64]

The Hollywood lobby's discrediting of government intervention on behalf of minorities stood in stark disjunction with motion-picture management's petitioning for government intervention on behalf of the industry's business interests at this time. Industry leaders and governor Ronald Reagan pressured the federal government to develop protectionist measures to assist the ailing Southern Californian film industry, and in March 1971 Nixon met with an array of Hollywood leaders, including Valenti and Charlton Heston (a meeting organized by MCA/Universal executive Taft Schreiber, who had headed Nixon's fund-raising campaign for California in the 1968 election).[65] At the meeting in San Clemente, the studio leaders described the film industry's dire financial straits to Nixon, while insisting, as the minutes recorded, that "U.S. films deserve support as they prove U.S. freedom." They lobbied for such measures as federal tax relief and the imposition of import duties on foreign films to enhance their own competitive advantage.[66] "Two major developments assisting recovery [of the film industry] . . . were expedited by the Nixon administration at the urgent request of industry leadership," explains the film historian David Cook: income tax credits on losses, which created profit shelters, and, written back into legislation, an investment tax credit on domestic production.[67] The Revenue Act of 1971, which rapidly followed the Hollywood meeting with Nixon, had a built-in provision to allow for the creation of offshore studio subsidiaries that avoided taxes on profits made from exports if these profits were reinvested in domestic production. These new tax arrangements helped independent film producers, discussed later in this book, as well as large studios. But the fact remains that at the same time as corporate film executives such as Valenti and Heston were rejecting minority "special treatment," they also sought and won their own corporate special treatment through massive government subsidies that funded their domestic and international operations. According to one entertainment lawyer's estimate, the corporate-welfare shelters alone amounted to some $150 million in film funding between 1973 and 1976.[68]

When Charlton Heston, president of the Screen Actors Guild, testified at the New York State Division of Human Rights investigations in 1968, he prefigured Valenti's rhetoric. In trademark style, he amiably discounted the claims made by aspiring minority actors to state regulators who were scrutinizing employment practices in the New York film sector. In answer to the question whether "the movies accurately reflected American life as it is in ethnic composition," he said, "By and large, I think they do."[69] Heston, like his friend Valenti, followed the classic neoconservative trajectory from liberal to conservative in the 1960s. His earlier role in the March on Washington, detailed in the introduction, was important in that it represented an

FIGURE 3.1 Film-industry leaders lobby President Richard M. Nixon at the western White House in San Clemente, California, April 5, 1971. Jack Valenti is seated at the far corner of the table facing the camera.
Source: Courtesy of the Richard Nixon Presidential Library and Museum, Yorba Linda, Calif.

endorsement from the center ground of American culture. Heston was also interested in workers' rights and had spoken out in the early 1960s about the widespread practice of income tax avoidance by Hollywood's top talent, who, making many "runaway" productions overseas, moved their permanent residency abroad to avoid tax.[70] However, despite these progressive imperatives, Heston's shift rightward started a while before his coming out as an energetic "Democrat for Nixon" in 1972.[71] The star stated in his memoir that as early as 1964 he had a moment of conservative awakening ("almost an epiphany") when he saw a billboard for segregationist presidential candidate Barry Goldwater reading, "In your heart, you know he's right." Heston recounts saying to himself, "Son of a bitch . . . he *is* right!"[72] Another signal moment in his conservative turn was the San Clemente meeting between film-industry leaders and Nixon in 1971, resulting in the exceedingly generous Revenue Act. Heston, in fact, had been lobbying politicians, including governor Ronald Reagan, for such subsidies since the mid-1960s as the head of the Screen Actors Guild.[73]

FIGURE 3.2 Charlton Heston and Jack Valenti are among the industry leaders who wait their turn to address President Nixon at San Clemente. The Revenue Act of 1971 that followed this meeting provided government subsidies and tax shelters for the film industry. Heston credits this meeting with helping to trigger his turn to the Republican Party.

Source: Courtesy of the Richard Nixon Presidential Library and Museum, Yorba Linda, Calif.

Heston had also adopted a labor-modernization stance as the president of the Screen Actors Guild from 1965 to 1971 (he was voted in an unprecedented seven times)—prefiguring his later aggressive antiunion activism. When facing questions about unemployment in the guild, he often blamed what he saw as unsustainable wages and conditions of workers in Hollywood that made California uncompetitive. He also remarked, developing his facility for gently pro-corporate utterances, "It seems to me a basic premise of enlightened trade unionism that our prosperity is tied to the prosperity of the industry as a whole."[74]

At this stage, the Screen Actors Guild president was distancing himself from the black struggle while still trying to draw on its moral capital in decidedly conservative terms. At a dinner honoring Coretta Scott King in 1969, eighteen months after her husband's assassination, Heston's introductory speech captured his repudiation of collective action and black power: "I believe in great men. I think most of the important work in the world is done by great men. Now that's not a fashionable opinion these days. We live in the age of the common man, the age of the victim." His masculinist and individualist critique of the apparently celebrated common man, whose work should be judged as "unimportant," jarred with his role as the representative of eighteen thousand actors, whose remuneration rates differed vastly between a few Heston-style self-employed stars and vast numbers of under-employed and under-remunerated actors. Moreover, his statement was also of course diametrically opposed to the organizing efforts of the Southern Christian Leadership Conference and its slain leader, whose Poor People's Campaign and organizing efforts during the sanitation workers' strike in Memphis the previous year envisaged a transracial movement of the poor. Heston's "great man" speech offers another early example of Hollywood's powerful domestication of the King project. Doubling down, Heston described black nationalists as "tiny, bitter men who stand shouting in the void [King] left behind him"—words redolent of William Styron's tirade (quoted in chapter 2). He added, "You get nothing from decent men with threats, except their anger"—thus mobilizing provocative backlash discourses about the limits of white tolerance.[75] Heston's journal account of this part of his speech showed that it clearly pleased him: "I made my point about black racism . . . to applause."[76]

Where Emilie Raymond and Steven Ross, in their detailed scholarly accounts of Heston, correctly read the star's speeches and actions at this time as consistent with the later rehabilitation of conservatism, they seem in part to support the self-construction of the neoconservatives as "liberal[s] mugged by reality," in Irving Kristol's famous phrase. Kristol implies that neoconservatives basically stayed constant during the 1960s and early 1970s as the Democratic Party, the New Left, the antiwar movement, and the freedom struggle radicalized, bringing America's turmoil and trouble with them.[77] But this reading, which certainly fits with Heston's own enduring self-construction as a reasonable-sounding pragmatist occupying the center ground, misunderstands the racial project of neoconservatism around the turn of the 1970s. As many scholars have shown, the neoconservatives were, along with Heston's friend William Buckley, early architects of the conservative revolution. They found a new centrist-sounding language to mobilize a wholesale assault on workers and minorities, laying the groundwork for the inequality economics and depleted democracy to come. Heston, like the other neoconservatives, was not politically constant during the 1960s but instead was turning into a powerful conservative communicator, preparing the discursive field for what Nancy Maclean explores as "the radical right's stealth plan for American."[78] Race was a powerful component of this field. Heston's speech at the dinner for Coretta King (as in Valenti's lunch for Wilkins) is in fact evidence not of his continuing commitment to the freedom struggle, but, by contrast, of his backlash against King's project. He was using King to progress laissez-faire, pro-business conservatism through the story of an individual "great man" (which reflexively, of course, refers also to Heston himself) who had apparently settled the racial-justice question back in the mid-1960s. Heston, like Valenti, increasingly backed pro-management discourses and stridently anticollectivist rhetoric that coalesced with his evolving white-patriarchal screen image.[79]

The affable, racially meritocratic language—Valenti's characterization of the industry's "open doors" and his friend Heston's proposition that movie screens are "by and large" racially representative—stood in rhetorical contrast to the response of Hollywood's union leaders to the EEOC charges. IATSE head Richard Walsh, the industry's top union boss, sounded much more racially trenchant, rejecting the EEOC's "biased and false report." In a *Hollywood Reporter* cover story titled "Walsh Rips Race Bias Charge: IATSE Topper Blisters Detractors for Own Bias," he asserted that there was "no discrimination in any of the laws and policy of the IATSE, and where any charges are made we intend to defend the IA to the extreme."[80] In contrast to management's soft-power approach, the craft unions took "a barely-disguised racist position," according to Cliff Frazier.[81]

Although the tones differed sharply, the content of the statements by management and union bosses were more or less the same: a denial of discrimination and a defense of the realm. Studio management, however, saw the strategic advantage of creating distance between itself and labor by exploiting the latter's more embattled tone. A *Los Angeles Times* article in October 1969 titled "Film Executive Blames Hiring Bias on Unions" typified management's public-relations framing. The piece quotes the industrial-relations director for Columbia Pictures, Howard Fabrick: "I'm the last guy in the world who would try to maintain that Hollywood has clean hands in the question of minority group employment. But it's not the fault of the studios. The real question for the Justice Dept to handle is challenging a union seniority structure that has for twenty years prohibited a studio in hiring in the manner it might, in all good conscience, want to."[82] The disarming phrase "last guy in the world" directs attention away from the stark moral order emphasized in the statement: the unions have dirty hands, whereas the studios have a "good conscience." Heston later reiterated this false narrative: "Though the actors, writers, and directors had been historically almost totally free of bias, the technical unions had up until that time been closed shop."[83] As Clifford Alexander later remarked, "All that violently opposing [by the unions] was exactly the same as the polite corporate executive who has all the lingo down but still doesn't employ or doesn't promote [minorities]."[84]

The aggressively anti-affirmative-action position of some of the unions in Hollywood fed into the increasingly negative image of organized labor. This was a time when, as scholars have stressed, the class interests of working people, constructed as "heavies," were beginning to be systematically repudiated by both business and political elites.[85] The economist Robert Brenner influentially dated to this moment the very beginning of the U.S. "long downturn," characterized by sharp falls in profits, growth, and productivity, leading to periods of recession that brought wage cuts and unemployment.[86] Although these trends in most industries did not fully set in until around 1973, in the film industry they had started earlier, during the 1960s. Overall U.S. employment rates, which had risen consistently over the course of the 1960s, started to fall in 1969, but by that year film-industry jobless rates were already soaring.[87] The overcapacity, technological changes, and internationalizing trends that Brenner suggests were responsible for the nation-wide recession were already causing crises in cinema in the late 1960s, leading to flexible specialization and the rapid corporate restructuring of takeovers and mergers (described in chapter 2).[88] Thus, while other industries, in the economic historian Judith Stein's words, continued "to live complacently with postwar assumptions" into the 1970s, the film industry did not.[89] Falling profits (resulting from long-term declining ticket sales with the rise of television) meant that Hollywood corporates were already regrouping. Using race as a wedge in labor disputes was one tactic they quickly latched onto.

Overriding all other considerations in its battle with the Justice Department, studio management in 1970 sought to avoid the threatened suit. As late as the fall of 1969, the department notified the industry that it was seeking a consent decree to prevent discrimination by management and labor, which could have led to court convictions.[90] In an ironic turn, however, the pressure on unions to integrate their labor force and the attention directed onto IATSE's business agents to explain potential violations could be used to aid management's primary struggle. Such measures deflected attention from studio hiring practices, and there were other potentially unintended opportunities. If unions were forced by government agencies to open their hiring halls to minorities, it might help dismantle the crafts' good wages and strong bargaining position, maintained by restrictions on labor supply and criticized by the likes of Heston and Valenti.[91]

Following protracted negotiations in Hollywood and the industry's aggressive lobbying and public-relations campaigns, the Justice Department finally announced in April 1970 that it was backing down. It dropped its threatened legal action and agreed instead to a two-year voluntary process of minority training and hiring—a settlement in essence devised by the industry. Paralleling the resolution of the Philadelphia Plan episode—where construction-industry race targets were all but abandoned following an abrupt shift in government policy—a conciliatory Justice Department settled on the ambitious-sounding but nonbinding goal of 20 percent minority employment in the film business. The dispute was, reported Dave Kaufman in *Variety*, "resolved in a manner sought by the industry" because the targets were not to be enforced. After the one- or two-year terms, the studios and unions could resume operations as they had before the agreement. "While no one involved claimed any victory, and the official release was couched in diplomatic terms, there is no question that government acceptance of the voluntary agreement represents a triumph for the industry," wrote Kaufman.[92] To meet the voluntary targets, studios were asked to employ more minorities mainly in clerical and administrative roles (a clear win for the studios). Brought into line by the AMPTP, all of the studios came round, at least rhetorically, to endorse these temporary targets—even Walt Disney and Twentieth Century-Fox, the two majors that had initially refused to cooperate with the federal investigators.[93]

Hollywood's craft unions got to retain their seniority roster system. But because they had somewhat tougher targets than those stipulated for the studios, they were asked to set up minority labor pools from which, for a limited period, a minimum of 20 percent of union referrals to the studios should come. The agreement also asked craft unions to set up a program to train seventy minority members in various crafts. Even though these targets were short term and nonbinding, Hollywood unions were still by no means fully on board.

Labor Responds

Nancy MacLean's chapter title "From 'Massive Resistance' to 'Color-Blindness'" in *Freedom Is Not Enough* captures the broad trajectory of conservative racial politics from the 1960s to the 1970s.[94] But in some quarters of film-industry labor, massive resistance never really dissipated. During the two years when the settlement terms were in place, many rank-and-file union members were openly hostile to the racial targets—angered and aggrieved about the idea of training new minority workers to join their close-knit ranks. The union executives at IATSE, which together with the AMPTP had negotiated hard with the federal government, basically went along with the voluntary targets once the favorable deal was struck. But the settlement's terms of placing and training minority workers had to be operationalized farther down the chain in the union locals. "Strictly focusing on the summit is liable to suggest that a change of attitudes at that level would solve the problems of racism in media," warn Downing and Husband, who stress that any analysis of change to employment relations has also to attend to on-the-ground working codes and practices.[95] The nine union locals singled out for special attention by the Justice Department were Cameramen Local 659, Costumers Local 705, Film Editors Local 776, Grips Local 80, Laborers Local 727, Lamp Operators Local 728, Makeup Local 706, Propmen Local 44, and Soundmen Local 695.[96] On the ground, the business representatives and technical workers of these locals were tasked with implementing the targets; they held a range of views, and some pushed back against the targets in toxic ways.

Achieving racial change in these Hollywood locals might have been easier had the film industry not gone into full recession in the last quarter of 1968, just before the EEOC hearing. Profits had been declining for nearly two decades by the turn of the 1970s, due in large part to dropping attendance at movie theaters in the age of television. In 1969, the motion-picture industry experienced a convulsion. United Artists suffered the biggest loss of $85 million, followed by MGM, $72 million, and Twentieth Century-Fox, $65 million. Columbia came close to going into receivership.[97] Soaring unemployment rates were worsened by the accelerating trend of American films being made abroad, where production costs were lower. While 40 percent of American-produced films were "runaways" in the mid-1950s, this portion had jumped to 65–70 percent by the late 1960s.[98] Thus, it was a cruel coincidence that at the very moment of some movement against discriminatory practices in Hollywood, jobs were in short supply. As Judith Stein explains, state antidiscrimination policies "worked best when supported by the strong labor demands of growing industries"[99]—the opposite of conditions in the film business from 1969 to 1974. Film-industry unemployment was also structural. Ever since the collective-bargaining disputes of the activist 1940s, employers had won the demand that all locals have enough technicians on their rosters to be able to supply labor needs at peak production. This requirement led to many craft unions having surplus workers. In 1970, around 43 percent of all the film and television industries' workforce (approximately fourteen thousand people) were without work.[100] The federal government could have had some influence over the demand for minority workers via the settlement, but it had no leverage over job supply. One union executive explained the zero-sum terms in which his white members viewed the settlement: "Experienced vets would be expected to teach minority workers jobs so that they could replace the veterans."[101]

Despite endemic job insecurity, it is worth emphasizing that some locals in Hollywood tried to comply with the settlement's terms. The Soundmen, Costumers, Cameramen, and Film Editors Locals demonstrated a degree of racial openness, in part predicated on the realization that going along with these nonbinding and limited-term conditions was not onerous.[102] The Cameramen Local displayed the most robust support for the federal action. Its business representative, Doyle Nave, explained that "we signed the agreement in good faith with the Justice Department, first obtaining approval from our executive board, then presenting it to the membership at a meeting, where they voted in favor of the action taken by their business agent."[103] Such deliberation by leaders and members, leading to democratic decision making at the local level, offers a model of how to foster buy-in from members in order to operationalize employment targets. More evidence of racial openness came from the business representative for Laborers Local 727, Orval Brown, who defended the policy of employing minority summer workers even in the face of opposition from other unions. Equally, the Costumers Local, as detailed earlier, had "a good record" of minority employment, according to Clifford Alexander, and its business representative, William Howard, had declared his support for the EEOC's work.[104] Some white workers and union leaders thus embraced a more social activist unionism. As

Peter Levy stresses in his monograph *The New Left and Labor in the 1960s*, labor at the end of this decade was contradictory and ambivalent rather than monolithically inflexible and protectionist, as it is usually described.[105]

Nonetheless, inflexibility remained the dominant posture, with many white craft workers and their representatives deeply antagonistic toward civil rights implementation. This was evident in the most short-term, low-status employment roles even before the settlement. In the summer of 1969—following the EEOC hearing but before the Justice Department agreement—IATSE Laborers Local 724 protested against initiatives by Metro-Goldwyn-Mayer to hire just six minority workers to its summer program as part of a drive to help local youth. The union's business representative, Richard Jarrard, who headed the protest, had managed to overturn the modest program the previous summer. Similar protests from union locals attended Universal's attempts at hiring for its minority summer program, claiming that the hiring was against labor regulations.[106]

Cliff Frazier explains that in the face of union rigidity the new black filmmakers who were attempting to persuade unions to take on nonwhite trainees, including some from his Community Film Workshop, tended to argue in terms of mutual benefit. Rather than appealing to social conscience, which often didn't work, he would try to leverage the new commercial interest in black-oriented film to get the unions on board. His pitch to them was "to exchange jobs for union cards": "If we're going to hire your people, you're going to hire our people."[107] Following this logic, when Harry Belafonte and Chiz Schultz started preproduction on *The Angel Levine* in 1968 and wanted to bring on minority trainees, they submitted an apprentice program proposal to the unions to take on a number of interns. However, as Belafonte explained, the unions "not only rejected [the proposal] but . . . rejected it belligerently," capturing the hostility of many back-lot craftspersons at the time.[108] When the Ford Foundation went on to accept Belafonte and Schultz's apprentice proposal, they were able to employ fourteen interns (two Hispanic and twelve black) to assist on the production.

However, the white crew continued to be hostile, even though the apprentices were shadowing—not replacing—them and were not being subsidized by the unions. According to Belafonte, "The first couple of weeks on set, it was hell. The [interns] were not allowed to touch anything, they were not allowed to participate in any way under the threat of having the union walk out. . . . The kids just stood silently up against the wall, some of them with note pads, they said nothing." Things improved as the shoot progressed: "During coffee breaks the [interns would] bump into the union guys, and a black guy'd be holding a cup ... and this dialogue began to develop, and eventually the program was accepted by the union."[109] Thus, time and exposure eventually led the white crew members to recognize the interns and begin to share some skills. But, it must be remembered, this project was produced and funded by HarBel, the film-production element of Belafonte Enterprises, and shot in Harlem just after King's assassination—that is to say, the project would not have been green-lit and underemployed white union workers would not have been hired without the creative, financial, and political impetus of its African American producer-star.[110] Even under the watchful eyes of Schultz and Belafonte on a film about the need for interracial comity at a time of crisis, white workers were still very reluctant to open up to minority apprentices. More bleakly, perhaps it was precisely the idea of a black producer that stoked the white workers' resentment. This example, despite Belafonte's ultimately positive spin, suggests a pessimistic outlook for the diversification of the craft unions' communities of practice.

Following the Justice Department settlement, some union locals ramped up their resistance to antidiscrimination efforts. The Group for Union Equality (GUE) was formed, seeking to challenge "the legality of the racial hiring agreement as hurtful to Caucasians," summarized Variety's business writer Dave Kaufman.[111] Of the nine IATSE locals highlighted in the agreement with the Justice Department, five openly mobilized behind the GUE: Grips, Laborers, Lamp Operators, Makeup, and Propmen.[112] "We are fighting with the strength of rank and file members, and we have their backing," declared Allen Hill of the Propmen Local, one of the GUE leaders, stressing grassroots resistance concentrated in the lower-skilled crafts.[113] The GUE used litigation to thwart the regulators, mounting a class-action suit on the grounds that the agreement was unconstitutional and violated the Civil Rights Act. "We feel that the outrageous demands of the Justice Dept. are in direct opposition to the premise of Title VII of the Civil Rights Act which provides that there be no discrimination in employment and upgrading because of race, color, creed, national origin or sex," stated Hill.[114] Given the embattled language of white victimization, it is important to remember that the terms of the agreement were voluntary and temporary due to the powerful lobbying and negotiation by the AMPTP, the MPAA, and IATSE. GUE's class-action suit was ultimately unsuccessful. However, the litigation dragged on for many months and was unquestionably an effective strategy in forestalling the drive for fair employment that was already losing political steam in national politics.

By invoking the terms of Title VII to defend white workers as victims of discrimination, the GUE offered a trenchant, early example of *reverse-discrimination* politics that would become very powerful thereafter. It developed both the rhetoric and, through litigation, the policies of this emergent political project. "Minorities are receiving 'special privileges,'" accused the laborers local business agent Donald Zimmerman, while white "industry workers are not obtaining equal opportunity—ironic since the avowed purpose of the program is to establish equal opportunity for minorities."[115] Such claims totally discounted the fact that for hundreds of years, through slavery and Jim Crow, whites had been the official beneficiaries of a preferential racial employment system. It also ignored continuing entrenched and pervasive exclusion.

Responding to the GUE's reverse-discrimination accusations, the Justice Department pointed out that this type of minority settlement had been approved in other industries across the country. But the attorney for GUE, David Daar, contended (paraphrased by a reporter) that "a 'pat' formula introduced elsewhere successfully cannot apply when one deals with a depressed industry, [and] that instead something fitting the mold of the film industry should be devised because the industry's situation is unique."[116] Film workers constructed their depressed labor market as exceptional and their industry as above the normal law. GUE's powerful reverse-discrimination cries—in tandem with the corporate statements about "open doors" described earlier—were believed by many white film workers. As media scholars Downing and Husband explain, "Given the fierce competitiveness of the industry, there is a great deal of resistance to any sort of 'leg-up' in employment that is perceived not to be based on merit, indeed to anything that could be dismissed as 'affirmative action.'"[117] However, such white workers denied their own racialized advantages—even when compelling arguments were put forward in a moment of heightened antiracist activism—which amounted at a structural level to white (male) affirmative action. As the sociologist Deirdre Royster found in her study *Race and the Invisible Hand: How White Networks Exclude Black Men from Blue-Collar Jobs*, the greatest cause of differential work trajectories of black and white men is at the level of access to the contacts and networks that help in the job search-and-entry process (that is to say, precisely the "leg-up" stage, casually and routinely enjoyed by white men).[118]

As the historian Trevor Griffey argues, the arrival of organized resistance to affirmative action in employment is often dated to around 1980, when Ronald Reagan was elected president. However, there was actually "no heyday for attempts by federal regulatory agencies to impose affirmative action on US industry," states Griffey. Opposition from labor unions emerged "well before the more overt backlash against affirmative action became ascendant in the US political culture of the 1980s and 1990s."[119] The case of film labor bears this out. By challenging both the legality and the fairness of affirmative action, such "new right" film-industry activism fomented backlash politics and successfully constrained federal agents' ability to enforce new civil rights laws long before 1980. As with the MPAA's anti-EEOC lobbying of Everett Dirksen, the GUE reached out beyond the film industry. To build political traction for its attacks on minority hiring, it sent communiqués to politicians, including Senator George Murphy and Governor Ronald Reagan—both actors and erstwhile film-industry union leaders turned high-profile Republicans.[120] Conservative politicians were then just beginning to "romance the new right worker," in Jefferson Cowie's phrase, electrified by George Wallace's antigovernment, race-baiting platform in the 1968 election (when he had won 13.5 percent of the national vote), from which Nixon and other Republicans, including Reagan, learned a great deal.[121] The new coalescence between blue-collar whites and the Republican Party that helped to consecrate the move rightward in the years that followed was in part gestated in the film industry.

For union locals asked to work toward targets that they didn't believe in, it was easy to sabotage the minority labor-pool program. For instance, by hiring underqualified minorities they could tick the numeric boxes requested by the Justice Department. But then they could give the new workers none of the support needed to make a success of the traineeships. Indeed, it was often grist to the mill of white-worker racism if the trainees underperformed because of the lack of training and were humiliated in the process. Cliff Frazier explained that the minority program was "set up to fail" because people were just "pushed into jobs" rather than "a setup [being used] by which you are able to choose people."[122] The experience of many young aspirant minority workers must have been a bitter one when even under the stewardship of someone like Harry Belafonte they were left to languish on the sidelines. As in the case of the construction workers in the Philadelphia Plan, many whites simply refused to teach black apprentices, and because implementation of the settlement was voluntary, they were free not to meet the goals.

Once the minority labor targets (which in many cases weren't met) were lifted after one or two years, there was very little moral pressure to continue with diversification efforts. Indeed, for many unions there was a lasting sense, as in the case of the GUE, of white racial vindication and resentment (see chapter 5). George Lipsitz goes so far as to state that, "contrary to their stated intentions, civil rights laws have actually augmented rather than diminished the possessive investment in whiteness, not because civil rights legislation is by nature unwise or impractical, but because these particular laws have been structured to be ineffective and largely unenforceable."[123] Although it might be hard for white wage workers to take out their grievances against antilabor policies by management, runaway productions, and the transition to television, it was only too easy for them to shift blame onto disempowered and already often disliked minorities. As the race scholar Eduardo Bonilla-Silva has found, one of the "major story lines of color-blind racism," which was prefigured and fomented in these early post–Civil Rights Act years, is "I did not get a job (or a promotion) because of a minority." This story line is "extremely useful to whites rhetorically and psychologically," despite the scant evidence to suggest that it has much concrete foundation (given the persisting low level of minority employment in areas such as film from the 1970s on).[124]

In motion pictures, a small number of minorities were successfully trained and hired because of the federal activism around the turn of the 1970s. At the end of the agreement, the Soundpersons, Camerapersons, Film Editors, as well as Costumers Locals had made efforts to work out how to integrate some minority trainees into their rosters to meet the terms and perhaps the spirit of the deal.[125] However, those locals with heavy GUE membership had not, having openly repudiated and legally challenged the settlement terms. African American labor lawyer Basil Patterson explained at the time that the unions' cooperation was rarely obtained voluntarily: "Most unions will not accept any significant number of presently qualified black workers or graduates of training programs without the threat of legal action or an absolutely firm stand on the part of the major producers."[126] Binding laws were needed.

• • •

This chapter has charted the high moment of post–Civil Rights Act antidiscrimination initiatives by the federal government in the film industry. With its entrenched white workforce and as the producer of hugely influential films, Hollywood was a natural target for the mobilized EEOC under Clifford Alexander. The EEOC's efforts captured the feeling of possibility and qualified hope expressed by black assistant director and president of the Hollywood–Beverly Hills NAACP unit Wendell Franklin: "There is a new horizon in sight. But it is going to take concerted effort by the beautiful-thinking people to get us there."[127]

However, this concerted pursuit of a new horizon gave rise to formidable discursive and policy retrenchment. Precisely because of the film industry's heightened importance as America's preeminent image factory at home and abroad, the attack against it galvanized virulent forces of reaction. Senator Dirksen and President Nixon saw in the Title VII challenge to the motion-picture industry an opportunity to defang the EEOC. The industry lobbied Dirksen, the architect of the Title VII amendments, and Jack Valenti assisted with the war of ideas. Corporate Hollywood's neoconservative interpretation of its "open doors" for minorities painted a picture of an industry that was fast moving toward a level playing field—and thus in no need of federal reform efforts to "force doors." By stigmatizing organized labor as die-hard discriminators, industry executives positioned themselves as centrist liberals in ways that valorized their bid to ward off integration and reduce union organization. Although in material terms this latter attempt was unsuccessful in that the experience rosters were not dismantled, in discursive terms it worked well by neutralizing attacks on the studios. Organized labor responded in various ways to the federal activism. Some workers constructively changed practices, while others chose to thwart and reject diversification efforts. During these early years of affirmative action, both the formation of new "color-blind" laissez-faire discourses by management (drawing on and feeding into the budding language of racial neoconservatism) and the GUE's arch references to "reverse discrimination" (crystalizing new-right, blue-collar politics) were in very early evidence. While other industries were still basking in the relative prosperity of the liberal-consensus years, the film industry's early economic downturn helped spur discursive and policy reconfiguration driven by a reenergizing management class. Here and elsewhere, the rhetoric employed by Hollywood management and labor provided at once a rationale and a cover for the industry's attacks on state intervention and black activism—the impact of which, epitomized by the firing of Alexander as head of the EEOC, was felt far beyond cinema.

With federal reform efforts not proving effective—at the same time as being cruelly construed as an unfair leg up for African Americans—many black filmmakers turned to more self-determined, black-power-informed projects and narratives in the early 1970s. African Americans working in the film arena became increasingly cynical about the possibility of collective and cross-racial efforts to accomplish change through engaging with and pressurizing the state. New black film producers and the related surge in entrepreneurial black screen heroes offered a very different kind of symbolic and material "solution" to persisting and morphing practices of film-industry racial exclusion.

4

"GETTING THE MAN'S FOOT OUT OF OUR COLLECTIVE ASSES"

Black Left Film Producers and the Rise of the Hustler Creative

We are in the weakest area because we are just performers and a few of us are technicians. All of the projects that are taken to the distributors are taken by white people who make the deal. [We] have to wait until a white producer thinks there is something interesting commercially in a black idea. Then he goes to the parent company and tries to put this thing together. Now when the fucking axe falls and these guys are convinced that there is no other way to get activity on the subject matter, we are left out there waiting for phone calls. . . . My point is it is imperative that we have producing units now.

—Sidney Poitier, interview by Ruby Dee (1969)

op-down federal attempts to address job discrimination in Hollywood, described in the previous chapter, were only one important strand in efforts to bring about meaningful racial reform in cinema during these years. Even if the federal action had been successful, its scope did not extend to the core business culture of Hollywood. All of the distributors, producers, executives, and agents who made the film deals and pulled the strings in Hollywood were white. These decision makers were not forced into racial self-awareness by pressure to diversify their own ranks, and they were unaccustomed to film pitches that worked beyond their white racial frame and unattuned to those pitches' potential if they did see any. The new black filmmakers knew this only too well. Thus, African

American film creatives, sensing the limits of the industry's interest in wider and more varied forms of black and minority ethnic storytelling, strove to broker deals by becoming film producers. As Poitier stresses in the epigraph quotation, the emphasis was mainly not on economic benefits in themselves—with film being a risky business, in which all hits are flukes, producing movies was a dicey and demanding endeavor. The production of black films was propelled by a desire to augment artistic control, to influence staffing decisions, to move beyond the relative powerlessness that even very successful black actors possessed, and to install some agency in the cultural economy.

I begin the discussion of this effort by returning to Harry Belafonte (who had already become the first black film producer in Hollywood in the period before my story starts), Sidney Poitier, and Ossie Davis (with Hannah Weinstein) to consider how they variously seized on their creative capital and tried to convert it into production, financing, and deal-making clout in film. They had watched with great interest Gordon Parks Sr. be equipped with and exploit his creativity authority on *Learning Tree* and wanted to follow suit. As with Parks, I show their activities to be informed, to lesser and greater degrees, by the collectivist race and labor precepts of cultural-front politics. I then turn to the extraordinary production story of Melvin Van Peebles's experimental, black-power-informed, and ghettocentric hit *Sweet Sweetback's Baadasssss Song* (1971). Though radical in his praxis and critique of white "liberal" Hollywood, Van Peebles was also the blueprint for a more individualist and macho entrepreneurial creative archetype—what I call in this chapter the "hustler creative." His iconic success mobilized long-standing black working-class aesthetics that had not been presented on cinema screens before in that way, and these aesthetics spoke not only to a rising youthful African American political radicalism but also to its cynicism. After *Sweetback*, the final two sections of this chapter turn to the rise of iconic black (sub)cultural producers and entrepreneurs onscreen. In the immediate wake of *Sweetback*, the films that most strikingly developed dissident hustler-creative enterprise onscreen were *Super Fly* (Gordon Parks Jr., 1972), about Harlem cocaine dealers, and *The Mack* (Michael Campus, 1973), about Oakland pimps. Though both films were produced by white men, they had substantial creative input by African Americans that bore reflexive relation to the representations of blacks onscreen. I consider the production of these influential films before moving on to their narratives of black wealth creation and subcultural stylization.

I argue that the filmic representation of risk-taking street entrepreneurs—
the damaging wealth generation of the drug dealer and the stylized exploitation of the pimp, both operating within white-dominated economic arenas in a hardening social climate—became compelling tropes for African
American cultural-industries activity at the time and thereafter. The chapter
shows continuities between the filmmaking activities of black left film producers and the dynamic black entrepreneurs before and behind the camera
in iconic ghetto action features. Nevertheless, the shift I map in this chapter
is from black filmmakers' emphasis on pressuring and partnering with
white institutions to bring about change to an increasingly ad hoc, individualist black cultural-industries imperative, behind the scenes and onscreen.

Black Left Producers in Hollywood

Many in the first wave of black Hollywood filmmakers discussed in chapter 2 were steeped in labor conscious and antiracist political struggles. Harry
Belafonte, Sidney Poitier, and Ossie Davis had been politically educated by
and participated in New York radical circles since the 1940s. They all had
performed at cultural events to fund-raise variously for labor, civil liberties,
antisegregation, black arts, and black-liberation political causes, including
some events organized by groups affiliated with the U.S. Communist Party.
Belafonte, Poitier, and Davis were formatively connected to leading black left-
affiliated performers such as Paul Robeson, Lena Horne, and Canada Lee,
who spoke out not only against domestic inequality and injustice but also
against anticommunism and U.S. imperialism as the Cold War developed.
The stakes were high: Robeson's and Lee's careers were dramatically halted
and Horne's severely hampered by the anti-Communist repression and
harassment by the U.S. state. Belafonte's and Poitier's activities in the 1940s
made them vulnerable to anti-Communist accusations in the 1950s, sometimes losing acting jobs, while stage and film actors Davis and his wife, Ruby
Dee, along with James Edwards and black writer and filmmaker Carlton
Moss, were more aggressively targeted, together with a host of other symbol
creators who were deemed dangerous and un-American.

Performers Belafonte, Poitier, and Davis had developed materialist perspectives on racism in the mainstream cultural industries such as film,

perspectives that pushed their agendas beyond simply combatting immediate labor and representational exclusions (discussed in previous chapters) into the film industry's shadowy financing and distribution arrangements. As aspiring black filmmakers, they knew they were reliant on loan guarantees and distribution agreements from white institutions to fund projects. In this capital-intensive industry, the distributors and their lenders assumed the financial risk and in turn could recoup any profits, which they would then split with the producers of successful films. Black people were keen cinemagoers, but their economic role in consumption was wholly unmatched by any role in production and distribution. Davis provided a provocative class and race analysis of these dynamics in a keynote speech to the newly formed Congressional Black Caucus in 1971: "I directed a motion picture called *Cotton Comes to Harlem*, which grossed $6.5 million to date. Now 60 or 70 percent of the money that went across the box office came from black people. Money that came from the Harlems of all our cities, the Harlems of all our country, money that goes to Hollywood, and it's one-way—ain't coming back. I have been instrumental in helping rob—well, not rob exactly—*borrow* from my people money that we need in our own community."[1] Belafonte, Poitier, and Davis wanted to find ways to pay back this "debt." They were thinking deeply about how to make the films they wanted to in order to expand representations for black viewers, get more black labor into filmmaking below and above the line, and return money to the black community.

Off the back of his extraordinary musical success, Harry Belafonte had in the late 1950s become the first African American of the sound era to form his own film-production company. Taking control of his own management, he had set up Belafonte Enterprises, first establishing a music-publishing company so that he could own his own music, recoup more of his publishing fees and royalties, and strike favorable deals for his hugely successful music performances. Then in 1957 he launched the HarBel film-production unit as a subsidiary of Belafonte Enterprises—one of the star-fronted, independent production companies that sprang up in the period.[2] The formation of HarBel was a significant racial landmark in cinema. It allowed Belafonte, as he later recalled, "to scout for good scripts and to pitch them to the studios, not just as some supplicant on bended knee, but as a business—a black business—coming at them on their own level."[3] The mainstream film business, already notoriously risky because of the expense of films and unpredictability of audience responses, was even more challenging for Belafonte because he sought to get financing for projects made by black and left creatives that in part challenged cinema's dominant textual priorities. Despite little insider knowledge in an environment that was generally hostile to black creatives, he had made two HarBel films, the sci-fi drama *The World, the Flesh, and the Devil* (Ranald MacDougall, 1959), distributed by MGM, and the racial crime drama *Odds Against Tomorrow* (Robert Wise, 1959), distributed by United Artists.[4] Studio-forced compromises and mixed commercial results on these features, combined with his prioritization of political activities in the freedom struggle, turned him away from filmmaking for a number of years, until he briefly returned to film production around the turn of the 1970s, first with *The Angel Levine*, discussed in chapter 2.

Through his various production units, Belafonte was set on owning his own cultural material. He was not driven by personal wealth building but instead hoped to wrest more creative and financial control from the cultural industries and to use the profits from his musical performances to support the black movement. He did the latter formidably, becoming the "movement's chief fundraiser," in the historian Steve Ross's words, as well as a major donor.[5] But he did this mainly through his music recordings and performances and the staging of benefit concerts. Film production proved tougher for Belafonte. *Angel Levine* did not engage a substantial audience, and Belafonte failed to recoup costs on the film, in which he had invested creatively and financially. Although this loss was disappointing, the film was nonetheless seminal in the development of black creative and technical talent. One of its black apprentices, Drake Walker, developed a story idea that would become *Buck and the Preacher* (1972). Once Walker had shared his vision of a cinematic rewriting of America's racial history in the West, Belafonte approached his two long-standing friends Ruby Dee and Sidney Poitier to star, and the film was coproduced by HarBel in partnership with Poitier, both stars putting their own money into the film. Scripted by white leftist Ernest Kinoy, *Buck and the Preacher* came to be directed by Poitier, his first time directing. The resulting racially transgressive Western was also an allegory about housing discrimination and wealth injustice in the present. Made for around $2 million and with box-office grosses of $5–6 million, the film just about broke even, according to Poitier.[6] Following the commercial disappointment of *Angel Levine* and the lack of profit for *Buck and the*

FIGURE 4.1 Publicity still of Harry Belafonte, Ruby Dee, and Sidney Poitier in *Buck and the Preacher* (1971), Poitier's first film as director and coproduced by Poitier and Belafonte.

Source: Courtesy of the Academy of Motion Picture Arts and Sciences.

Preacher, Belafonte mainly retreated from a primary focus on filmmaking and financing, finding its mode of production too out of kilter with his political ideals and skills.

Belafonte's friend Poitier also recognized the need to engage with cinema's business practices to forward black creative and economic self-determination. Before Poitier became an actor and even during times of unemployment as an actor, he had worked as a dishwasher to support himself and his family and had a keen sense of wanting to escape exploitative labor. Like Belafonte, he had first developed business skills in catering when he used early earnings as a performer to set up a tiny New York eatery in the early 1950s. Poitier put the $5,000 he made from his first major feature *Blackboard Jungle* into Ribs in the Ruff in Harlem. Though the eatery failed and left him indebted, it was indicative of his yearning for workplace and economic self-determination.

As Poitier and Belafonte developed as filmmakers, they hired skilled white people to advise them in their quest to be more financially self-determining, and in Poitier's case his main collaborator was his agent, Marty Baum. But more than Belafonte, who worked with many white allies and institutions, such as Chiz Schultz and the Ford Foundation, Poitier had a strong sense of the importance of self-sufficient black enterprise and tailored his film content to meet this imperative. He cleaved to less-challenging content than Belafonte in order to pursue his primary political aim of proving black film business viability. When in 1968 Poitier not only returned more money to the industry than any other star (per Quigley's chart) but also managed to get paid more than any white actor, this success spoke to his (and Baum's) financial acuity.[7] His huge earnings that year resulted, above all, from the contract he and Baum had struck with Columbia for *To Sir, with Love*, a film made for just $640,000, and about which the studio apparently had quite low expectations. Poitier had given up most of his upfront salary payments in exchange for a "healthy percentage" of the $42.5 million gross (this was an unusual deal because studios normally give points on profits, which they can minimize through creative accounting, rather than on raw box-office take).[8] It is thus important to note that even as Poitier was playing the consummate, salaried professional helping white people onscreen (for instance, as Virgil Tibbs), he was actually emerging as the keen, well-remunerated creative entrepreneur in his industry dealings. And through various activities, including fund-raising, benefit concerts, documentary premieres, and the funding and housing of new film writers, he returned money and resources to budding minority filmmakers.[9]

Poitier was later than Belafonte in setting up his own production company, but once he did so, he tenaciously leveraged his star power to secure profits and develop influence. He set up E&R Productions, named after his deceased parents, Evelyn and Reginald, which would produce Poitier vehicles for release by Columbia Pictures, including *Buck and the Preacher*. Under the agreement with the studio, both Poitier and Columbia would look for story material that was mutually agreeable, and that material would then be packaged with input from Poitier. This gave him considerable creative authority. At the same time, Poitier joined forces with Barbra Streisand, Paul Newman, and Steve McQueen to launch the star-fronted production company First Artists Corporation. These liberal actors agreed to make tightly costed pictures, giving up higher budgets in favor of more agency, in a nonexclusive deal with distributors. As Poitier explained later, "From an economic point of view it seemed like a good deal, but the main advantage to us over and above financial considerations was the complete artistic control we would have, provided we made each of our films for $3 million or less."[10] Such a deal was surely especially important to Poitier, given the racist constraints of Hollywood. His First Artists films were produced by Verdon Cedric, another Poitier film company, named this time after his two deceased siblings. His First Artists debut, which he directed and starred in, was *A Warm December* (1973), distributed by Warner Bros.. Though it lost money, it was one of the first major studio-produced black romantic dramas, which Poitier reportedly made with his four daughters in mind. This commitment to opening cinematic space for representations of black love and romance (departing from his widely critiqued interracial romances) had already been evident in his first move into taking more control of film content when he had coscripted and starred in *For Love of Ivy* (Daniel Mann, 1968).

Poitier's film-producing capability, like Belafonte's, stood as a counterproposal to the white economic theft of black creative capital, which had, for instance, left Chester Himes, another veteran of the cultural front of the 1940s, with a small flat fee for the film-adaptation rights to all of his Harlem detective novels (see chapter 2). Black-determined productions were in some ways a kind of material revenge for the political-persecution-induced penury the state had exacted on Poitier's friend Canada Lee, with whom he had costarred in *Cry, the Beloved Country* (Zoltan Korda) in 1951. Lee had been an inspiring political and professional guide to Poitier during filming in South Africa. Blacklisted and stripped of his livelihood, Lee was reduced to shoe shining to survive and then died at forty-five years old in 1952, just weeks before he was due to face a House Un-American Activities Committee hearing. As part of the government's anti-Communist crusade, Poitier had been asked to publicly denounce Lee as well as his mentor and friend Paul Robeson as "dangerous." Though forced into publically distancing himself from them, Poitier, like Belafonte, under enormous pressure from the U.S. state and its entertainment industries, had not betrayed either of them.[11]

Prioritizing the establishment of a viable black film-producing unit, Poitier experimented with different kinds of content. Following the commercial disappointment of *A Warm December* and the only break-even earnings of *Buck and the Preacher*, he set about producing and directing a string of highly successful black-cast, black-made family comedies in the mid-1970s.

The two highest-performing Poitier-produced and-directed films would be *Uptown Saturday Night* (1974) and *Let's Do It Again* (1975), in which he staked out a new successful black mainstream comedic buddy formula, which he then refined in *A Piece of the Action* (1977), already discussed in this book's introduction. With these comedies, Poitier would become the most commercially successful black film director and producer, creating opportunities for black film workers and spaces for black and interracial filmic representation. When Belafonte would make disparaging remarks about the content of these black family comedies, Poitier would retort by saying that at least they, unlike Belafonte's output, proved the commercial feasibility of black-oriented film fare and did so without relying on liberal-reformist private organizations such as the Ford Foundation. As the film scholar Keith Corson, who has examined Poitier's comedies, rightly insists, his "work as a director is rarely invoked in summaries of his accomplishments in Hollywood,"[12] nor is his role as a producer.

FIGURE 4.2 Director-producer Sidney Poitier on the set of *Uptown Saturday Night* (1974), a black-cast family comedy.

Source: Courtesy of the Academy of Motion Picture Arts and Sciences.

Following the success of *Cotton Comes to Harlem*, Ossie Davis teamed up with film executive Hannah Weinstein, media organizer Cliff Frazier, and a host of black and left actors and artists to launch the Harlem-based independent film company Third World Cinema Corporation in 1971. Its ambitious purpose was to increase employment in the media industries for underrepresented and low-income groups and to gain more control of representation and finance. Having experienced firsthand how resistant film's labor organizations were to taking on minority recruits (as discussed in chapter 3), Davis and Weinstein, like Belafonte, sought to produce their own films. They announced the intention to make five features that could stoke demand for the new Third World Cinema pipeline of minority trainees. The training programs were truly multiracial—one audit of Third World trainees found them to be 60 percent black, 30 percent Puerto Rican, 5 percent Asian, and 5 percent poor white. By 1975, it had trained up several hundred film technicians and creatives.[13] The film-production side of Third World was led by Weinstein, one of the only female executive producers in the film and television industry at the time. A long-standing left activist and producer, she had worked extensively with blacklisted and ostracized American talent in the 1960s from her base in Europe before her return to the United States. There, in 1970, she had produced a Madison Square Garden rally to fund-raise for the election of U.S. senators opposed to the Vietnam War.

Ten of the fifteen stockholders in Third World were black and Latinx, and some were longtime political and artistic collaborators with Davis. The members included Ruby Dee, Diana Sands, Rita Moreno, James Earl Jones, Brock Peters, Sidney Lumet, John Killens, and Godfrey Cambridge, all of whom, like Davis and Weinstein, gave their professional services either for free or at very reduced rates. Third World found a way to be financed in part by public funding. New York City's Manpower and Career Development Agency in the Department of Employment committed $400,000 to train minorities in craft jobs at Third World. The federal Model Cities Agency also funded the company by buying nearly half of Third World's stock through the Harlem Commonwealth Council. Model Cities was a community-development venture, obligating Third World to make "commercial features," from which 40 percent of any profits would be returned to the Harlem Commonwealth Council for local economic development.[14] Weinstein and Frazier thus squeezed some of the last resources from

FIGURE 4.3 Cliff Frazier, Sidney Lumet, and Ossie Davis of the Community Film Workshop in 1970. The following year Frazier and Davis would launch Third World Cinema with Hannah Weinstein.
Source: Courtesy of the Dwyer Cultural Center.

these Great Society initiatives before the strategies of "benign neglect," launched in the Nixon era, fully set in.

Such activity moved beyond the mainstream/independent and reformist/radical dichotomies, modeling ways of organizing and financing film production that were at once alternative, entrepreneurial, community oriented, and state funded. As Davis told the Black Congressional Caucus, "I need your help in structuring a way that when the money goes to Hollywood it only stays for a little while; it doubles and comes back to the black community."[15] Third World would go on to make two commercially successful films, *Claudine* in 1974 (explored in chapter 5) and the interracial comedy *Greased Lightning* (Michael Schultz, 1977), starring Richard Pryor and Beau Bridges. Davis's project with Weinstein and Frazier at Third World, combining elements of Belafonte's and Poitier's approaches, emerges as the most politically serious and consistent of the three black production-unit interventions detailed in this section.

All of these black Hollywood Renaissance–era producers understood that to start influencing filmic discourses onscreen, they would have to engage deeply, often reluctantly, with financial and organizational matters. Poitier, as one journalist recounted, was "not really interested in being a producer (except to exert that much more control over the material in which he appears)."[16] Belafonte, though the earliest black Hollywood producer, was unwilling to deny his political orientations in his dealings with the film business—a posture aided by his interests in other less-constricting cultural-industries platforms. Ossie Davis stated that film producing, though much needed, "is a highly technical skill that I want nothing to do with."[17] At heart a writer and actor, Davis became a producer because he grasped the determining influence of money over creativity. He always insisted that "the Struggle isn't only a matter of action, it also involves knowing about things—like power, for instance, about money."[18] These movement stalwarts became producers in order to bring about organizational change and to be allowed to tell different screen stories, finding alternative sources of financing, both black and white, and in many cases taking on the risk.

In some cases, these producers lost their own money and that of their communities. Perhaps the saddest example was the failure of *Countdown at Kusini* (1976), an action film shot and set in Nigeria, directed by Ossie Davis, starring Davis and Dee, and produced by Davis with Nigerian filmmaker Ladi Ladebo. Davis had funded it in part through a loan from the Harlem bank Freedom National and by the African American sorority Delta Sigma Theta, with each sorority member asked to contribute $50. "Its funding came out of the pockets of the thousands of black women who believed in us and in the project," recalls Davis.[19] Though the film was made independently of Hollywood, it was distributed through conventional channels by Columbia and initially opened in only a few U.S. theaters. It lost money for the sorority members and for Davis, crystallizing the risks of trying to make inroads into unpredictable, high-cost filmmaking. The independents' reliance on orthodox distributional and exhibition structures, which strongly determine success through promotion and theater bookings, made matters only more challenging.[20]

Aside from these three black left film producers and their white and black allies, there were very few other African American producers in the renaissance years. One exception, who came out of a black capitalist rather than a black left tradition, was Motown music mogul Berry Gordy. He made a very successful foray into film, producing the Diana Ross vehicle *Lady Sings the Blues* (Sidney Furie, 1972), leading Ossie Davis to remark, "He put so much money into that production that I could kiss him!"[21] It was a major crossover hit, grossing nearly $20 million, and was the year's tenth-highest earner, and Gordy went on to produce and direct another successful Ross vehicle, *Mahogany*, in 1975.[22] Like Belafonte, he used his primary career as a leading creative entrepreneur in music to push his way into the more deeply exclusionary and expensive film-production arena. Another aspiring black producer who ploughed all his savings into his own project showed most strikingly how self-determined, alternative film producing could sometimes be extremely successful. Melvin Van Peebles took some of the most influential next steps in this story of black economic and creative self-determination in early post–civil rights cinema.

Van Peebles as Hustler Creative

Like Gordon Parks Sr., whose second directorial feature following *Learning Tree* was *Shaft* (1971), and Ossie Davis, whose second studio-distributed film as director after *Cotton* was the gritty *Gordon's War* (1973), Van Peebles turned, after his Hollywood debut *Watermelon Man*, to ghetto action themes and to the provocative repudiation of black-respectability politics. Practically single-handedly, he made *Sweet Sweetback's Baadasssss Song*: directing, coproducing, scoring, coediting, and starring. It centers on sex hustler Sweetback (Van Peebles), who early in the film converts into a proto-revolutionary when he comes to the rescue of a black nationalist who is being brutally beaten by two corrupt white cops. The film narrates the hero's protracted and ultimately victorious flight from the authorities. Though commentators and scholars sometimes reduce *Sweetback* to the launch of the so-called black-exploitation, or "blaxploitation," film cycle, this characterization misses its strong European new-wave narrative and stylistic framing, married to black working-class and radical aesthetic traditions. Film scholars Allyson Field, Jan-Christopher Horak, and Jacqueline Stewart are right when they position *Sweetback* as formative of LA Rebellion movement filmmaking of the 1970s in that it offers an experimental exploration of aspects of "the lifeworlds of Black working-class and poor people." Like other LA Rebellion films, it presents "a black-oriented cinema more firmly grounded in black aesthetic traditions and less dependent on white models."[23]

Van Peebles wanted the project to be "a living workshop," with "50 percent of my shooting crew to be third world people," expanding on Belafonte's ambitions for *Angel Levine*.[24] He pitched the project to Columbia producer Stanley Schneider, with whom he had made *Watermelon Man* as the first of a supposed three-picture deal. According to Van Peebles, Schneider had protected him from too much interference, helping him to achieve *Watermelon Man*'s black-power ending. But because of the new script's politicized violence and explicit, interracial sex sequences as well as Van Peebles's hiring plans, which would contravene union roster agreements, Columbia rejected it.[25] Unwilling to compromise and unable to find a mainstream backer, Van Peebles took on a great deal of the financial risk to make the film. Using all his savings and earnings from *Watermelon Man* plus $50,000 from Bill Cosby and funds from other black and white contributors, he made the film for around $300,000 (estimates vary). Many independent filmmakers are forced to use alternative funding arrangements, including self-funding, because they fail to get a deal. What makes Van Peebles distinctive is that as a marketable Hollywood Renaissance director he chose to walk away from a major multipicture contract rather than compromise on production and content. This choice adds credence to his politicized anti–Hollywood establishment assertion that "I didn't do it for money in the first place. I made the picture because I was tired of taking the Man's crap and of having him define who we were to us."[26] Making *Sweetback* on his own was his provocative, race-conscious form of resistance to Hollywood's filmmaking and mythmaking hegemony.

Van Peebles achieved his "living workshop": a majority black and Latino crew. His team included Clyde Houston, a black production manager of pornographic features, as assistant director and Jose Garcia, a Puerto Rican who came from Cliff Frazier's Community Film Workshop, as cameraman and assistant director. Van Peebles struck a deal with a distributor of exploitation and pornographic films, Cinemation, owned by producer Jerry Gross, to coproduce the film with him. He then marketed the production as a pornographic film, which it was in part, with its lengthy, reportedly unsimulated sex scenes. The porn sector was traditionally nonunionized, allowing Van Peebles to bypass the employment rules of organized labor. As he remarked at the time, "The Unions don't trouble themselves over smut films . . . which I suppose they consider beneath their dignity."[27] This anti-organized-labor posture stands as one of the big ways that Van Peebles departs politically from the cultural-front-influenced black left producers discussed earlier in this chapter.

Thus, in the year that the Justice Department backed away from impos-ing binding employment commitments on the Los Angeles film industry amid mounting race backlash from management and unions, this LA-based black film auteur, intent on having a multiethnic crew, managed to circum-vent the AMPTP-run roster system. Also, by using mainly nonprofessional actors ("the black community," as the credit title claimed), with himself in the lead role, he faced down the employment requirements of the Screen Actors Guild. Furthermore, Van Peebles avoided traditional exhibition channels by initially relying on grindhouse theaters to screen the film—"an entire parallel distribution circuit," in his words.[28] As well as a pragmatic move, this decision offered a layer of transgression—a subversive means of occupying an alternative, demotic, "smut" space in the cultural industries. He locked out the major studios and many exhibitors from making any profit on the film, while affronting their mores. *Sweetback* opened slowly in a hand-ful of theaters, publicized by word of mouth and by the Black Panthers newsletter, which printed the widely read Huey Newton article subtitled "A Revolutionary Analysis of *Sweet Sweetback's Baadasssss Song*," which really helped the film gain traction.[29] The leading black film critic of the time, James Murray, described "the euphoric joy of many black men and women leaving 'Sweetback' during those first days following its Harlem premier[;] . . . community identification was intense."[30] It went on to be a major hit with black and youth audiences, eventually grossing in the region of $15 million and returning $4.1 million in rentals: one of the most successful U.S. films of its decade in terms of the ratio of profit to investment.[31]

Freed of interference but on a very tight budget, Van Peebles made his ghettocentric celebration of LA-style working-class black life in Watts and South Central. As he remarked, "The thing that kept occurring to me was that I could delve into the black community as they [Hollywood filmmak-ers] would never be able to do because of their cumbersome technology and their lack of empathy."[32] His experimental film broke taboos, even within the context of the relaxing standards and politicoaesthetic innovation of the Hollywood Renaissance. The film's black politicized aesthetic energies, far removed from those of Belafonte and Poitier, crystallized what the leading cultural theorist Stuart Hall would later describe as "black diasporic cultural repertoires." These repertoires, which had not been shown on widely screened films theretofore, were marked by "linguistic innovations in rhetorical stylization of the body, forms of occupying an alien social space, heightened expressions, hairstyles, ways of walking, standing and talking, and a means of constituting and sustaining camaraderie and community."[33] Indeed, the very title of Van Peebles's film indexes what Hall describes as this repertoire's three main dimensions, all of which would prove black-representational preoccupations in the post–civil rights cultural industries to come. First, the title *Sweet Sweetback's Baadasssss Song* foregrounds the centrality of style, with the term *baadasssss* flagrantly announcing black linguistic innovation. "Within the black repertoire," Hall explains, "*style*—which mainstream cultural critics often believe to be the mere husk, the wrapping, the sugar coating on the pill—has become *itself* the subject of what is going on."[34] Van Peebles explained that he decided on this avowedly antibourgeois title "instead of some phony shit with a subtitle about it being made for brothers and sisters. With that title they would KNOW."[35] That is, they would know that exuberant black vernacular style is the subject.

Second, Hall describes how, "displaced from a logocentric world[,] . . . the people of the black diaspora have . . . found the deep form, the deep structure of their cultural life in music."[36] Hence, the film is Sweetback's *song*, borne out by the film's heavy reliance on music, composed by Van Peebles and by then emerging soul-funk group Earth, Wind, & Fire, to drive the narrative forward. Again, Van Peebles was self-conscious about his distinctively black-diasporic use of music in film: "Very few look at film with sound considered as a creative third dimension"—in part because, he added, "most directors can't carry a tune in a fucking bucket." Van Peebles had already released his first record, *Brer Soul*, in 1968, on which he rapped poems over jazzy soul beats. Understanding music to be "an integral part of the film" led to aesthetic innovation and marketing opportunities, when Van Peebles put out a soundtrack single on his own record label, Yeah, Inc., ahead of the film's release to generate publicity.[37] In this regard, he shares ground with many other black film artists since then in that he used music to make inroads into exclusionary film.

Third, Hall asks readers to "think of how these cultures have used the body—as if it was, and it often was, the only cultural capital we had. We have worked on ourselves as the canvases of representation."[38] Sweetback's body as canvas is predominantly and insolently sexual—used for pleasure, prestige, payment, and control. Foregrounded in the title, the hero is named for his legendary *sweetback*, established at the start of the film when the credits are "superimposed over a montage of shots of Sweetback's back pumping, women's faces, and Sweetback's legs running," as the script puts it.[39] Through its fetishization of the black male body as sexual canvas, *Sweetback* controversially appropriated the "buck" imagery with which white cinematic culture had long oppressed black men and did so in a manner that offered a secondary rebuke to the representational strategy of undersexualizing black men, as captured in Poitier's "Saint Sidney" Hollywood roles. Like writer and director Bill Gunn with *Landlord* and *Stop*, Van Peebles was a new black-diasporic filmmaker encapsulating the confidence of Hollywood Renaissance maverick directors and lacing it with racial transgression, critique, and revolt. Both filmmakers threw off black-respectability discourses in a move to validate black working-class tastes and dispositions, while marrying this validation to Black Arts Movement and European art-house sensibilities in the creative flux of the early 1970s—a time when exploitation, independent, and mainstream priorities came to be melded.

Much more could be said here and has been said elsewhere about *Sweetback*'s aesthetic experimentation, its unprecedented portrayal of politically motivated black violence toward police, and its portrayal of hedonistic and troubling black and countercultural sexuality. The point I want to pursue continues with my focus on reflexivity: this landmark release was self-conscious about cinema's institutional politics, and Van Peebles mobilized a sense of Hollywood racism to help define and market his product.

It was common wisdom that filmmakers needed a rating from the MPAA's new Classification and Ratings Administration (CARA) for their film to succeed, which led them to "voluntarily" self-regulate their content before submission for classification. Films that did not self-censor and were rated X barred viewers younger than eighteen, which made them more difficult to book and exhibit.[40] But Van Peebles circumvented the industry by not submitting his film to CARA (avoiding the fee in the knowledge that it would have got an X anyway) but nonetheless using the film's outré status for marketing purposes. He did his own marketing, printing the slogan "RATED X BY AN ALL-WHITE JURY" on the film poster and promotional T-shirts, exposing the fact that the CARA board had no minority members. This is a counterstorytelling move, racializing an industry that liked (and still likes) to work under a normalizing cloak of whiteness. Van Peebles communicated the rebellious political relevance of this film and, in turn, the lack of relevance of the industry's gatekeepers in a marketing-through-negative-publicity move that would be much repeated thereafter, especially in hip-hop's marketing of its "dangerous" products.[41]

When the film scholar David Cook describes *Sweetback* as "manifestly threatening to whites," those "whites" include many in the film industry.[42] Van Peebles's activities offer a strikingly early example of how in cinema's asymmetric battles outsider symbol creators can generate interest and attendance by discursively framing their productions as salvos in a cultural-political war with the establishment. As such, Van Peebles should be positioned (though very rarely is) as one of the maverick auteurs who bucked the system in the film-renaissance years, embodying the creative individualism that, as Jeff Menne argues, fed into the emerging post-Fordist cinematic landscape.[43] After Sweetback escapes to Mexico, the ending intertitle tells the audience to "Watch out! A baad asssss nigger is coming back to collect some dues." As well as political dues, this warning holds the literal meaning of collecting payment despite and ironically also because of industry obstacles—making some material amends for what Ossie Davis provocatively called the "robbing" of black cinemagoers' dollars.

In addition to marketing his black-diasporic product explicitly through its relationship to the industry's regulatory frameworks, Van Peebles further built his publicity image by releasing a notable diary book about the film's making—what the production studies scholar John Caldwell would call an "industrial meta-text."[44] Published at the same time as the film and with the same title, the book performed several functions. First, many aspirant "guerrilla filmmakers" of all races used this making-of diary as a manual for independent filmmaking in the 1970s. As Van Peebles described it in the book, such politicized symbol creation is "a workshop situation where people carry the fight onward while at the same time they're gaining the necessary technical knowledge."[45] Van Peebles schooled his readers in the link between economic and creative self-determination, reiterating statements by black left producers quoted earlier: "The Man can pull the economic rug right out from under you" if your film project is "too relevant for the particular taste of the funding group." Thus, a degree of financial control, so difficult to achieve in this capital-intensive sector, was essential. Van Peebles offered potent black-power statements about film as an ideological battlefield: "The Man . . . has colonized our minds. We've been violated, confused and drained by this colonization and from this brutal, calculated genocide the most effective and vicious racism has grown, and it is with this starting point in mind and the intention to reverse the process that I went into cinema in the first fucking place." Van Peebles suggested that his desire to gain self-determination within the industry came to be the very subject of the film: "Story-wise, I came up with the idea, why not the direct approach. Since what I want is the Man's foot out of our collective asses, why not make the film about a brother getting the Man's foot out of his ass."[46] Thus, he self-consciously spelled out the reflexive politicoaesthetic dimensions of his film.

Despite his structural critique of the racist industry, represented by "the Man" and "the Unions," Van Peebles nonetheless described his pragmatic, informal partnering with individual industry whites—for instance, Columbia head of production Johnny Veitch ("a film man from . . . his fingertips and a no shit guy"), who set up deferral arrangements for equipment and laboratory costs in exchange for points on profits. Consistent with the argument of this book, Van Peebles distinguished the practices of actual white individuals in film—describing progressive as well as racist experiences he faced in his personal dealings—from the structural practices of Hollywood that he critiqued.[47]

Although some black film producers, such as Harry Belafonte and Cliff Frazier, had been trying to work with the unions, striving to get apprenticeships and union cards for minority technicians by appealing to and bolstering organized labor's social activist elements, Van Peebles was disdainful. This disdain is indicative of an important political departure from a major strand of the black left social activism, epitomized by the projects of A. Philip Randolph and Bayard Rustin and also pursued by Ossie Davis, which sought to organize black workers and demand union solidarity as a resource for African American labor. Van Peebles staked out territory away from these historic stances. Yet because *Sweetback* was set and shot in the Los Angeles area (unlike most of the films discussed earlier in this book), the rejection of organized labor in its production model and in the "making of" diary held particular charge. Van Peebles's repudiation of LA's craft unions and guilds—home of the racist Group for Union Equality, which emerged the same year this film was made—remains understandable. The film's quasi-realist Watts setting offered exciting new perspectives on an area that had experienced the deadly rioting in 1965 that set off powerful white-backlash currents against the antiracist struggle, including the election of actor Ronald Reagan as California's governor in 1967 (a post he held until 1975). Through the manual and in the making and marketing of this extraordinary film, Van Peebles variously rejected and affronted both Hollywood's racist politics as well as, to be sure, certain strands of the black freedom movement.

Though forming a powerful treatise on alternative, black-nationalist-informed film culture, Van Peebles's diary and film nonetheless construct him as a troublingly macho, individualist symbol creator. The book starts with him driving out of Los Angeles into the desert, where he begins to masturbate in order to spark his creativity—his account of this "semen shock" is quite extensive. Thus, the book starts with "smut," shadowing the film, which opens with a very controversial scene of Sweetback's brothel-sited sexual initiation as a child (played by Van Peebles's own son, Mario). The film features scenes that are often countercultural and bohemian—for instance, Sweetback's burlesque sex show in which a woman wearing a dildo morphs into the hero.[48] At other points, as with the opening, the film is disturbing. As Mark Anthony Neal and other critics have suggested, later sex scenes, including two quasi-rape scenes presented as mere tactics to evade the authorities, are very problematic in their validation of sex as an act of domination.[49]

Van Peebles's stud image in the making-of book, though hedonistic, is more normative. Van Peebles casually remarks at the outset, "Maybe I could have brought a girl or a couple of girls with me to ball but that would have meant dividing my attention. That's why I decided on using my good old childhood Mrs. Thumbs-and-her-four-daughters method."[50] This presentation of the macho black entrepreneurial creative—who feeds this cool-pose publicity image into his film text—would become very influential in the post–civil rights period. In S. Craig Watkins's assertion that "arguably the most persistent problem in the Blaxploitation film was the superstud characteristics used to code black masculinity,"[51] Van Peebles and his self-creation Sweetback, even more than John Shaft, are the ur-texts.

Van Peebles's script introduces Sweetback as "a young up-and-coming small-time big shot. His clothes fit beautifully but the expression on his face seems out of place. . . . It's impossible to be sure what his state hides. Some would say intelligence, some would say sensuality. . . . [E]veryone's first thought is to try to get on his good side."[52] Because Van Peebles the filmmaker

FIGURE 4.4 Melvin Van Peebles (Sweetback) and Rhetta Hughes (Old Girlfriend) in *Sweet Sweetback's Baadasssss Song* (Melvin Van Peebles, 1971).
Source: Courtesy of the British Film Institute National Archive.

plays Sweetback, the equivalence between hero and creative is fully materialized. The male dominance in film-thematic priorities of the early 1970s is well known, and as film scholar Mia Mask suggests, this new black macho should be read alongside portrayals of "tough white cops who confronted and controlled inner city crime" in films such as *Dirty Harry* (Don Siegel) and *French Connection* (William Friedkin), released in the same year as *Sweetback*.[53] Nonetheless, Van Peebles's macho heroics onscreen, underwritten by his publicity image canonized in the making-of book, consecrated the image of the new black superstud. The film and book remain, in many ways, radical. But they also marked the beginning of the shift toward the championing of a charismatic, risk-taking, street-inspired black male archetype and as such represented the dawning of the cinematic hustler creative. Although Sweetback's black-diasporic sex hustle is used to evade the authorities, it is not yet monetized, which stands in contrast with the most iconic hustler creatives in the ghetto action films that ensued.

Producing Ghetto Action Films

Along with *Sweetback*, *Super Fly* and *The Mack* were among the most avidly viewed films by black youth audiences in the 1970s. These two features were, contends the critic Darius James in his book *That's Blaxploitation! Roots of the Baadasssss 'Tude*, the "two defining films of the 1970s blaxploitation cycle" because they were "mentioned most frequently" by black people as he conducted the research for his book.[54] *Super Fly* was a runaway hit in urban theaters, inspiring very high levels of repeat business, and went on to gross more than $12 million. *The Mack*, which came out a year later, though less of a hit (grossing about $6.5 million), enjoyed a very long shelf life.[55] As the actor Dick Anthony Williams, who stars in *The Mack* as Pretty Tony, remarked, "Almost everyone's got a copy, most bootlegged. It hit something."[56] Both Williams and James highlight the importance of films that chronicled and mythologized black subcultural enterprise.

Despite their popular-cultural importance, *Super Fly* and *Mack* have tended to be treated negatively and summarily by film scholars, who cast them as part of the period's deleterious black-exploitation production trend. One reason for this treatment is that, unlike *Sweetback*, both films had white producers. Film scholars such as Mark Reid are right to point out that behind the "mythology of black control" projected in marketing campaigns of such films were white executives and entrepreneurs.[57] Yet such arguments risk underemphasizing the black creative input in the making of these black-germinated films. They were, in different ways, interracial collaborations with substantial black creative input that made money also for black creative workers, investors, and organizations. *Super Fly* was made by mostly black symbol creators, and *Mack* grew out of significant interracial collaboration. In both cases, these important, if problematic, ghetto action films captured black production advances, political contestation, and representational value, strikingly furthering the dramatization of black-diasporic cultural repertoires. Mapping these films' production histories and film themes demonstrates the reflexive development of the new masculinist hustler creative as post–civil rights archetype.

Super Fly, a story about a Harlem cocaine dealer who struggles to get out of the life, was first developed by African American advertising executive Philip Fenty from Cleveland. He wrote the script in his late twenties with input from his friend Ron O'Neal, who plays the lead character, Youngblood Priest, and the film was directed by Gordon Parks Jr. The African American writer, actor, and director were not from the places they portrayed. Fenty was part of the new hip marketing culture of the 1960s and early 1970s that Thomas Frank chronicles in *The Conquest of Cool*, which grasped "the vast popularity of dissidence."[58] Though Fenty "knew not much about" the Harlem scene, he had noted the "tremendous creative energy" of this "exciting, interesting subculture."[59] Parks Jr.'s professional journey before *Super Fly* encompassed art school in Paris and working with celebrated French documentary maker Pierre Gaisseau, who had made a film about New York. Thus, like Van Peebles, Parks Jr. was a European-influenced Hollywood Renaissance–era filmmaker. He had also just finished working as a stills photographer on *The Godfather* (by far the most successful film of 1972), which powerfully mythologized illegal white ethnic enterprise. It was, ironically, *Super Fly*'s white producer Sigissmund Shore who actually hailed from Harlem. Growing up there and in the Bronx, according to one journalist, he was "familiar and sympathetic with the problems of the ghetto foreign-born, black, and minority groups."[60] Shore described his own fascination with "the way [blacks] got into being hustlers on the street." Unlike for white hustlers, for black hustlers "it was a competition of style," averred Shore—admiring black style as *itself* the subject of what was going on, according to Hall.[61] Thus, by combining the advertiser's and the documentarian's eye—overseen by the "White Negro" Shore[62]—Fenty and Parks produced a film that was far from an unmediated slice of ghetto life but also far from a simple exploitation film.

Super Fly was in fact a landmark in minority participation in major-distributed filmmaking. Picked up by Warner Bros. only after its completion, it marked two racial precedents: the first major-studio-distributed film to be financed predominantly by black limited partnerships and to have a majority nonwhite technical crew.[63] The filmmakers went directly to the Harlem business community (the milieu of the film's setting) to raise the initial production costs, and Parks Sr. contributed $5,000,[64] a funding arrangement that prevented, recalling Van Peebles, "the Man [from] pull[ing] the economic rug right out from under" the filmmakers. *Super Fly*'s black-community funding enabled its makers to avoid the external interference of white studio representatives, whose approval is normally required at each stage of production.

The agenda of the film's bankrollers, who had never before invested in film, differed sharply from that of conventional industry sources of capitalization, and they pressed for labor redistribution behind the camera.[65]

The makers recruited aggressively among New York's minority groups, with technicians and apprentices coming from Third World's training program, and in this way were able to put together a majority black and Puerto Rican crew.[66] The local black investors also enabled an unusual degree of access for location shooting. While ghetto action sequels *Shaft's Big Score* (Gordon Parks Sr., 1972) and *Come Back Charleston Blue* (Mark Warren, 1972), both financed in-house by major studios, were forced to re-create Uptown elsewhere following security problems, *Super Fly* "quietly wound eight weeks of almost all-Harlem locationing [*sic*] with no trouble whatsoever," reported *Variety*.[67] The investors guaranteed the shoot safe passage, paving the way for the film's celebrated scenes of craps games, eateries, and tenement blocks, leading Donald Bogle to assert that "*Super Fly* looks authentic: the Harlem settings, the streets and alleyways, the bars, and the tenements all paint an overriding bleak vision of urban decay," which was "new terrain for commercial cinema."[68]

The Mack, a rise-and-fall story about a stylish Oakland pimp called Goldie (Max Julien), was independently made by first-time white producer Harvey Bernhard, whose background was in television documentary (where one of his collaborators had been David Wolper, the producer behind the failed *Confessions of Nat Turner* project). The film was distributed by the independent West Coast company Cinerama Releasing and was made for about $400,000, which the producer raised and then took a hands-off approach. The story was first conceived by an African American, Robert Poole, during a long prison term—his first drafts were reportedly written on toilet paper. On Poole's release, he told the story to his barber, who passed it on to Bernhard. The sites of the prison and barbershop in this film's development capture the classic spaces of performance and exchange of twentieth-century black vernacular "toast" culture, including pimp lore. The script was further developed by the film's main actors, Max Julien and Richard Pryor (during the shoot Pryor stayed with his Oakland-based friend Cecil Brown, the acclaimed black writer who had spoken out against *Confessions of Nat Turner* and worked with Hal Ashby), and by its white director, Michael Campus, as they resided for several months in Oakland. Campus was born and raised in Manhattan, the son of a doctor who worked in a Harlem hospital. He recalls that as a child he would go and "sit with my father on a Saturday night," and "we used to weep together" at the consequences of poverty and racism.[69]

The Mack filmmakers, like those who made *Super Fly*, had a great deal of control over creative development, and the project came to be embedded in its locale. When New York–based director Campus and star Julien arrived in Oakland, they soon met with the Ward brothers, who, according to Campus, "kind of ran the Oakland underworld."[70] This gang, in particular its leader, Frank Ward, came to work with the filmmakers, offering technical advice, props, script input, and access. The ten Ward siblings had moved to Oakland from Alabama, and as Michael Campus recalls, Frank "was ashamed of the fact that he couldn't read or write well and he became a mack [pimp] because that was all he felt he could do."[71] The Wards were in dispute with the Panthers when the filmmakers arrived, and Oakland-based Panthers Huey Newton and Bobby Seale soon also held meetings with the filmmakers. The Panthers' involvement led to rewrites, beefing up the black-nationalist themes, and following negotiations with producer Harvey Bernhard, Newton also took over the hiring and paying of local people as extras.[72]

Furnishing some quasi-realism, some of the films' investors and creative contributors appeared as characters in both films. In *Super Fly*, the Harlem hustler KC plays a pimp, and his ostentatious, locally renowned black Cadillac El Dorado features prominently as Priest's car ("My El-D and just me / for all junkies to see," croons Curtis Mayfield on "Pusherman"[73]). Nate Adams, who plays a dealer and served as the film's lauded costume designer, owned a Harlem employment agency that recruited personnel for the film. Similarly, members of the Oakland underworld appear in *The Mack*, which features two classic cinema vérité scenes. The first is the memorable barbershop sequence featuring the unscripted boasting exchange between Frank Ward and Pretty Tony (Dick Anthony Williams)—a real-world hustler and an award-winning actor—about their hustling exploits (repeatedly sampled in rap music since then). The second famous scene comes from the actual Players' Ball, an annual gala for the Bay Area black subcultural scene. In an interview, Campus describes these shots as documentary rather than fiction, instigated by both a desire to capture "the life" on camera and to work within his straitened budget: the Players' Ball offered fantastic and free filmic spectacle. These scenes emerge as particularly "visceral and real," according to the director.[74] The whole film was shot on location, with the main set housed in a downtown Oakland nightclub. Local inhabitants and locales thus traveled into the diegesis of both films, materializing connections to the local black subcultural, business, and activist communities depicted in the films. In several important ways, the financing arrangements, hiring practices, and creative input for the films directly facilitated the racial redistribution of labor behind the camera and the black-diasporic content of images on screen.

The films' marketing and release campaigns captured both credible local dimensions and deliberate commodification of "ghetto authenticity." Major studios hired African American public-relations and advertising companies: in the case of *Super Fly*, Warner hired James Booker Associates.[75] Prescreenings were held, according to one Booker executive, "not for the kind of cultural elite usually found on those white 'opinion makers' advance screening lists at the majors, but for Harlem bartenders, hairdressers, barbers and street people who have immediate impact within the black community."[76] Campus and Bernhard publicized *Mack*'s community engagement in a different way by announcing that all the profits from the opening full-house screening in Oakland would go to the Panthers Milk Fund—a political move in 1973 given the state's full-blown repression of that organization. Campus is thus largely persuasive when he claimed in the face of heated criticism, "We're not exploiting anything. We're talking about something that exists. It's not like someone sitting in a deck chair in Hollywood with a typewriter saying how are we going to rip them off. The story came from the ghetto itself."[77] Because the two films were in different ways embedded in the urban enclaves they represented, the employment of black marketers, recourse to local opinion makers, and politicized fund-raising efforts were consistent with production principles—preferable to the alternative of relying on white outsiders. At the same time, such selling strategies enhanced these films' images of ghetto realness, which with their stylish and subversive imagery helped maximize interest among the youth audience consisting of insiderist blacks and thrilled whites.

However creatively open the racial production relations were for *Super Fly* and *Mack*, whites still stood to profit enormously from these productions. The James Booker marketing strategy was highly effective, and in one night *Super Fly* had cleared the weekly operating expenses of salaries, insurance, taxes, and rent at the packed, white-owned and run Loew's State II in New York in August 1972, leaving all the rest of the week's income as clear profit. *Super Fly* cleared more than $10 million within three months of release and went on to generate rentals of $6.4 million (Warner's break-even figure to be recouped was reportedly around $2.5 million).[78] Though the black investors got significant cuts, producer Shore got by far the biggest pay-off, claiming in a *Variety* interview that he had negotiated for himself a 40 percent profit share.[79] One journalist described him as "[lighting] up like downtown Las Vegas at the mention of *Super Fly* and immediately [converting] into a veritable human computer spilling out amazing gross figures."[80] No doubt, a slightly grotesque image. *Mack* grossed more than $2 million in its first five weeks of release in about twenty-two urban theaters, with producer Harvey Bernhard and Cinerama enjoying the highest earnings from the film's rentals of $4.3 million.[81]

However, African Americans also made money. On *Super Fly*, the black director Gordon Parks Jr. and star Ron O'Neal divided a 10 percent cut of profits—much less than Shore but not insubstantial.[82] Most significantly, if we include the massive additional revenue generated by the film's soundtrack, Curtis Mayfield emerges as by far the most well-remunerated African American on this project about black business enterprise. Following the powerful musical scores of *Sweetback* and *Shaft*, black action films continued to find their "deep form" in music. This resulted in critically acclaimed and highly successful soul–funk soundtrack albums. Earnings from performance rights and royalties fed back to Mayfield because, like Harry Belafonte with Har-Bel and Van Peebles with Yeah, Inc., he owned his own publishing company and independent record label, Curtom Records, which he had founded in 1963.[83] Each of the hit singles "Super Fly" and "Freddie's Dead" sold more than one million copies, and the crossover soundtrack album went on to sell twelve million units, with Mayfield ultimately earning more than $5 million, surpassing even Sig Shore's profits. This payoff contrasts sharply with, for instance, Isaac Hayes's experience of writing the iconic Oscar-winning *Shaft* score, for which he received a flat fee of $20,000.[84] Hayes ended up signing away all rights to future royalties when he faced bankruptcy by the mid-1970s (his compositions for the film were owned by MGM). His experience foregrounds the continuing theft of black culture, against which Mayfield's hard-fought black self-determination must be understood.

In the case of *Mack*, the black creatives who got points on the film were its top-billed stars, Max Julien and Richard Pryor. The Black Panthers also negotiated a share of profits, and the soundtrack was produced by the songwriter and singer Willie Hutch, generating two hit singles, "Brother's Gonna Work It Out" and "Slick," released on Berry Gordy's Motown Records, the leading African American recording company.[85] These racialized creative and financial negotiations behind the scenes at a time of heightened black nationalism fed into narrative priorities onscreen as film producers started to understand the vast marketability of dissident black identity politics.

Representing Ghetto Producers

In many of Hollywood's black-oriented films of the postwar years, as already suggested, the theme of racial discrimination was dramatized through stories of blacks' exclusion from and attempts to enter the workplace. From the important critique of racist working-class job sectors in *A Raisin in the Sun* and *Nothing but a Man* (Michael Roemer, 1964) to Poitier's upstanding professionals of the 1960s, race-themed films variously staged the exclusion from and entry into labor markets. However, there had been little serious thematic engagement with black business culture—themes that had dropped off the cinematic landscape with the demise of black-made race films in the early decades of the twentieth century.[86] Nor indeed did black enterprise feature much in the earliest black-oriented films of the 1970s. With the exception of Van Peebles's film *Watermelon Man*, in which the hero sets up his own black insurance business, impasse-era films tended to present race and class critiques of small businesses and precarious work in the informal economy. *Cotton*'s beset black detectives work hard for their modest public-sector salaries, while preacher Deke O'Malley's attempts at underground wealth creation ultimately amount to extortion. Angel Levine's numbers running—an illegal enterprise that had a long history as a source of underground wealth generation in Harlem, as Belafonte well knew—is presented as basically a dead-end hustle. Mrs. Copee in *Landlord* is frustrated by her tiny tenement-sited beauty salon. *Shaft*, in 1971, presented an early post–civil rights businessman as a slick, self-employed private detective operating in both black and white worlds. But narrative emphasis rests on his lone sleuthing, at least one step removed from the black community. Further powerful stirrings arrived with *Sweetback*, as I argued earlier in this chapter: though his currency is sex, not money, the sense of black economic self-determination was powerfully warranted by the hero being played by Van Peebles.

However, it was *Super Fly* and *Mack* that most influentially engaged the thematic terrain of black subcultural enterprise—albeit through the socially harmful businesses of drug dealing and pimping. These films narrated the barriers to and adaptive chances for black male business activity within white-dominated power structures, projecting onscreen the predicaments, mindsets, and fantasies of black subcultural youth. Acclaimed film *Black Caesar* (Larry Cohen, 1973) is the other iconic film that contributed to the flowering of portrayals of black underworld entrepreneurs at this moment. But as a remake of the classic 1930s white ethnic gangster film *Little Caesar* (Mervyn LeRoy, 1931), it was far less socially embedded in subcultural black business culture than the two main case studies here.

Super Fly tells the story of four Harlem cocaine dealers: Eddie (Carl Lee), Scatter (Julius Harris), Freddie (Charles McGregor), and Priest (Ron O'Neal). Priest and Eddie are business partners who, starting from nothing, have expanded their distribution operation, and the narrative focuses on Priest's attempt to pull off a huge $1 million drug haul so that he can go straight. In their classic investigation of racial inequality, the sociologists Melvin Oliver and Thomas Shapiro explore the shortage of self-employment and wealth-generation opportunities for black Americans. They argue that the marginalization of black entrepreneurs by white finance and white consumers has greatly exacerbated the wealth gap.[87] *Super Fly* brazenly flips this racial script. As the commentators James Parish and George Hill have summarized, Priest and Eddie have "fifty men out on the New York City street all pushing dope (mostly to white people)."[88] In a sequence partway through the film, there is a three-minute montage of split-screen stills depicting the distribution, sale, and consumption of cocaine, propelled by the backbeat of Mayfield's song "Pusherman." The montage is markedly multiracial, showing the interaction of blacks, whites, and Asians, but in general cool blacks are selling to whites from all walks of life (business executives, construction workers, etc.). Cocaine is problematically constructed as a hip, prestige product (in implicit contrast to heroin), enhancing the dealer's image. The high-stakes entrepreneurialism of Priest—who penetrates white markets, generates jobs for minorities (however precarious these jobs may be), and operates above the law—constitutes a highly pleasurable signifier of black pride and success, which was of course dangerously far from a realist portrayal. As Nelson George remarks, "Ron O'Neal's Priest was a glamorous vision of the commonplace drug wholesaler. No one I saw or knew in Brownsville was as fly as Priest."[89]

Along with interracial trade, *Super Fly* stages black intergenerational investment. Priest turns to the father figure Scatter for help to pull off his big score. Scatter is a former drug distributor who had gotten Priest started in the business. Now an established small businessman, Scatter reluctantly agrees to help, willing to risk everything for his protégé because he understands the crucial importance of passing on resources to the next generation. As Priest's partner Eddie remarks incredulously to the hero, "You want that man to give up the little time he got left and lay it on the line for you. And you know he *wanted* to do it for you!" Scatter has a hard-won appreciation of the fact that "family assets expand choices, horizons, and opportunities for children," which can counteract what Oliver and Shapiro call the "socially layered accumulation of disadvantages" that compound the racial wealth gap across generations.[90] Scatter describes Priest's underworld apprenticeship as an alternative schooling within a context of deprivation: "I gave you one scholarship, Youngblood. No-one ever gave me nothing." Facing death near the film's end, with his capital now of no use to him, Scatter switches to third person: "All the money Scatter done made." Racial oppression deepens the family melodrama, with real pathos in Scatter's sacrifice for his "son."

Much of the film's tension revolves around the different worldviews of business partners Priest and Eddie. Priest sees the drug economy as a pathway to mainstream success, expressing an aspirational desire for expanded life chances. Asked what he would do after the big score, he responds, "It's not so much what I'd do as having the choice." He rejects the menial jobs available: "Working some jive job for chump change, day after day. If that's all I'm supposed to do then they're gon' have to kill me because that ain't enough." Priest emerges as a hip rendering of the American entrepreneurial hero, ready to seize post–civil rights opportunity. His climactic speech, in which he triumphs financially and rhetorically over the white drug kingpin and police deputy commissioner, is an exhilarating rap, beginning "You don't own me, pig!" Priest's crossover bootstrap charisma certainly excited white film commentators at the time. For Vincent Canby of the *New York Times*, Priest "succeeds in his last big deal, rather gloriously"; another reviewer described him as "downright glamorous."[91]

By contrast, sharp-dressed, hip-talking Eddie views the underground economy as an end in itself. Tension arises because he sees no reason to

FIGURE 4.5 Publicity still from *Super Fly* (Gordon Parks Jr., 1972) featuring partners Youngblood Priest (Ron O'Neal) and Eddie (Carl Lee).
Source: Courtesy of the British Film Institute National Archive.

terminate their drug-dealing operation. Eddie's limited horizons express a self-conscious internalization of racial inequality: "That honky's using me," he says of their white drug wholesaler. "So what? You know, I'm glad he's using me. . . . People been using me all my life." Eddie's vernacular insight expresses exploitative dynamics and curtailed life chances. When Eddie finally betrays his partner, it may appear to be a simple act of treacherous short-sightedness, but the cycle of social constraint mires Eddie in ways that have more salience than Priest's glamorized aspiration. He crystallizes the film's defense of the socially damaging business of drug dealing: "I know it's a rotten game, but it's the only one the man left us to play." Eddie's statement seductively positions such activities as the only option available due to historic and ongoing exclusion. In the film's most quoted speech, he describes the good life they have achieved: "You're gonna give all this up? Eight-track stereo, color TV in every room, and can snort half a piece of dope every day. That's the American dream, nigga! Well, ain't it?" Explaining the subcultural logic of black hustlers, Robin Kelley sheds light on Eddie's outlook: "Possessing capital was not the ultimate goal; rather, money was primarily a means by which hustlers could avoid wage work and negotiate status through the purchase of prestigious commodities."[92] Eddie's speech thus provides insights into the resistive styles and pleasures of the life.

Super Fly's contested entrepreneurial imagination, negotiated through Priest, Eddie, Scatter, and the tragic Freddie, invites a reexamination of the role of Curtis Mayfield's soundtrack—according to the leading critic Nelson George, "arguably, the single greatest black pop effort of the decade." With its lyrical complexity, vocal sincerity, and instrumental dynamism of guitars, horns, and flutes, the album is movingly and adeptly "at odds" with the drug dealers on screen, but at the same time, as I have argued elsewhere, the music also affirms the pleasures and perils of black subcultural enterprise.[93]

The less-accumulative mindset represented by Eddie is also developed in the subcultural entrepreneurialism of *Mack*. The film's main protagonist, Goldie, languishes in prison at the start, where, overhearing pimp tales, he first comes up with his idea to enter the Life. Once out, he builds his street reputation and "stable" of women until he is crowned "Mack of the Year" at the Players' Ball. Presenting both the glamor and the dubiousness of pimping, *Mack* charts the story of Goldie's rise and fall. Because of the strong influence of his black-revolutionary brother, Olinga (Roger Mosley), and following the murder of his mother (*Imitation of Life* actor Juanita Moore), Goldie finally turns his back on pimping. Pimp culture had circulated and evolved in black communities not only through the pursuits of a few actual pimps but also much more widely through the sartorial styles, toast poems, and vernacular language of poor and working-class black men across the twentieth century. Pimp culture was passed on in the predominantly male spaces of the street, barbershop, and prison and became emblematic of black stylization and verbal exuberance. Thus, though a misogynist social malefactor, the pimp had long been fetishized as a subcultural "heroic hustler."[94] In the late 1960s and early 1970s, pimp culture came to be transmitted in new ways and to spatially removed audiences through fiction, the most influential book being the violently misogynist *Pimp: The Story of My Life* by Iceberg Slim (Robert Beck), first published in 1967.[95]

Mack was the first text that concertedly transposed this lore onto film screens, if in relatively hippie-inflected, Bay Area terms. Goldie's hustle, like Eddie's in *Super Fly*, is far from a simple ode to capitalism. The film's white drug wholesaler describes Goldie's business as a "penny-pushin' pimp scheme," indicating the difficulty and danger of this "artisanal" subcultural mode of earning a living. Indeed, *Mack*'s rendition of Oakland pimps extends further the idea of the "competition of style" that first attracted *Super Fly*'s makers. Heavy emphasis rests on Goldie's image, which can be explained on the functional level of impression management, as the folklorist Bruce Jackson explains: "A doctor in jeans is still a doctor, but a pimp without flashy clothes and a sharp car is nobody at all."[96] But it must also be understood in symbolic terms, whereby the dandified display of Goldie and the Players' Ball participants pleasurably rejects the dominant society's typecasting of working-class black people as subordinate. Racially encoded dandyism and hedonism present a symbolic affront to a dominant social order founded on the tenets of a forbearing Protestant work ethic. Goldie instructs his prostitutes to think of themselves as "ladies of leisure," and in a later film, *The Candy Tangerine Man* (Matt Cimber, 1975), the pimp hero is the "the black baron," tapping into aristocratic anti-American models associated with rentier wealth, indolence, and public display. Pimp antiheroes thus conflate upper- and lower-class identifications; through their style politics and occupational pursuits, they brazenly repudiate the "square world," serving as heroic totems for the rejection of unfulfilling, mechanized labor.

Although pimp texts such as *The Mack* privilege lifestyle over employment or style over substance, the refusal of work is not to be taken at face value. The pimp trickster's ostentatious pose masks an underlying narrative of street education, entrepreneurial endeavor, and rhetorical dexterity. Like Priest's relationship to Scatter, Goldie is mentored by Blind Man (an Iceberg Slim–informed figure)—the central relationship between the established old head who teaches the "rules of the game" to the young aspirational hustler. This teacher–student connection is exemplified in the famous barbershop scene, when Goldie listens to established pimps rap about their work philosophy. Conventional education has failed Goldie, as it did the illiterate Frank Ward, and the emphasis on alternative schooling is clear. Because pimp lore is based on rhetorical skill and psychological manipulation, all texts stress the difficulty, discipline, and intelligence associated with being successful. With its confluence of work and leisure, pimp culture of the 1970s presented a suggestive and misogynist pop-cultural take on what Robin Kelley has influentially described as the "struggle to carve out a kind of liminal space between work and play, labor and performance" among underemployed black men.[97] This first cinematic dramatization of the pimp

FIGURE 4.6 Publicity still from *The Mack* (Michael Campus, 1973) featuring Goldie (Max Julien) and Slim (Richard Pryor).
Source: Courtesy of the British Film Institute National Archive.

antihero's fusion of work and play would stand as a powerful blueprint. It would take on more pop-cultural salience as permanent underemployment grew for African Americans in the post–civil rights period.

The superstud coding of black masculinity described by S. Craig Watkins and powerfully consecrated in *Sweetback* and *Shaft* was further developed in the hustling milieus depicted in *Super Fly* and *Mack*. These films romanticize the black masculinist cool pose, with many reviewers admiring in particular Priest's "smoldering, virile presence."[98] Pimp culture—which celebrates tricking and abusing women and making money through commodifying their sexual activity—is of course an egregiously masculinist and sexist form of subcultural business practice. The homosocial bonding within the male peer group in *Mack*, typifying ghetto action films of the 1970s, is privileged over relations with women: the men teach each other and celebrate how to psychologically manipulate women for profit. Although Goldie plays a nonviolent pimp, foregrounding his emotions (he cries in several scenes), the only woman he embraces in the film is his mother, foregrounding the heroic pimp's sexual restraint and rejection of heteronormative love and sex in favor of homosociality. As with much of mainstream film culture in the early 1970s in which women are portrayed in passive and victimized roles, *Mack* stood as part of a rejection of the second-wave feminist movement. At the same time, it stood as an insolent rendition of and rebuke to Daniel Patrick Moynihan's vision of the dysfunctional black family (discussed further in chapter 5).

In different ways, through these masculinist subcultural entrepreneurs, these films staged the glamorous but precarious circumvention of restrictions on African American male social and economic agency. Through their production relations and thematic content, they brought into the cinematic spotlight subcultural style practices and alternative wealth-generation models that had evolved over a long history of marginalization. Their action-genre conventions were tailored to black interests and expectations, dramatizing the injuries of the racial wealth gap and the turn to alternative opportunity structures in a bid to gain pleasure, status, and cash—aided by the creative and economic input of African Americans behind the scenes. According to the film critic Lindsay Patterson, such films "presented an important message about the failure of American society to freely provide legitimate opportunities for its bright but impoverished young black men."[99] But to what extent did the powerful message about society's failure in these films support the antiracist movement of radicals and reformists during these years?

The Politics of Hustler Creatives

Classic civil rights mobilization had been built in part, as Nancy MacLean describes, on reforming the state to support "the belief that those who worked hard at honest callings, whatever their origins, could better themselves and lift their children's prospects."[100] Popular culture was seen to play a vital role in this quest by projecting positive and sustaining images to selves and others, like those presented totemically by Sidney Poitier. However, continuing in a path laid out by *Sweetback*, the street-identified heroes in *Super Fly* and *Mack* stood as an affront to such a project. Pop-cultural representations of heroic hustlers were energized by a sense that promises of decent jobs for black people who were ready to work at "honest callings" were not being kept—not least in the film industry. The pervasive liberal discourses of rights and opportunities proved dubious and even detrimental for many poor and working-class blacks with rising expectations in a still-exclusionary job market. The profane glamorization of black *dis*honest callings in *Super Fly* and *The Mack* thus encapsulated widespread feelings of cynicism and anger about the racial distribution of jobs and wealth.

If both films reject integrationism, they differ fundamentally in their negotiation of black-revolutionary politics. *Super Fly*'s portrayal of black nationalists is very negative. In a pivotal scene, three "black militants" approach Priest and Eddie and challenge them to give something back to the community: "We're out here trying to build a new nation for black people. It's time for you to start paying some *dues!*" Priest's response comes off as far more virile, eloquent, and even militant as he says he will offer his allegiance only when they start "killing whitey": "Until you can do that, go sing your marching songs somewhere else." Begrudgingly impressed, the militants retreat, constructed as just another interest group on the take. This scene has been lambasted. The scholar William Lyne laments, "As they leave with their tails between their legs, the 'militants' have not only bowed to Priest's superior masculinity, they have also relinquished any claims on effective resistance."[101] After *Super Fly*'s release, Roy Innis of the Congress for Racial Equality, which had moved its offices to Harlem, castigated *Super Fly* as "anti-struggle, anti-revolutionary (so-called Black revolutionaries are usually portrayed as bungling idiots), and anti–direct involvement,"[102] and Black Panther leader Huey Newton complained that black action films "leave revolution out or, if it's in, they make it look stupid and naïve."[103]

The classic black-nationalist mission was to mobilize the hustler, to convert cynicism into radicalism. Newton described the Black Panther mandate "to transform many of the so-called criminal activities going on in the street into something political."[104] This conversion process had been staged in the narrative of *Sweetback*. In his very widely circulating autobiography, published in 1965, Malcolm X represented himself as a totem of such conversion, and Ossie Davis describes how the black radical leader had a "redeeming effect on the disaffected masses" in Harlem, where *Super oFly* is located.[105] *Super Fly* shockingly reverses such political redemption:

channeling political energies away from activism and toward stylish and business-savvy individualism.

The scene between Priest and the black nationalists may be legible in terms of the ebbing of black- revolutionary politics in the early 1970s. Widespread grassroots radicalism was still vital, but it came up against an intractable and resentful white majority and extremely repressive state apparatus that had no appetite to deliver de facto racial equality to minorities. As Howard Winant summarizes, "The result was that the movement's relatively manageable demands were incorporated within the status quo, while its radical demands for social justice and black power—with their disruptive, participatory, and redistributive content—were systematically rejected."[106] Nonetheless, why would the *Super Fly* filmmakers choose to promote this rejection, especially given the production's substantially black-determined enterprise? Progenitors *Sweetback* and *Shaft* opted to show some degree of collaboration between individualist heroes and activists. Accounts of the making of *Super Fly* suggest that this decision may have come down to experiences during the shoot. *Super Fly*'s makers were repeatedly approached by local Harlem political groups, who demanded funding, jobs, and politically conscious imagery in exchange for access and protection.[107] Street gangs, according to actor Julius Harris, also "wanted their taste." The makers refused to "cough up. We were street cats too. We said no, no."[108] Fenty and Parks incorporated these disputes into script development, conflating activists and gangs in its figuring of "militants." Priest and Eddie emerge as the superfly stand-ins for the black investors and filmmakers dramatically refusing to pay their dues to these groups in Harlem. Sadly, the only major-release film to come anywhere near the ambitious goal of "95% black crews on pictures made in the black community," demanded by Harlem activists, lampooned black neighborhood political groups.[109] The genuine social critique mounted through the film's realist images of urban poverty and disinvestment, through Mayfield's lyrics (above all "Little Child Runnin' Wild"), and through the insights spoken by Eddie, Scatter, and Priest does not prompt collectivist solutions. This critique instead tends to sanction the hustler creative's turn to individualism and enterprise.

Mack offers a very different perspective, and, again, this difference was determined in part by the conditions of its filmmaking. Set in Oakland, the birthplace of the Black Panther Party, the film sets Goldie's lumpen entrepreneurial imagination against his brother Olinga's revolutionary one, underscored by the classic Willie Hutch soundtrack single "Brother's Gonna

Work It Out." Both brothers see the American system as racist and exploit-ative, but they differ markedly in their responses to it. For Goldie, the racist system justifies his hustling individualism, whereas Olinga, wearing Afro-centric clothes, tries, as he asserts, to "convert the false consciousness of all oppressed people" through grassroots political action. Olinga's transforma-tionist rhetoric has authority, and he emerges as one of the most compelling black-nationalist portraits on mainstream film screens in the 1970s. His charismatic black transformationism in the film and the low-key ending (which is very unusual for a ghetto action film of the 1970s) can be explained by the substantial creative input by the Panthers, notably Huey Newton; the complex critical politics of actors Richard Pryor, Max Julien, and Carol Speed; and by the left-leaning politics of director Michael Campus.[110]

The film is dedicated to Frank Ward, who was found murdered in Berke-ley just before the film was finished, adding further weight to the depiction of the dangers and desperation of hustling.[111] *Mack* ends with Goldie, alone and stripped of his pimp garb, taking a bus bound for Alabama. Thus, New-ton's Panther mandate of converting criminal activity into political con-sciousness is staged in part through the film's resolution.[112] When Robin Kelley argues that Malcolm X's "participation in the underground subculture of black working-class youth . . . was not a detour on the road to political consciousness but rather an essential element of his radicalization," the same might be intimated for Goldie.[113] Campus remarked, "I didn't want people to walk out and say they wanted to be a mack. I wanted to show the tragedy."[114]

However, Campus's mission for the film mainly backfired. Certainly, the film offered multiple points of identification for audiences, and there was room for radicals and progressives to see their views well represented and ultimately narratively vindicated. But there can be no doubt that the film's seductive pleasures encouraged identification with Goldie's and Pretty Tony's stylish, homosocial individualism over Olinga's grassroots communalism. As the *Los Angeles Times* reviewer Kevin Thomas asserted, the film's "high-light is the authentic pimp's ball, in which handsome men and beautiful women fairly glow in their dazzling finery. It's a sight as spectacular as it is ephemeral and is likely to linger in the memory long after the movie is over."[115] The ephemeral spectacle, once captured on film, not only lingered but was endlessly replayable. Despite the producers' best intentions, the inequality-warranted black-pimp archetype only grew in dazzling pop-cultural and subcultural stature thereafter. Pimp culture encapsulated the mesmerizing style politics associated with spectacular youth subcultures and black-diasporic cultural repertoires, both of which proved so commodifiable and lucrative in the post–civil rights cultural industries.[116]

Because of *Super Fly*'s flagrant repudiation of transformative politics and *Mack*'s dazzling spectacle overpowering its robust black radical themes, it would be hard to argue that these films were not in many ways politically demobilizing. Their onscreen fetishization of harmful black entrepreneurialism served mainly to undermine communal action. Through their transmission of hip fashions, they encouraged consumerism among youth audiences nationwide—including, in the case of *Super Fly*, drug consumption. The title of a *Jet* magazine cover story in December 1972 pronounced somewhat sensationally: "'Super Fly' Film Is Changing Behavior of Blacks."[117] In his autobiography, the black journalist Nathan McCall asserts that *Super Fly* "influenced the style, thinking, and choices that a lot of young black men began making around that time. I know it deeply affected me."[118] The ethnographer Mary Pattillo-McCoy found that the film "consumed" black youth. "I grew up with *Super Fly*," recalls interviewee Lauren Grant. "That picture had a profound effect on my life." The film influenced occupational choices, enticing some ambitious black youth into drug dealing, including McCall and Pattillo-McCoy's interviewee Grant, who "decided to stop mimicking the costumes and mannerisms of the movie characters in *Super Fly*, and instead started reproducing the behaviors of the actual drug dealers in her own environment."[119] The films' glamorization of ghetto entrepreneurs, it seems, helped pull some young people toward the underground economy.

However, these films' mythologizing of black entrepreneurial hustlers also offered cues for work in the cultural industries. Rhetorical and embodied black stylization, long circulating in black-diasporic subcultural scenes, lent itself hugely, it turned out, to popular-cultural appropriation. *Super Fly* and *Mack*, like *Sweetback*, capitalized on and contributed to the immense currency of black urban culture in the early 1970s, a period of proliferating ethnographies and press features on "authentic Negro culture," as Kelley has compellingly critiqued.[120] In the year before *Mack*'s release, the white ethnographers Christina Milner and Richard Milner had published *Black Players: The Secret World of Black Pimps*, a sympathetic study of Bay Area hustlers.[121] Thus, white commentators were busy chronicling, exoticizing, and (in the case of Moynihan) disparaging urban communities for mainly white and middle-class consumption. The creators of these films and their soundtracks responded by drawing on this topicality to construct their own versions of stylized ghetto masculinity that catered primarily to black appetites but that also found a lucrative, secondary white youth audience. Black cultural industry—specifically the conversion of black-diasporic style politics into marketable cultural practices and products—became an expanding route to and dream for self-determined labor for post–civil rights black youth as other kinds of work disappeared.[122] Hustling practices and narratives became powerful tropes and tactics for young people aspiring to careers in entertainment. Cultural-industries employment offered both the dream of legitimate opportunities that rejected menial and low-pay jobs as well as a potential way out of the precarious informal economy narrated in the films. Thus, in many ways these iconic film projects, *Sweetback*, *Super Fly*, and *Mack*, serve as allegories for post–civil rights black pop-cultural production.

A parallel emerges between partners Priest and Eddie and their fifty foot soldiers in front of the camera and the film's black makers, Parks Jr. and Fenty, and their Third World apprentices behind the camera. If father figure and drug dealer Scatter invested in Priest, likewise actual father Parks Sr. and underground businesspeople invested in Parks Jr.'s film, constituting a literal show of nepotism and alternative finance arrangements that stood as a tactical response to Hollywood's white structures. With *Mack*, Robert Poole was the hustler turned writer, a conversion narrative into creative labor that is also staged onscreen when real hustlers such as KC and Frank Ward play themselves, revealing the immense potential for pleasurable and lucrative pop-cultural commodification of black subcultural styles and behaviors. The films' narratives revolve around black economic activity operating inside intractable white-dominated power and profit mechanisms, which is also the story, as we have seen, of the films' making. Ossie Davis presciently grasped the redolent cultural conversion-narrative possibilities: "If you would give me the five biggest pimps and pushers in this country, the black ones , and I could persuade them for one year to drop their hustle on the corner, if I could say, 'Look, for one year I want you to take that same push, that same organizational ability, and put it in films'—well, at the end of that one year black folks would take over the whole film industry.[123] Where *Mack* shows that ultimately the exploitative system is stacked against black collectivist and business activity, emphasizing its costs and precarity, in *Super Fly* the final "You don't own me, pig!" scene in which Priest walks away with all the money emerges as a particularly egregious ghetto fantasy.

When Eddie states that the "rotten game" of drug dealing is "the only one the Man left us to play," he could be talking about the "game" of Hollywood film acting for minorities. The idea of shifting a tainted yet exciting product speaks not just for the deleterious drug trade onscreen but also for performing the role of a drug dealer within cinema's racist representational regimes. Eddie's statement reads as a lament for the historic marginalization of minority talent in the film industry and perhaps as an apologia for taking on an acting role that glamorizes drug dealing. Carl Lee, who plays Eddie, was the son of Sidney Poitier's friend Canada Lee, whose career and life were demolished by racism and McCarthyism, a connection that lends extra resonance to the oppression-determined opportunism of his son's statement as Eddie. A look at the career profiles of *Super Fly*'s two partners is salutary in terms of progress narratives. Talented, award-winning theater actor Ron O'Neal failed to establish himself thereafter, despite his widely touted star qualities, and the iconically hip actor Carl Lee was unable to maintain his career and, like his father, died early, perhaps indicative of the ongoing and deeply entrenched structures of racial exclusion in the film industry that this film both exposes and dangerously conceals.[124]

Although such reflexive narratives of ghetto entrepreneurs onscreen did not lastingly benefit O'Neal or Lee personally, they proved influential and far-reaching in the post–civil rights cultural arena. "Hustler creatives" have since gained great traction, not least in hip-hop culture. Given the historic barriers to black entrepreneurial opportunity and the increasingly pessimistic course of black–white relations in the 1970s, these films' subversion of business norms emerged as problematic but resonant enunciations that potentially offered new roadmaps for conversion into black creative labor.

■ ■ ■

This chapter began by tracing how early post–civil rights black left producers and their collaborators used their considerable creative and organizational resources to try to make inroads into the white corporate concentration of the film industry. Informed by civil rights, black-nationalist, leftist, anticolonial, subcultural, and black-capitalist ideologies, they grappled with the industry's status quo and staked out a range of economic, organizational, and discursive alternatives, becoming producers not primarily to accumulate capital but instead to bring about various forms of economic and symbolic redistribution. When Van Peebles, the archetypal seat-of-the-pants black radical creative, stated in his making-of book, "*Sweetback* made me a rich man. NO, not in money, I blew that a thousand times. I am speaking of rich in contentment—the feeling that comes with the knowledge of having been instrumental in striking a blow for justice," his assertion is credible because of the financial risks he assumed to augment his autonomy, rejecting Columbia's conventional, highly prized source of capitalization. However, when Van Peebles went on to claim that making *Sweetback* was a "triumph of the individual over a stifling social system,"[125] a note of enticing maverick individualism creeps into his entrepreneurial image, militating (along with his hip macho posturing) against his otherwise valid rhetorical claim that this film was made by the black community. Through Priest in *Super Fly*, we start to see a cinematic vision of this hip black business individualism. The parable of *Mack* seems to be that whatever the filmmakers' collectivist and alternative intentions, these aims were overwhelmed by the sheer spectacle of enterprising black-diasporic stylization on film screens. Within a hardening climate, the proto-liberationism innate in such powerful subaltern narratives could too easily be commoditized and displaced.

The ambitious black left producer creatives who tried to develop new programs for filmmaking did not have a lasting impact on cinema's racialized political economy. Their rhetoric was often authoritative and their efforts determined, but these ideals proved very difficult to translate at the time into a viable new cinematic infrastructure, beyond pockets of independent activity. However, though precariously positioned in real-world terms, the arrival of new black producers (onscreen and behind the scenes) were seized on by growing forces of cinematic white backlash. They were cast as totems of *black privilege* by whites gripped by a stirring politics of resentment. Against this supposed new African American racial entitlement, white male "disadvantage" was increasingly measured and mobilized.

5

COLOR-BLIND CORPORATISM

The Black Film Wave and White Revival

Rocky (John Avildsen), the smash hit of 1976 (grossing $117 million at the box office), presented a very different model of enterprising black masculinity than had Priest in *Super Fly* or Goldie in *The Mack*.[1] In contrast to these projections of dissident black entrepreneurialism of the early 1970s, *Rocky* was premised on a notion of black cultural pre-eminence represented by the self-made boxing champion Apollo Creed (Carl Weathers), against whom the unassuming white ethnic underdog hero Rocky Balboa (Sylvester Stallone) was positioned. At the end of the film, Rocky loses the climactic boxing match on points in an outcome that captures the idea that showboating, physically superior blacks now have the upper hand. The dice are loaded against racially benign, even beset, white men such as Rocky. The seeds of soft white backlash, planted in films such as *In the Heat of the Night*—when scene-stealing Chief Gillespie bows to Virgil Tibbs's hyperprofessionalism—had grown by the late 1970s into a full-blown white reaction founded in part on the specious notion of black (male) privilege. The scholar Matthew Frye Jacobson influentially calls this reaction "white ethnic revival."[2] The revival fomented onscreen was also mobilized in industry politics as the 1970s progressed, including by another prominent Italian American with whom we are already familiar. MPAA head Jack Valenti, who had been instrumental in thwarting the implementation of civil rights laws in the film industry, continued to undermine attempts to bring racial change to Hollywood. When black workers and advocacy groups mounted campaigns in 1972 for more jobs and control, he cast their demands as unwarranted and illiberal: "I'm deeply concerned not just about the movie business, but about any part of the society when, with threats of any kind, some group or some organization demands something that nobody else has."[3] Black industry advocates, he suggested, were racially overentitled, demanding something that nobody else had—including scrappy Italian Americans such as himself (and, later, Sylvester Stallone and Rocky Balboa). Yet, of course, in *Rocky*—conceived and coscripted by Stallone—it is the white ethnic hero/filmmaker who comes out on top morally as well as financially through the film's enormous, franchise-spawning success. This chapter shows that imbricated film narratives and industry politics of white resentment and revival, accompanied by changes to film financing and production trends, led to an almost total shutting out of black people from the film business after 1976.

However, before the door closed, many black-oriented films did get made. The film industry of the early 1970s seized on the demand for and marketing excitement about African American material, leading to a brief but

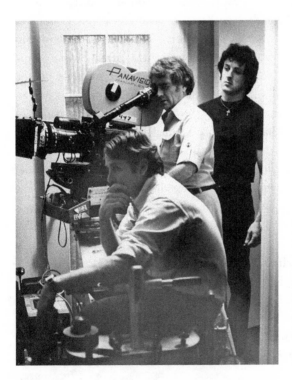

FIGURE 5.1
Director John Avildsen (*behind camera*) and writer Sylvester Stallone during production of the runaway hit *Rocky* (1976), in which Stallone stars.
Source: Courtesy of the Academy of Motion Picture Arts and Sciences.

unprecedented "boom" in black films.[4] Much of this chapter charts this important film wave from 1972 to its end in *Rocky*-dominated 1976. First, I extend the arguments of chapters 2 and 4 to consider some of the rich political and creative dimensions of black-oriented cinema of the time, which extends well beyond the delimiting, charged term *blaxploitation*. I examine a range of projects and thematic priorities, including the surprisingly rich and varied representations of black women, as the second section details. I then turn to the black film wave's decidedly blaxploitative dimensions, explaining why and how the industry opened the floodgates to so many cheaply made and luridly scripted and marketed black-themed products, which often fed into racial backlash politics. Finally, the last section spans the whole period 1972–1976 to consider the industry politics that largely determined the rise and fall of the black-oriented film wave. This chapter continues my book's argument that a fuller understanding of racial politics in cinema necessitates a careful consideration of whiteness and that white, not black, separationist practices powerfully determined patterns of racial continuity and change. Interracial collaboration as well as contestation and containment are widely evident.

Through an examination of representation onscreen as well as of battles over jobs and resources in Hollywood, I extend my story of how cinema was a powerful national arena in which the interventionist approaches to racial justice, particularly surrounding employment and economics, were negotiated and increasingly repudiated. New black film-representational codes and conventions had been established. But film's racial politics in the 1970s were also bound up with a resurgent corporate sector underpinned by a rehabilitated white identity politics. By the late 1970s, the wholesale rebuttal of the politics of racial redress and the withdrawal of funding for minority-made films by the industry, especially after the ending of the lucrative tax-shelter funding regime in 1976, had been somehow recast as a racially meritocratic state of affairs.

Reevaluating the "Blaxploitation Era"

Immediately following the racial-impasse films of 1970, most of which had not made money, the industry's integrationist rhetoric in the wake of King's assassination and the Kerner Commission report had proved hollow. Executives and producers largely withdrew from black-oriented film projects, so that, according to one account, the year 1971 saw the release of just nine black-focused features.[5] Two of these features, however, were enormously successful: independently produced *Sweetback* and major-studio-made *Shaft* (which grossed $17 million off a moderate budget, with more than $7 million returned to the ailing studio MGM).[6] Both were powered by exciting and lucrative cross-promoting soundtracks, installing a model that could be readily replicated, and their success led majors and independents alike to dive into black subject matter. The period from 1972 to 1976 saw a massive upsurge in black-oriented productions: according to the film scholar Keith Corson, an average of thirty-seven (mainly low-budget) black-themed releases per year.[7] Part of the attraction of making black-oriented pictures was the concentration of African American and youthful cinema audiences in urban areas. With whites moving to the suburbs and market research showing that people of color were much more frequent cinemagoers (in a period that was only just beginning to come out of long-term declining cinema attendance overall), urban theaters were high value. Following the success of *Sweetback* and *Shaft*, exhibitors believed they could market black-oriented films to packed urban houses, driving demand for content.[8] B. J. Mason, writing in *Ebony*, captured the synergistic possibilities of the style-oriented and music-propelled new black film wave, detailing such ancillary markets, following the release of *Shaft*, of "suits, watches, belts and sunglasses, leather coats, decals, sweatshirts and night shirts, beach towels, posters, after shave lotion and cologne."[9]

The surge of black film releases after 1971 was also propelled by financing trends. That year's new Revenue Act, which Hollywood had helped instigate, gifted substantial income tax credits on film losses and reintroduced investment tax credits for domestic film productions. The film historian David Cook stresses the importance of these new tax arrangements to filmmaking in the 1970s, becoming "the key mode of production finance" for most of the rest of the decade.[10] In a notoriously risky industry, producers could make money through tax write-offs even on officially loss-making film projects.

It is worth stressing that these conditions—the demographic changes affecting exhibition trends, the marketability of black identity politics, and the generous tax environment—made for quite an open production environment in comparison to film-industry norms. They created opportunities for a range of black-themed films, along with many other kinds of films, to be

COLOR-BLIND CORPORATISM   171

made. The majors distributed about one-third of these black-film-boom features, many of which, like *Super Fly*, were not made in-house but were picked up for distribution afterward, during a period of heightened cross-fertilization between studio-made films and independently created films. However, the majority of the black-focused films were made and distributed by smaller film companies and independents. Because black versions of stories were needed by an industry keen to capitalize on the new production trend, some African Americans were drawn into production, with quite a number of the releases written or directed by African Americans. In 1972 alone, five studio films had first-time black directors: Parks Jr. directed *Super Fly*; actor Ivan Dixon made *Trouble Man*, picked up by Twentieth Century-Fox; Sidney Poitier took over the direction of *Buck and the Preacher*, a joint enterprise for Columbia Pictures, Belafonte Enterprises, and Poitier's E&R Productions; film editor Hugh Robertson directed *Melinda*, made by MGM; and television director Mark Warren helmed the *Cotton Comes to Harlem* sequel *Come Back, Charleston Blue*, distributed by Warners. These five directors were accompanied in 1972 by a larger cohort of first-time black directors working outside of the major studios (including film school graduate William Crain [*Blacula*], actor Yaphet Kotto [*The Limit*], theater director Michael Schultz [*Together for Days*], actor Christopher St. John [*Top of the Heap*], and writer Oscar Williams [*The Final Comedown*]).[11]

It was unquestionably a creatively fertile period for black filmmakers. Quite a few films offered narratives of political awakening, organizing, and insurrection, capturing the period's black-power imperatives of community control of economic and neighborhood institutions as well as armed self-defense. For his second feature, Ivan Dixon finally got enough funds together (some of his own money and small donations from many black people in limited partnership) to start shooting the adaptation of Sam Greenlee's novel *The Spook Who Sat by the Door* (1969), picked up and ultimately funded in part by United Artists. Released in 1973, the film stages the political conversion of the "spook," a soft-spoken black social worker who is recruited into the Central Intelligence Agency to become a token of workplace integration, kept at the office ("sat by the door") rather than in the field in order to escort white sightseeing parties through the building. Workplace denigration and white hypocrisy lead directly to his radicalization.[12] This black-made film, in which the hero organizes and takes up arms, seems to offer a militant response to accommodationist narratives about black employment integration. It offers, for instance, an anti-assimilationist rejoinder to

Poitier's screen image of the black professional striving to integrate work-places, which led to color-blind resolutions.

A comparable film production was *Gordon's War* (1973), directed by Ossie Davis, about a Vietnam veteran (Paul Winfield) who upon returning home from war assembles a black and Latino group to take on the Harlem drug trade. In an answer text to the glamorization of black cocaine dealers in *Super Fly*, *Gordon's War* casts the charismatic Carl Lee as fighting (rather than dealing) drugs in Harlem. Made by Twentieth Century-Fox, it was shot on location and featured many actors from the Negro Ensemble Company, with heavy involvement from the community, including security from Harlem's black Muslims.[13] Davis and the film's producer, Robert Schaffel, contacted unions directly to request that craft locals, including East Coast Camera Local 644, grant waivers to enable the employment of black and Puerto Rican technicians not yet on union rosters, using Third World Cinema recruits and securing minority jobs in the areas of production, camera, and makeup.[14] On these film productions, community self-determination onscreen and behind the scenes ran in tandem.

The Education of Sonny Carson (1974) was another important and reflexive narrative about the genesis of black insurrection. After making *The Mack*, Michael Campus—perhaps chagrined by his inadvertent romanticizing of Oakland pimp culture—turned to making this screen adaptation of Carson's memoir of growing up in Brooklyn in the 1950s (published in 1972), a childhood attended by poverty, racism, police brutality, gangs, prison, political conversion, and civil rights activism. Carson was the film's technical adviser, and he had been very active in the struggle for community control of the Oceanville/Brownsville Brooklyn School District in the 1960s. He also became head of the Brooklyn chapter of the Congress of Racial Equality and critiqued the organization's national leadership for its black-capitalist orientation.[15] The resulting film, which stars Rony Clanton (who had featured in Shirley Clarke's film *The Cool World* [1963]), was the first producer credit for Irwin Yablans (who would go on to make hits such as *Halloween* [1978]) at Paramount. Irwin and his brother, Frank Yablans, who was the boss of Paramount, put up a substantial $1,300,000 production budget for *Sonny Carson*. Like Carson, the Yablanses had grown up in a poor tenement block in Brooklyn, and both, according to Campus, were closely involved in the planning of the film, which came "from the bowels of Bedford-Stuyvesant." Campus claimed that the brothers ceded creative control to the director: "I

FIGURE 5.2 Rony Clanton as Sonny Carson (*third from left*) and others in a scene from *The Education of Sonny Carson* (Michael Campus, 1974).
Source: Courtesy of the Academy of Motion Picture Arts and Sciences.

was prepared for one of those infamous creative battles; I had my speech prepared. But Frank never laid a glove on me."[16] Though a union picture made by a major studio, the film had eight minority crew members, a black scriptwriter (Fred Hudson), and fifteen minority interns. As in *Super Fly* and *Gordon's War*, many local amateur actors coming from local social clubs and street gangs played fictionalized versions of themselves.[17] The film's scenes shot on location in the Essex County Correctional Center in Caldwell, New Jersey, and at Sing Sing Prison in Ossining, New York, lent credibility to the film's critique of the criminal justice system in the dawning moment of the "race to incarcerate."[18] *The Education of Sonny Carson*, like *Gordon's War*, typified the continuing racializing of the Hollywood Renaissance: one of the biggest studios, with new-generation production heads, working with a black activist and a white leftist to produce social-realist yet experimental content rooted in the community.

Some features of the black boom were produced by Black Arts filmmakers and new film school graduates, capturing a different kind of creative ferment. Writer-director Bill Gunn, who had written racial-impasse films discussed in chapter 2, went on to write and direct the surreal and expressionistic black vampire love story *Ganja and Hess* in 1973. It starred Duane Jones (the lead actor of George Romero's indie classic *Night of the Living Dead* [1968]) and Marlene Clark, who recalls that it was made by a "totally mixed" crew.[19] The film centers on a young doctor who becomes addicted to blood after having been afflicted with an obscure, ancient disease. Though poorly reviewed in some of the mainstream press at the time of its release, the black film critic James Murray described it as "the most important black-produced film since *Sweetback*," and it was named one of the Ten Best American Films of the Decade at the Cannes Film Festival in 1973.[20] At the same time on the West Coast, the University of California at Los Angeles (UCLA) film school was incubating black filmmakers, who would go on to make important films that rebelled against the codes and conventions of both mainstream and exploitation cinema. According to the acclaimed filmmaker Charles Burnett, "LA Rebellion" films were complex aesthetic and thematic "response[s] to false and negative images that Hollywood films were promoting."[21]

Capturing another Hollywood Renaissance trend, new black film directors came from the worlds of theater and acting. *Five on the Black Hand Side* (Oscar Williams, 1973) was an adaptation of the play from 1969 by Charlie Russell, a member of the Harlem Writers Guild, who also wrote the screenplay. The film is a comedy about a black middle-class family headed by a self-made community businessman (L. Errol Jaye) of a very different mold than *Super Fly*'s Priest. He is a conservatively dressed barbershop owner whose faltering patriarchal grip on his family gives rise to conflict and comedy as he is challenged by his wife and children. The film's marketing campaign seized on its contradistinction to ghetto action pictures with the following pitch: "You've been Coffy-tized, Blacula-rized and Superflied—but now you're gonna be glorified, unified and filled-with-pride . . . when you see *Five on the Black Hand Side*." The film, picked up by United Artists for distribution, made money, returning more than $2 million (though its first-time interracial producers, actors Brock Peters and Michael Tolan, saw none of the profits).[22]

The need for black creatives to helm projects—sought after because they could enhance content and provide marketing credibility—continued to give rise to opportunities for black symbol creators in the first half of the 1970s. Though there were no guarantees of the ideological moorings of textual outcomes, greater minority involvement in filmmaking, as I have been arguing throughout this book, opened valuable employment opportunities and in general paid textual dividends. Take the example of film editor Hugh Robertson (who had been the first nonwhite American to be nominated for the Best Editor Academy Award for his work on John Schlesinger's film *Midnight Cowboy* [1969]). When Robertson moved into directing with the genre picture *Melinda*, he was taken aback by the MGM executives' intentions, explaining: "I had to fight and fight for any human elements in the story. They kept pushing for all sex and violence." Along with writer Lonne Elder and actor Rosalind Cash, Robertson achieved substantial changes to the studio's original script.[23] To be sure, as detailed in subsequent sections, some blacks were brought on in tokenistic ways to *sit by the door*, leading to the *Ebony* magazine writer B. J. Mason's "nagging suspicion that white filmmakers only use black craftsmen to lend authenticity."[24] But because of this critique, many commentators have failed to comment on actual employment diversification and content changes achieved, seeing them as at best inconsequential and at worst helping to lend credibility to ideologically problematic material. Such stances risk losing sight of the ways in which African Americans such as Robertson, Elder, and Cash, along with countless other minority symbol creators, sought to gain some agency over the content on which they worked. Like Poitier and Davis, they were committed to the challenging task of creating space within popular-genre formats that many audiences, including many blacks, favored. The relevance of input from African Americans, over and above a sense of marketing authenticity, helps explain why, although the majority of black-focused film directors of the period were white, many of the most influential directors and writers were African American.

Indeed, although film scholars have recognized and discussed black indie auteurs such as Melvin Van Peebles, Bill Gunn, and LA Rebellion directors as important, they have often sidelined the black creative input on genre films. Take, for instance, the black-exploitation film *Blacula*, which has undergone a scholarly recuperation and is now widely recognized as a racially generative and transgressive text. But in many scholarly accounts, with the exception of the one by Novotny Lawrence, the black creative labor involved in this horror picture is neglected.[25] The film scholar Leerom Medovoi has written a highly regarded scholarly article on the film, drawing out its surprising genre subversion and development of alternative models of black heroism and historicity.[26] But the film's production, which might explain some of the determinations of its racially productive content, is absent from consideration, and no mention is made of the fact that it was directed by an African American, William Crain. Indeed, Crain was one of the first graduates of UCLA's celebrated film program, at which Charles Burnett, Larry Clark, Haile Gerima, and Jamaa Fanaka were then gathering, thus making the discrepancy between lauded indie black auteurs and ignored genre-film directors all the more egregious. Ignoring the production histories on mainstream, exploitation, and nonauteurist film fare closes off important questions to do with the racial negotiations over cultural and economic resources behind the scenes that fed into film content.

Though the black directors of ghetto action films have been neglected, the black makers of their films' music soundtracks have not, often because they are seen as one step removed from the tainted films.[27] Powering the popularity and iconicity of many of these features were, of course, their extraordinary soundtracks, produced by many of the most influential soul-funk artists. Again, Earth, Wind, & Fire's soundtrack for *Sweetback* and Isaac Hayes's score for *Shaft* (for which he won the Oscar for "Theme from Shaft") were the main progenitors of this trend. There followed, along with Curtis Mayfield's extraordinary *Super Fly* score, Bobby Womack's *Across 110th Street*, which provides the plaintive music-scape for the impasse-era heist drama of the same title, starring Anthony Quinn and Yaphet Kotto; Marvin Gaye's *Trouble Man*; and James Brown's *Black Caesar* (with its edgy, percussive refrain "paid the cost to be the boss"). Typically, as in these cases, the finished film would be screened for the musicians, who would then compose the music, but in some cases the musicians were on set, as were Willie Hutch for *The Mack* and Curtis Mayfield, who performs "Pusherman" diegetically in *Super Fly*. These ghetto action-film soundtracks were certainly a heavily exploitable dimension of the film packages and are central to popular and scholarly understandings of the so-called blaxploitation era—not just because these often spellbinding soundtracks offered some critical commentary on the films but also because their transmission extended well beyond film watching and into the soundtrack of everyday life in the 1970s.

Even the pictures made by the notorious company that produced the most black-exploitation features, American International Pictures (AIP), nearly all directed by whites, should not be prejudged as self-evidently "blaxploitative" in their production and content. AIP was thriving in the early 1970s, capitalizing on the freedoms that followed the introduction of the self-regulatory CARA system in 1968. In his memoir, AIP's president Sam Arkoff explains his company's aggressive and opportunist policy: "We recognized a fad that we seized upon and rode to success."[28] Riding the black fad involved not only the promulgation of all kinds of crass racial and sexual stereotypes but also at times creative and representational openness. The racial complexity of its highest-grossing black horror film, *Blacula*, has already been noted, and its most successful black gangster film, *Black Caesar*, a remake of *Little Caesar* written and directed by successful white television screenwriter Larry Cohen, was also striking and innovative. The hand-held camera shooting in New York for *Black Caesar* was done with one camera without a permit by *Super Fly*'s director of photography James Signorelli. Its closing scenes included shots of the gorgeously besuited but wounded Black Caesar (Fred Williamson) walking down Fifth Avenue in front of Tiffany's jewelry shop, capturing some of the shocked reactions of passers-by, who thought the situation was real—"like it was a documentary," Cohen explained.[29]

Facing mounting criticism for its black-themed fare, AIP turned to some nonexploitation texts especially toward the end of the black film wave. *Cornbread, Earl, and Me* (Joseph Manduke, 1975) was a coming-of-age courtroom drama that *New York Amsterdam News* described as "about as close as we'll get to a realistic portrayal of ghetto life in relation to Black youngsters."[30] It stars Moses Gunn as an attorney (in a role contrasting to the Harlem mobster Bumpy Jones he played in *Shaft*), Lawrence Fishburne in his debut performance as the wrongly accused child, and Rosalind Cash as the child's mother in one of the period's nuanced portrayals of black working-class motherhood.

AIP also made *Cooley High* (1975), which was a substantial hit (returning $4 million to AIP in rentals), scripted by black playwright Eric Monte, creator of the hit television series *Good Times*, and directed by Monte's friend Michael Schultz, a young filmmaker who would go on to be one of the few black directors who managed to sustain his career after the black film wave.[31] A well-regarded high school drama set in Chicago in the 1950s, *Cooley High* eschews most of the set pieces of black-exploitation films. Though *Cornbread, Earl, and Me, Cooley High*, and most other AIP black-focused hits had men

FIGURE 5.3 Laurence Fishburne (in his debut screen role as Wilford Robinson), Thalmus Rasulala (Charlie), and Rosalind Cash (Sarah Robinson) in *Cornbread, Earl, and Me* (Joseph Manduke, 1975).
Source: Courtesy of the Academy of Motion Picture Arts and Sciences.

in lead roles, the black-oriented film that made the most money for the company, *Coffy* (Jack Hill, 1973), is, perhaps surprisingly, centered on a woman—representative of an underacknowledged turn to filmic representations of African American heroines of this period.

Representing Black Women in the Shadow of Moynihan

Black film culture of the early 1970s was decidedly male: all the new directors of mainstream and exploitation films were men. It would take into the 1980s for a black female director to get a commercial film release when Kathleen Collins made *Losing Ground* in 1982, costarring Bill Gunn.[32] Furthermore, in film texts such as *Sweetback* and *Shaft*, the misogyny onscreen runs deep. But this period nonetheless afforded substantial screen roles for black women. For all the justifiable concern about the new black superstud heroes surrounded by permissive, expendable women, there also emerged a number of black female heroines. They included strong mothers in dramas, such as Cicely Tyson in *Sounder* (Martin Ritt, 1972) and Rosalind Cash in *Cornbread, Earl, and Me*; romantic leads, such as Cash in *Melinda* and Vonette McGee in *Thomasine and Bushrod* (Max Julien, 1974); and action babes, such as Pam Grier in *Coffy* and *Foxy Brown* (Jack Hill, 1974) and Tamara Dobson as a karate-kicking federal agent in several higher-budget films starting with *Cleopatra Jones* (Jack Starrett, 1973), made by Warner Bros. Female-led films also encompassed notable biopics, including the Diana Ross vehicles *Lady Sings the Blues*, based on the life of Billie Holiday, and *Mahogany*, as well as comedy-dramas such as *Claudine* (John Berry, 1974), starring another singer-actor, Diahann Carroll. Strong black women also featured in independent releases such as *Georgia, Georgia* (Stig Bjorkman, 1972), starring Diana Sands (from a Maya Angelou screenplay); *Black Girl* (Ossie Davis, 1972), the screen adaptation of the off-Broadway play, featuring Peggy Pettit in an ensemble, mainly female cast; and *Bush Mama* (Haile Gerima, made in 1975 though not released until 1979), starring Barbarao. Nearly all these films made money, a signal that they resonated with audiences at a moment when black American women were enjoying unprecedented popular-cultural visibility, which was also evident in television shows such as the influential sit-com *Julia* (1968–1971), starring Diahann Carroll as a working single mother. In light of the history of misrepresentation and underrepresentation faced by black female screen performers from Ethel Waters to Lena Horne and from Hattie McDaniel to Beah Richards, this was a significant moment for black actresses and black audiences.

Of course, black female actors of the early 1970s still struggled to move beyond the stultifying stereotypical Jezebels, mammies, and matriarchs. For instance, Ivan Dixon, directing his first film *Trouble Man*, had to call in the NAACP to negotiate changes to the script he had been given by Twentieth Century-Fox, particularly to develop the portrayal of the leading black female character (played by Paula Kelly). In the original script, the character is "jumping in and out of bed like a cat in heat," which Dixon and the civil rights organization successfully challenged.[33] It was the portrayal of black women that most exercised Robertson, Cash, and Elder when they signed up to make *Melinda*, as the director explained: "I had to insist on the dinner scene between Melinda (Vonette McGee) and Frankie (Calvin Lockhart) so we could see some kind of relationship between them, not just bring her into the story and suddenly have her dead the next morning." He also recounts the fight to keep a scene scripted by Elder between Frankie and Terry (Cash) that "shows her as a black woman who's strong and a real person." They managed to prevent the scene from being excised. After *Melinda* was released, Cash noted the many positive comments she got for her role as Terry: "When I go up to Harlem, the hard-working soul sisters come up to me and say 'you were for real in that part; I know what that character was all about."[34]

Such hard-fought progress in the screen representation of black women was particularly striking when set against dominant filmic trends of the period. "Hard-hat" cinema of the 1970s has been widely interpreted as extremely masculinist—fomenting backlash against the feminist movement and the real-world progress then being made by women. As Molly Haskell summarizes in her classic work *From Reverence to Rape*, "There were no working women on the screen, no sassy or smart-talking women, no mature women, and no goddesses either." In his examination of the biggest hits of the Hollywood Renaissance period, the film scholar Peter Krämer concurs, suggesting that almost all the films "revolve around the experiences, desires, and actions of men," with women "on all levels . . . sidelined (or vilified)."[35] The machismo and misogyny of the lauded Hollywood Renaissance were very influential in filmmaking themes then (and have continued to be since then). This onscreen marginalization and vilification of women intersected with profound behind-the-scenes underrepresentation of women of all colors in film-industry jobs. The hearing held by the EEOC in Hollywood in 1969 had uncovered an almost total lack of women in studio management, in the craft unions, and among filmmakers as well as a pervasive sense of complacency about this patriarchal status quo.[36] Clifford Alexander, who headed the EEOC committee, later reflected that, relative to racial discrimination, "it was not as 'fashionable' then to be on the side of protecting employment rights, or pension rights, or right-to-work rights on behalf of females."[37]

In light of this pervasive marginalization, the black screen heroines of the 1970s are notable. Many of them were, to lesser or greater degrees, hardworking and respectable in normative ways, from the hard graft of Louisiana sharecropper Rebecca Morgan in *Sounder* (a role for which Cicely Tyson got top billing) to the black-power-inflected respectability of FBI ace Cleopatra Jones, the impoverished, hard-working dancer in *Black Girl*, and the rags-to-riches fashion designer Tracy Chambers in *Mahogany*. Some of the film roles were more provocative, including two important ones—in *Coffy* and *Claudine*—that I now consider. The two films could not be further apart in terms of their genesis. *Coffy* was written and directed by white "sexploitation" filmmaker Jack Hill, who had never before made a black-focused film and was given his brief by AIP. The lead role launched Pam Grier as a star, grossing around $13 million at the box office off a $500,000 budget. For one week, this vigilante flick, about "the baddest one-chick hit-squad that ever hit town!," as the poster's tagline put it, was the top-grossing film in America—a first for a film in which a black woman had top billing.[38] *Claudine*, by contrast, was made by the radical filmmaking outfit Third World Cinema, which chose this "tender, inner-city romance-comedy," made and set in Harlem, as its first in-house production.[39] Distributed by major studio Twentieth Century-Fox, *Claudine* was produced by Hannah Weinstein and directed by the previously blacklisted white filmmaker John Berry. Though not on the same scale as *Coffy*, *Claudine* was also successful, grossing $6 million off a moderate $1.3 million budget. Commenting on its success, James Murray remarked that "all those who had invested in the debut production for Harlem's Third World Cinema Corp would certainly reap a psychologically lifting reward."[40]

In very different ways, both films present ambivalent portrayals of black female heroism, negotiating debates over black respectability and the pathologizing discourses about working-class black women that had been circulating inflammatorily since the publication of Daniel Patrick Moynihan's report *The Negro Family: The Case for National Action*. Deploying graphs and florid language, "the Moynihan Report," as it became known, contended that "at the heart of the deterioration of the fabric of Negro society is the deterioration of the Negro family." Poor black families headed by single mothers were apparently trapped in a self-perpetuating "tangle of pathology."[41] Among the many who critiqued the report was the psychologist William Ryan, who lambasted its portrayal of the "all-time favorite 'savage,' the promiscuous mother who produces a litter of illegitimate brats in order to profit from AFDC [Aid to Families with Dependent Children]."[42] Such was the discursive legacy of the report that black film heroines of the late 1960s and early 1970s were all, to some extent, configured in its shadow.

Some films attempted an ideological rehabilitation of black women by reinstating the patriarchal family to mollify Moynihan-influenced discourses. For instance, *Mahogany* follows such a containing logic in its treatment of family values and black females' work aspirations. As the scholar Miriam Thaggert has detailed, the heroine, a department-store secretary from Chicago's impoverished South Side, studies art at night school to work her way up and become a top fashion designer, only to give up her career to get married and start a family at the film's resolution.[43]

On some levels, both *Coffy* and *Claudine* chime with striving pro-Moynihan narratives of black women as hardworking, thrifty, and aspirational. Coffy is a nurse. When she turns vigilante, weaponizing herself through the guise of a high-class prostitute, Mystique, it is to avenge the abuse suffered by her drug-addicted young sister. Her sister got the money for her drug habit from an unsuspecting Coffy, who had been working extra nursing shifts to pay for her sister's music classes—Moynihan would surely approve of this striving industriousness in the pursuit of generating both economic and cultural capital. Thus, in this setup, Coffy is both connected to an impoverished (if sensationalized) urban experience through her family and is on the way to joining the ranks of the black middle class. However, her counterfeit persona, Mystique, serves as pretext for lots of racialized, exploitational scenes of sex and violence. In a screenplay written by exploitationer Jack Hill, Grier as Mystique performs a lurid "Jezebel" act to entrap male wrongdoers. This portrayal fits within Moynihan's neoconservative moral economy. Yet Coffy remains a sexually active black woman who isn't ultimately punished or contained for this activity (as was the norm in many film genres). And she is sexually active not just through her role play as Mystique but also as up-and-coming nurse Coffy. She has sex for pleasure and romance as well as using her sex hustle to forward her agenda and vanquish her male adversaries. Black female viewers certainly responded ambivalently to this performance, engaging enthusiastically with Grier's "funky downhome aggressiveness," as Donald Bogle puts it, but also shocked by the film's unfamiliar exploitation codes, as Stephane Dunn has ably explored.[44]

If *Coffy* transgressed Moynihan Report discourses in part by staging the financially independent, sexually assertive black female, *Claudine* rebuked the "tangle of pathology" discourses very differently. Grasping the nettle, it did so from the vantage point of a single-parent black mother on welfare. Heroine Claudine is well turned out and extremely hard working, thus on the surface positioned as part of Moynihan's deserving poor—seemingly ripe for cinematic rescue from her toil to the better life she warrants. But the film resists the ideological pull of this easy closure and, in the words of producer Hannah Weinstein, presents instead "a comedy-drama—not heavy—about the realistic problems of poor people for which there are no easy answers."[45] Indeed, Claudine is far from a sanitized iteration of the deserving poor, having six children ("a six-time mama," as the film's tagline announces) with no father present. Explaining the provenance of her kids, who range from eighteen years old to infant, she says she has had two husbands and "two almost marriages"—a nonnuclear state of affairs that, as Vincent Canby wrote for the *New York Times*, "may be taken as ammunition by people who are out to shoot down all welfare programs as corruptors of self-respect and ambition."[46] Indeed, the film directly invokes the Moynihan-fueled backlash against black mothers, with Claudine, echoing William Ryan, quipping provocatively, "You know us ignorant black bitches. . . . Grindin' out babies for the taxpayers to take care of."

The film interrupts this discourse by dramatizing lightly comedic family scenes as well as the challenges of Claudine's domestic work as she buses away from her family each morning to clean and wash for white people (in an early scene her pampered employer complains to a friend that her maid is late). Claudine and most of her friends are the working poor, and to make ends meet she does not declare her job so that she can claim welfare. When she falls for a sanitation worker played by James Earl Jones, this becomes another aspect of her life that she needs to conceal from the state. Avoiding what filmmaker Clyde Taylor calls the "sociological lens of Blackness as lack," the film parodies the predicament faced by the protagonists, including the prim white social worker who comes to inspect Claudine's apartment.[47] *Claudine*—and, in much more earnest terms a year later, *Bush Mama*, which chronicles the political awakening of a pregnant welfare recipient who is being pressured by the state to get an abortion—complicates conservative constructions of black mothers as the immoral instigators of a self-perpetuating culture of poverty. The black female sexuality in *Coffy* and the black female reproductive activities in *Claudine* worked ambivalently against the grain of the era's race/gender neoconservative project of family values and non-self-expressive female sexuality.

A look at these films' production relations once again sheds light on their gendered filmic themes. Both AIP's *Coffy* and Third World's *Claudine* had

FIGURE 5.4 Pam Grier in publicity still for *Coffy* (Jack Hill, 1973).
Source: Courtesy of the Academy of Motion Picture Arts and Sciences.

some important female and proto-feminist input. To be sure, *Coffy* was largely a white- and male-determined text, scripted and directed by Hill, commissioned by AIP boss Sam Arkoff, and overseen by AIP producer Larry Gordon. However, the making of *Coffy* was not exclusively male, in part because Hill had developed the role specially for Grier, whom he had cast earlier in her first proper acting role in the exploitationer *Big Doll House* (1971).[48] Deeply influenced by the Black Women's Manifesto of the Third World Women's Alliance in 1970, Grier had recently moved to Los Angeles, hoping to acquire resident status in California in order to qualify for lower film school fees at UCLA. Though not yet a student, she spent time on campus, then a hotbed of activism, with some of the students who were to become the LA Rebellion filmmakers: "I took a risk, striding onto the campus [and] act[ing] like I was part of the school. I found a group that was making films and pretended like I belonged there," remarks Grier regarding her entrance to the milieu of one of the most exciting film insurgencies in black American film history.[49]

When AIP approached Hill to make *Coffy*, Grier was already featuring in minor roles in several black action films, and Hill states that he "immediately thought of Pam Grier as the lead" and scripted the role "specifically for [her]." The lack of budget for quality actors is, according to Hill, the biggest drawback in fringe cinema, and so spotting and developing underexposed talent are crucial: "If I know actors and know I can get them, then I write for them."[50] Though Grier didn't get a writing credit for *Coffy*, she explained in an interview in 1973 that she came up with many "situations and characters" in the film, and, according to Hill, "Grier contributed very good ideas on a kind of life that I wasn't that familiar with and we worked together on things that she could do and I would write some of them into the script." This led him to emphasize an acting skill that would become crucial to Grier's screen persona: her ability to code-switch. Hill had noticed that "Grier was very good at making the shift from a very classy, cultured black woman to really getting down and talking tough. She was at home in both worlds—like a chameleon."[51] Adopting and dropping personas, allowing her to shift from nurse to prostitute to avenger, Grier could convincingly communicate a sense of identificatory fluidity in her performance that spoke intersectionally to working- and middle-class black female formations. Grier's portrayal of a heroine who is trying to negotiate some space in a sexist, racist world spoke reflexively to and was energized by the unequal gendered and racial power relations in the film's production story. In this way, *Coffy* fashioned a compelling, contradictory star image for Grier.

Creative input from women was more obviously central to *Claudine*—indeed, it was because of powerful women behind the scenes that this project became Third World Cinema's first in-house feature. The idea for the film came from Diana Sands, a partner in Third World, who was due to star in the title role, continuing with the kind of captivating working-class protagonists she had developed in theater performances and in Hal Ashby's film *The Landlord*. Hannah Weinstein, one of the most powerful women in the film industry at the time and a stalwart member of the Old Left, executive-produced the film, liaising with its producer Tina Pine (who also coscripted it) and casting agent Joyce Selznick (niece of *Gone with the Wind* producer David O. Selznick). Harlem-born actress Diahann Carroll—just before her

FIGURE 5.5 A modern family acted by (*left to right*) Yvette Curtis, David Kruger, Lawrence Hilton-Jacobs, Diahann Carroll, James Earl Jones, Tamu Blackwell, Socorro Stephens, and Eric Jones in a publicity still for *Claudine* (John Berry, 1974).
Source: Courtesy of the Academy of Motion Picture Arts and Sciences.

stint as cohost of *Black Journal*, the influential public-broadcasting television series that ran from 1968 to the late 1970s—took over the role of Claudine following Sands's terminal illness. She remarked, "I have been searching desperately for a role in a film that was not a sophisticated, well-dressed educated lady, which has been my image over the last 17 years. Claudine offered that opportunity."[52] Thus, Claudine, like Terry in *Melinda*, stood as a refreshing counterproposal to the respectability roles thanks to the strong female and leftist input into the film. The unusual portrayal of a black screen heroine was further accented by the Curtis Mayfield–scored soundtrack performed by Gladys Knight. As a result, *Claudine* had more female involvement in production than almost any other major-studio-distributed film of the period.

Like *Coffy*, *Claudine* includes suggestively reflexive elements having to do with questions of gender, work, and the role of the state in creative labor.

Claudine, like its eponymous heroine, was welfare assisted. Third World, as detailed in chapter 4, was full of committed creatives and technicians who were nonetheless dependent for their filmmaking and training programs on federal and state funds, such as the Model Cities program.[53] Created to train and find jobs for minority workers, Third World produced this film at a moment when public funds for the independent creative arts—like government funds for women with children—were drying up amid concerted discursive attacks on state entitlements and supports. As a consequence, *Claudine*, despite its moderate success, would be one of only two films produced by Third World, which soon ran out of money.[54] Not unlike working, single mothers, community film-training programs faced bleak prospects as neoliberal state policies set in.

I have added to the voices that insist on the creative and textual fertility of the black-film-boom years. By no means all the pictures were exploitation films, in the industry sense, nor were they all defined by racial exploitation in their financing, production, or content. Even full-blown exploitation features cannot simply be written off. The tax-sheltered, target-marketed, and politicized conditions in which these black-oriented productions were made led to a brief but vibrant cinematic subfield. However, whereas some creatives and companies responded to these conditions with texts that complexly negotiated ideas about political radicalism and reformism, others seized on the moment in much more problematic ways.

The End of the Boom

The term *blaxploitation* was coined in the outcry following the release of *Super Fly* in the summer of 1972, understandably alighting on its controversial romanticization of Harlem cocaine dealers. But the critique extended far beyond this one film, capturing mounting concerns over racial exclusion from decision-making roles and over film imagery amid the arrival of a flurry of black-themed film releases. In this section I explain why the critique was in many ways understandable, important, and effective, given the hyperracialization, depoliticization, and oversexualization of many film protagonists at a time when black people were coming into new kinds of self-representation and political empowerment. The film scholar Ed Guerrero, who has written the most influential scholarly account of "blaxploitation," though noting fertility, thus summarizes it quite negatively as "a diversionary period of violent 'superspade' caricatures masquerading as progress on the issue of black filmic representation."[55]

The basic political-economic critique of "blaxploitation" is interpretively forceful at any moment of U.S. film history, as this book has been arguing. Ossie Davis captured it well when he provocatively described a film industry "robbing" black cinemagoers of their hard-earned dollars because the industry's revenues, reaped disproportionately from black Americans, flowed overwhelmingly into the pockets of whites. But the term *blaxploitation* was especially powerful in the early 1970s due to particular production, textual, marketing, and exhibition elements in the industry. Despite the creative and financial openness of the period, the black film wave was also often marked by substandard production values and a cavalier approach to racial stereotypes in film content and marketing campaigns. Although the broad ghetto comedy of *Cotton Comes to Harlem* might have been safe in the hands of Ossie Davis, it also set a thematic precedent, opening the symbolic sluicegates for less-adroit and often racist renditions of black as well as white comic typologies. Or as the producer Warrington Hudlin pointedly remarks, "*Sweetback* had explicit sex, explicit violence and revolutionist politics," but many of the movies that followed it "left the sex and violence. Left out the politics."[56] Following *Super Fly*'s hip repudiation of black nationalism, some of the white-scripted films that followed further trivialized black politics by presenting nationalist rhetoric as an empty, boastful, race-envious cant to "beat whitey." Accordingly, Cedric Robinson pessimistically describes blaxploitation films as the "misrepresentation of liberation," and Howard Winant sees them as part of "the degradation of race-consciousness into a commodified and depoliticized form."[57]

Such sweeping arguments remain persuasive because of the way that many in the industry went about cashing in on the black film boom in a moment of mounting racial retreatism and backlash. AIP films typified these practices. Black-exploitation films *Coffy, Black Caesar,* and *Blacula*—as well as films such as *Slaughter* (Jack Starrett, 1972), starring Jim Brown as a former soldier out to avenge the murder of his father—had productive features and resonated in meaningful ways with their target audiences. Each was produced for AIP's budget of $500,000, and all made millions of dollars for the fringe film company. Massively enriched boss Sam Arkoff immediately set about commissioning sequels: *Foxy Brown*; *Hell up in Harlem* (Larry Cohen, 1973); *Scream, Blacula, Scream* (Bob Kelljan, 1973); and *Slaughter's Big Rip Off* (Gordon Douglas, 1973), respectively. Rather than increasing the budgets of these sequels in light of the original films' success, he maintained the $500,000 ceiling, which in real terms meant a budget decline because the now successful directors and lead actors, reprising their roles, commanded higher fees. "*Coffy* is much better than *Foxy Brown*," explains Jack Hill (who wrote and directed both); the latter's budget was "functionally less because they had to pay me more and they had to pay Pam Grier more so that left me with less money for the rest"—he had to resort in some cases to "stuntmen playing actors' parts."[58] Larry Cohen explains a similar pattern with *Hell up in Harlem*, released just ten months after *Black Caesar*, on which the writer-director had "no time to work on the script." He ended up scripting it on set as they went along.[59]

The audiences, excitedly returning for another instalment of films in which they had heavily invested, found a similar-looking but much-inferior product. According to Hill, in rapidly writing a sequel "you felt that you've already used up your best ideas on the first one and so you tend to use ideas that you originally rejected." To make up for the shortfall in acting, writing, and budgeting, he made *Foxy Brown* "more extreme and more outrageous."[60] Thus, the sequels typically had higher doses of more poorly rendered racialized sex and violence (including the shockingly salacious *Foxy Brown* scenes in which white men racially abuse, tie up, drug, and then rape the heroine). Arkoff, who took a $100,000 fee from every picture and then made a fortune in profits, had, according to Jack Hill, "a lot of contempt for the black audience."[61]

The audience's disappointment at the rush-order caliber of sequels was no doubt augmented by the substandard theaters in which the films were screened. Many downtown theaters, vacated by whites who were moving to the suburbs, had very poor facilities, some so dilapidated that they were closed down due to fire and building-code violations.[62] Only a miniscule number of these theaters were owned or even leased by people of color. Like Arkoff, the white exhibitors were pocketing rather than reinvesting the high profits from packed urban theaters in a moment of recession when, as Canby asserted in the *New York Times*, "black audiences may be in the curious position of possibly saving the commercial American Film industry that so long ignored them."[63]

If these racially charged films mobilized black-nationalist themes for their content, many did so in backlash terms. The extremely successful *Coffy* illustrates this point. The film into which Hill had put his "best ideas," including fashioning the class-permeable, new screen image for Pam Grier, also offered starkly pejorative representations of job advancement for black men. Its black male characters are ineffectual (Coffy's police officer exboyfriend, Carter, is ethical but weak and ends up paralyzed), buffoonish (the comical pimp King George ends up lynched by whites in an extended, comically rendered, and troubling spectacle), and pernicious (Coffy's politician boyfriend Howard Brunswick). The failure of Coffy's black male suitors to offer protection derives in part from the exigencies of genre: the film exemplifies the "vigilante revenge" narratives that proliferated in the early 1970s and in which populist heroes such as Coffy are forced, through others' failure, to take the law into their own hands.

Nonetheless, the portrayal of black men in *Coffy* is unduly negative. In an early scene, charismatic councilman Brunswick launches his campaign for Congress, giving a speech for the local black press, condemning the "combination of big business and government that has kept our sisters prostitutes and brothers dope peddlers," which is "a vicious example of the white power structure." But after Brunswick has drawn in his black audience (both on- and presumably offscreen) with this mobilizing speech, a white TV director appears in the frame to orchestrate cheers of "right on" from the small black crowd, saying, "Nice going, Howard. You were convincing." It later turns out that Brunswick is exploiting nationalist rhetoric to generate votes for personal gain and is actually using this political platform as entree into a crime network of drugs and vice. As he tries to convince his white criminal associates of his loyalty near the end of the film, he spells out his true motivations: "You've been listening to my political speeches. I thought you'd be more intelligent than to listen to crap like that. For chrissakes, black, brown, yellow? I'm in it for the green!"

The year of *Coffy*'s release marked a high moment in the election of African Americans following the Voting Rights Act of 1965, including four black mayors in major cities (such as Los Angeles, where this film was made and set).[64] It was a moment when, as Robin Kelley puts it, "there was a little less talk of revolution and more emphasis on winning local elections,"[65] and *Coffy* offered one of the first post–civil rights substantial screen representations of a black politician. Asked about his inclusion of the nefarious politician

Brunswick in the script, writer-director Hill said: "I had in mind a black congressman from Harlem" who was "really on the take." Hill had the sense that black politicians were "selling out as fast as they could," and he included Brunswick to "push certain buttons."[66] The white exploitationer readily alighted on a story that discredited the momentous new gains in black political culture. Although eager to write into the script unwarranted job advancement among blacks, Hill was much less assiduous in providing concrete opportunities for black film workers. The one African American crew member on *Coffy*, an assistant director, was, according to Hill, immediately "sidelined because he wasn't up to it"—the kind of damaging tokenistic hiring gesture described in chapter 3.[67] *Foxy Brown*, which followed soon after, had no black crew members. The irony once again is that the fictional film narrative suggests job progress for blacks had gone too far in a workplace context that had certainly not gone far enough in including them.

AIP films such as *Coffy*, with obvious selling features and well-established distribution channels, were easier to market than nonghetto action fare. Again, there were exceptions. For example, United Artists spent a generous $500,000 on the marketing campaign for *Five on the Black Hand Side*, a sum that was nearly as high as the production budget ($650,000), but it paid off with good business.[68] However, though the demographic concentration in urban theaters at the time meant that a range of black films got theatrical release, production and distribution conditions remained challenging.. Sidney Poitier recalls that if it hadn't been for the terms of his First Artists contract, which he had made sure was "free of tiny loopholes" and signed at the height of his star power, he would have been dropped after his poor-performing first film as producer, *A Warm December* in 1973. Had that happened, he would never have been given the money to make his second film, *Uptown Saturday Night* (which returned around $7.5 million to the industry, with a box-office gross of nearly double that amount).[69] When Poitier first screened the finished film of *Uptown Saturday Night* for its distributor, Warner Bros., he recalls that boss Ted Ashley said, "I don't understand it"—struggling to envisage how to package a black urban comedy that did not feature sex, violence, or a superstud protagonist and that did not draw on Poitier's signature liberal-reformist screen image (which, from here on, he ditched in favor of family comedy).[70]

If Poitier, with his contractual and star-power muscle, found it hard to make nonexploitative black-cast family movies, it was undoubtedly yet more difficult for filmmakers trying to produce politically and aesthetically challenging films. Scholars have ably uncovered how the state censored the release of *The Spook Who Sat by the Door*.[71] Or take the notorious case of Bill Gunn's art-house film *Ganja and Hess*, which, despite being celebrated in black and white art-house circles in the United States and Europe as an important film in the new American cinema, was not backed by mainstream critics. These critics, its star Marlene Clark would later remark, "believe that black people make very straightforward, literal movies. So Bill was really an enigma to them. They just did not understand what he had done."[72] Nor did the film's distributor, Kelly-Jordan Enterprises, understand *Ganja and Hess*, withdrawing it from cinemas after one week at one New York theater, reediting it down to two-thirds its original running time, and rereleasing it as *Blood Couple* in an attempt to make it fit the black-exploitation horror blueprint. As the film critic Richard Brody describes Gunn, he was "a visionary filmmaker left on the sidelines of the most ostensibly liberated period of American filmmaking," and after this experience he didn't try to make another feature until *Personal Problems* in 1980, which was never released.[73]

The industry was barely more receptive to new white directors searching to fund and distribute nonghetto action racial content. Television writer Larry Cohen got the call from AIP's Arkoff to make *Black Caesar* because he had already written, directed, and produced his first film, a dark comedy called *Bone* with an interracial cast that sent up white racist fears and fantasies about black sexual potency. *Bone* was based on the premise, according to Cohen, that "the core of racism was sexual" and starred Yaphet Kotto, whose warm, charismatic performance undercut the film's "black buck" white racist projections.[74] Shot for just $85,000 at Cohen's home in Los Angeles, the film had both a stage-play feel and a rich cinematic scope because it was filmed by then retired cinematographer George Folsey Sr. (who had received a full thirteen Academy Award nominations for Best Cinematography during his career). Although the resulting film was well reviewed— according to the film critic Robin Wood, it was "one of the most remarkable debuts in American cinema"[75]—Cohen struggled to sell it. Considered too risqué and low key by most distributors, it was eventually picked up by fringe producer Jack Harris and, like *Ganja and Hess*, sold as a black-exploitation film. Audiences expected a superstud action drama, just as they expected schlock horror when they went to Gunn's *Blood Couple*. In both cases, their expectations were not met, leading to disappointing ticket sales. "You can't deceive the audience," explains Cohen. "They've been misled. Like if you've ordered vanilla ice-cream and you give them chocolate. They don't want chocolate, they want vanilla. Even if it's the best chocolate they ever tasted."[76]

Such repackaging of race-themed films was based on the assumption that these provocative products could be sold only to the urban market. Sonny Carson was surprised and disappointed that Paramount decided to limit the opening of *Education of Sonny Carson* to black theaters because he felt that it was important for white people to see it, too (including members of the white judiciary, given its powerful critique of the criminal justice system).[77] Similarly, Cohen states that because of *Bone*'s message about racist white-liberal attitudes, he "never even thought of it [as being just] for the black market."[78] The freewheeling days of the Hollywood Renaissance may have brought in fresh new-generation executives and filmmakers, some of whom were more open-minded, but most of the distributors and exhibitors had not changed. According to Cohen, they "had the mentality of Carnival showmen. In those days, they were just hardboiled old guys, who didn't understand anything new, so you couldn't expect much from them."[79]

Notwithstanding broader renaissance appetites, even with the right packaging and distribution, films such as *Ganja and Hess, Bone,* and to a lesser extent *Education of Sonny Carson* might have always been niche films, given their off-beat generic and aesthetic parameters. But audience reach was further constricted by the assumptions of veteran white distributors, who opted for intense target marketing in the immediate post–civil rights period, gatekeeping racial divisions in a transitional moment of potential openness. Jim Brown expressed similar frustration and disappointment with the release pattern of *Slaughter,* AIP's second biggest hit of 1972: "I would like to know what was black about it. It was booked as a black movie. We shot it in Mexico, with Mexicans, 80% of the actors were white, we had four black people in it, and I was the lead. Man, I mean if a movie is black because I'm the lead we're in trouble."[80] Such films often did not make it much beyond urban theaters, where they flooded the program. Nearly half the box-office receipts in first-run urban theaters of major cities during 1973 and 1974 were from black-focused films.[81] Thus, in tandem with practices and policies of residential segregation, target marketing by whites in the pop-cultural realm furthered racial separation. Although this target marketing opened up urban theaters to a range of black-oriented products—reproducing some of the segregation-era protections enjoyed by the earlier "race film" movement—it also led to greater audience stratification. In light of the crass handling of identity politics screened to resegregating audiences (and in the case of urban audiences in substandard theaters), the resultant heightened rhetoric from protestors was understandable.

With black audiences increasingly tiring of the overplayed thematics, the box office for black films declined sharply in 1974—the year of the record number of black releases.[82] The mainstream industry suddenly declared the black film boom over. The boom had yielded only a few fully crossover hits—including *Shaft*, *Super Fly*, *Sounder*, *Lady Sings the Blues*, *Blazing Saddles* (Mel Brooks, 1974), and *Uptown Saturday Night*—since 1970. Without the lucrative white market—often shut out by the decisions of white funders, distributors, and exhibitors—there was an upper limit to box-office grosses, and so the major film companies turned away from black-oriented projects. Broader film-industry reconfiguration played an important role in this rejection. This was a moment when the motion-picture business was establishing a "new industry consensus," as David Cook puts it. With the majority of releases failing to turn a profit and profits concentrated in a very few high-revenue films, the major studios moved to slash the number of releases by half (from an average of 160 a year in the late 1960s to 80 per year by the mid-1970s). The Hollywood Renaissance was nearly over, and the new emphasis, as Cook explains, was on "films that were carefully packaged and laden with 'proven' elements, like pre-sold properties and bankable stars."[83] The focus shifted to more expensive releases with broad appeal, based on marquee-event releases in the wake of the blockbuster success of *Jaws* (Steven Spielberg, 1975), accompanied by a withdrawal by the majors from many modestly budgeted, niche-market productions. With the success in urban theaters of earlier films such as *The Godfather* and *The Exorcist* (William Friedkin, 1973), the majors were slowly developing a renewed awareness that black people's filmic tastes extended well beyond black-themed product, leading the studios to all but withdraw from black-oriented features by 1975.[84]

Smaller studios and independents, which had always made the majority of the films of the black film wave, continued to make black-focused films after 1974, offering some opportunities to black filmmakers. But this trend, too, soon halted abruptly, in part because of the elimination of tax-shelter financing with the Tax Reform Act of 1976.[85] The number dropped from thirty-three black-focused features in 1976 (the last year of the film boom) to just ten by 1978, before falling even further by the turn of the 1980s, according to figures from the scholar Keith Corson.[86] For the few African American film producers who had managed to establish themselves in the industry, this closing off of black-oriented pipelines marked the end. Indeed, by 1980 Pryor was the only black star working consistently in mainstream Hollywood.[87] As Poitier, who had previously inhabited Pryor's lonely racial-exception spot, would remark, calling out structural racism, "The industry doesn't set out to cultivate one person representing a particular minority. What it does, I think, is to react to minorities the way the general society reacts—which is, more often than not, in a racist way."[88]

To understand these shifting racial power relations in cinema and to understand what Stuart Hall calls its "concentration of cultural power,"[89] we need to turn back to industry discourses and practices during these years. The industry engaged with and fed into national racial discourses as pro-white, pro-corporate laissez-faireism took hold in the final years of the transitional decade, from 1972 on. Indeed, one of the more galling aspects of the crassly racialized representational and marketing strategies already outlined was how they were denied by an industry increasingly proclaiming itself a bastion of racially transcendent corporate color-blindness.

Hollywood's White Corporate Revival

By 1972, as the black film wave grew and Nixon enjoyed a landslide reelection victory, the serious federal drive to integrate Hollywood's studios and craft unions was over. As detailed in chapter 3, the expiration of the industry's two-year agreement with the Justice Department on minority employment marked the end of meaningful state activism in motion pictures. Despite some well-disposed individuals' efforts, the system could not be dismantled through voluntarism without a major shift in whites' attitudes and a firm stand from employers, backed by binding intervention. But with the threat of legal action overcome, the practices of often unintentional white crony-ism in employment could continue pretty much unabated. The end of fed-eral activism forced black advocacy groups and film workers to try to take matters into their own hands to reinvigorate the struggle for cultural jus-tice. In the outcry about the emergence of lucrative ghetto action films, many African American groups rounded on Hollywood, demanding more representational control. Protests came from Jesse Jackson's Operation PUSH and from an alliance that called itself the Coalition Against Blaxploitation (CAB), led by the Beverly Hills–Hollywood branch of the NAACP (though not fully supported by its national leadership), which included the Congress of Racial Equality, the Southern Christian Leadership Conference, and the Black Artists Alliance.[90]

According to CAB's head, Junius Griffin, the protestors were struggling "against the power exploitation of the black condition in America by the white owned, white controlled, and white financed motion picture industry."[91] He was the one to coin the charged neologism *blaxploitation* in August 1972. Although consternation about some of the films and the wider political economy of cinema was genuine and intense, the very controversy over "blaxploitation" also provided a platform for action. Through public statements, protests outside major studios, meetings with executives, and the threat of box-office boycotts, activists demanded more jobs for blacks, more meaningful storytelling about blacks, and a say in decision-making processes. The protests were accompanied by intense debates and critiques among black viewers, commentators, and intellectuals. [92] For many, remedying injustice would require a system of preference in industry financing, hiring, and creative decision making on black-oriented productions.

This heightened debate over cultural justice and the pressure from black activists led to many microlevel creative opportunities and concessions on individual film projects, spurring the arrival of new African American directors of feature films between 1972 and 1974, as detailed earlier. Having decided that "black is in" and amid mounting protest, the industry had to hire some black creative talent. However, the activists faced a mounting discursive onslaught from Hollywood management. The industry had already seen off the EEOC in 1970, through its corporate lobbying and public-relations messaging backed by emergent national neoconservative discourses. Then, in 1972, another key year in moves against the implementation of civil rights laws, President Nixon publicly eschewed proportional representation in employment policies and discourses as antimeritocratic: "Criteria for selection will be based on merit," read Nixon's far-reaching memorandum to departmental and agency heads. "Numerical goals . . . must not be allowed to be applied in such a fashion as to, in fact, result in the imposition of quotas."[93]

Within a month of this antiquota memorandum, in September 1972 a strikingly similar rhetoric of meritocracy was deployed by Hollywood management to reject blacks' demands for inclusion. In its first official response to CAB, the MPAA (i.e., its head, Jack Valenti) charged that its demands and those of Jesse Jackson's Operation Push amounted to a bid for unfair preference, a response covered in a *Hollywood Reporter* story titled "Valenti Calls Black's [sic] Bluff; Rejects 'Special' Treatment." Thus, rather than seeing the activists' calls for redress as reasonable demands to confront historic and continuing exclusion, Valenti and the MPAA instead construed them as requests for an unfair handout. In this press statement, he echoed the statement quoted in the introduction to this chapter, stating: "I feel uneasy about any segment of the population demanding for itself what other segments of the population don't have."[94] Here, Valenti signaled his participation in a broader debate then taking place: blacks' demands in the film industry were presented essentially as an assault on the national interests and liberal values "in any segment of society."

Valenti declared in his press statement, "I think it's bad to polarize a society by trying to segment it. I'm very much for integration because I think segregation is bad, segregation of anybody."[95] The slippage from *segmentation* to *segregation* is telling. By calling out black film activists as the segregationists, Valenti rearticulated the terms of debate. He inverted public understandings of "segregation," which in recent popular memory conjured shameful images of angry white southerners and police setting dogs on black people—images that had mobilized Americans of all races against Jim Crow. Perhaps the neoconservatives' single most powerful contribution was to rehabilitate conservatism from a low point in the 1960s through the renarrativization of the language of freedom, fairness, and civil rights. The most far-reaching example of this would be the rearticulation of the term *color-blind*, which Martin Luther King Jr. had popularized when in 1963 he famously envisioned a future built on substantial social reorganization in which his children would "not be judged by the color of their skin." As the historian Robin Kelley explains the rearticulation, neoconservatives "seized the language of the Civil Rights movement and turned it on its head."[96] By disarticulating color-blindness from its civil rights moorings and attaching it to opposing ones, neoconservatives stole a great deal of the movement's moral capital. They did so by deflecting attention from the actual practices of continuing white opportunity hoarding in the industry, which often amounted to continuing de facto segregationism. Jack Valenti, repeatedly stating in his speech that he rejected the activists' "basic premise" and did not "buy the notion" that you can divide filmmaking along racial lines, drew attention to the rearticulative force of his statement.[97] As he had done previously with his "open doors" rhetoric (chapter 3), he was coaching his executive peers, white film workers, and the media in a wholesale rejection of the color-conscious racial project—equipping them with a vocabulary that allowed them to defend white privileges and to express resentments without sounding racist.

Jack Valenti, a former Democrat adviser turned aggressive corporate leader, continued to catalyze the nascent neoconservatives' ethnicity-based identity politics. In their various writings, neoconservatives were gaining traction with their insistence that white ethnics had not shared in the historic "white privilege" on which the black-power critique was predicated.[98] Accordingly, in his press statement Valenti mused: "There are Italians, Catholics, Jews, Poles, Chicanos, Chinese, Japanese, blacks, northerners and southerners. I don't know where you draw the line."[99] With the arrival of the black film wave that year, his repudiation of black demands is partly legible, and no doubt the underrepresentation of Latinx and Asian Americans in filmmaking was, in relative terms, discursively deprivileged in this moment of heightened black struggle for screen representation. Nonetheless, at the heart of solidifying neoconservative discourses were reasonable-sounding reductions of race to ethnicity (and region). These reductions reinvigorated, as Michael Omi and Howard Winant have explored, an ethnicity-based paradigm of race that served to deny the persisting institutional discrimination faced by racial minority groups. The ethnicity-based paradigm was premised on *individual rights* in order to combat nationalist and class-based racial paradigms that were based on *group rights*.[100] With his populist roll call of pluralist America, Valenti rhetorically leveled out unequal power relations by reducing racial difference to merely a matter of competing ethnic and regional "segments" in healthy rivalry. Continuing inequality in the film industry (which affected all racial minority groups) was dubiously cast as a natural outcome of group competition, drawing attention away from the structural fact that all decision-making film jobs were still being performed by white people, who were also still overwhelmingly reaping the revenues from film-sector activity.

Neoconservative thinking thus drove what Jacobson calls "white ethnic revival in post–civil rights America," marked by skepticism toward state intervention on behalf of blacks, by individual (rather than structural) interpretations of racism, and by an image of America as a land of bootstrap immigrants in which newly empowered blacks should be treated as merely the latest wave of incoming strivers, to be interpreted "through the lens of Ellis Island's huddled masses."[101] The white ethnic group most associated with racial neoconservatism was ironically also the one most associated with civil rights activism: Jewish Americans,[102] and this group held many decision-making positions in Hollywood. Jews in general had been liberal and leftist in social and political terms and inside the industry of the early 1970s continued strongly to support the black freedom struggle, including the producer Hannah Weinstein and others who features in this story. Weinstein, along with Columbia executive Bert Schneider, was a key contributor to the Panthers fund and she went on, following *Claudine,* to produce two of the most commercially successful black-directed films in the postboom void: *Greased Lightning* (Michael Schultz, 1977) and *Stir Crazy,* an interracial buddy movie starring Gene Wilder and Richard Pryor and directed by Sidney Poitier that would become one of the highest-grossing black-directed films ever.[103]

However, in this period of dramatic racial transition, many white ethnics, including some Jews, cleaved increasingly to the melting-pot allegiances and resentments that were being propounded in neoconservative discourses of the day. Since 1969, Irish American neoconservative Daniel Patrick Moynihan had been briefing Nixon on the growing fractures in the black–Jewish civil rights alliance. Affirmative-action calls for proportional representation were often unwelcome, and white ethnic revival behind the scenes fed into onscreen portrayals. Many of the biggest films had, for the first time at this moment, come to be populated by white ethnic actors playing conspicuously ethnic characters, including the highest grossers of 1970, *Love Story* (Arthur Hiller) and 1971, *Fiddler on the Roof* (Norman Jewison). The latter was an epic ethnic-revivalist story of Jewish diaspora identity, which culminates with the mass emigration from the pogrom-ridden Russian Empire, many to America. The new investment in white minoritarian identity, modeled in part on the surge in black identity politics, held a range of political orientations. *Fiddler* was directed by Canadian WASP Norman Jewison (perhaps himself subject to viewing America with a kind of immigrant excitement), whose follow-up picture was *Jesus Christ, Superstar*, filmed in Israel. The runaway hit of 1972, *The Godfather*, was a towering text of white ethnic revival, mythologizing an Italian American crime family. It included the highly racist reference to black Americans and the drug trade: "They're animals anyway, so let them lose their souls." *The Godfather* paved the way for runaway hit *Rocky*, described in the introduction to this chapter, with the humble hero facing a puffed-up black nemesis (in a horrible caricature of Muhammad Ali). Indeed, if we consider both the film-textual and industry discourses of white ethnic revivalism in motion pictures in the 1970s, it is probably Italian Americans—from Valenti to the Corleones to Rocky/Stallone—who emerge as its most flagrant proponents.

Though this period marks the moment when "'white ethnic' and 'white backlash' became interchangeable terms," as the historian Bruce Nelson writes in his study of race and class in the workplace,[104] it is easy to overemphasize the role played by *ethnic* whites. In truth, the backlash was a white backlash in general. This point can be illustrated by returning to Charlton Heston, a WASP of mainly Scottish extraction. An increasingly archneoconservative, he explained his high-profile turn to conservatism in the 1970s as driven by the Democrats' welfare, defense, and foreign policies. Government help for working-class and poor Americans, like that narrated by Third World Cinema in *Claudine*, had helped radicalize this industry stalwart (who later cited the racist political scientist Charles Murray to decry the apparent "damage done to the black family by welfare programs").[105] The lavish tax shelters that Nixon had agreed to in San Clemente at the meeting attended by Heston (which amounted ironically to "corporate welfare," though Heston would hardly have seen it in those terms) were accompanied by Nixon's exhortations to the industry to make more patriotic, optimistic films. Heston favored these all-American themes, mounting critiques of Hollywood's left-liberal "doom-watchers and nay-sayers."[106]

Heston's conversion to the Republican cause made him—along with another Nixon Democrat, Sammy Davis Jr.—of particular strategic value, joining a camp already populated by veteran conservatives such as John Wayne, Clint Eastwood, Jimmy Stewart, and, of course, Ronald Reagan.[107] Heston's value in the rehabilitation of conservatism in the 1970s rested not just on his civil rights and labor-organizing past but also on his centrist screen image, from his early role as Moses in *The Ten Commandments*

(Cecil B. DeMille, 1956) to his messianic role in *Omega Man* (Boris Sagal, 1971). Heston, who read the Declaration of Independence at Nixon's second inauguration in 1973, became a hugely effective Republican spokesperson, fund-raiser, and campaigner. In his opposition to an interventionist state and his belief instead in unregulated markets (apparently except for the film industry and other corporate concerns), Heston powerfully fomented the race and rights discourses of the conservative revolution. He made the same rearticulative moves as Valenti, claiming that Martin Luther King Jr. had eschewed affirmative action. King, Heston claimed, had believed that "there is no indemnity due for the failures of the past." Daniel Moynihan later described this rearticulative process as " 'semantic infiltration': if the other fellow can get you to use his words, he wins."[108]

Following the storm about quotas in an increasingly hostile environment in 1972, and amid the arrival of a few more black filmmakers, the campaigning of such groups as CAB, Operation PUSH, Third World Cinema, and the Black Artists Alliance—though leading to the green-lighting of and constructive changes to black-oriented productions explored earlier—was ultimately overwhelmed by Hollywood's institutional intransigence. The meeting between CAB and industry management about film jobs, shortly after Valenti's press interventions, captures the enforced retreat. The industry was well represented at the meeting by the powerful Lew Wasserman, head of the AMPTP, close friend of Ronald Reagan, and earlier pioneer of Hollywood tax-avoidance schemes. He agreed, in the inordinately attenuated wording, to the activists' "demand" to "work toward establishing an affirmative level of minority emphasis of employment," reported the trade press.[109] With a few more minorities working in the film business in the first half of the 1970s, Hollywood management was more than happy to pay lip service to such a weak statement. The idea of a more formalized or lasting system of racial preference was so stigmatized as to be off the agenda at a time when, as the EEOC's Clifford Alexander remarked, "the politically sensitive term 'quota' [was] being used to pit Black against white, worker against worker."[110]

As black advocacy groups faced mounting opposition, many seized on business-oriented arguments that chimed with the turn to black film enterprise explored in chapter 4. The activist action star Jim Brown, who founded the Black Economic Union, asserted in late 1972: "The one approach that will work is to approach movies as an industry, as a business. Black people must stop crying 'black' and start crying 'business.' "[111] When Roy Innis, the director of the Congress of Racial Equality whose pro-black-capitalist leadership of the organization was critiqued by Sonny Carson, turned his attention to film—setting up with Ossie Davis an organization to train minorities for film jobs in Harlem—he foregrounded the power of the black box office: "We're 40 percent of the dollar. This is money. Those are capitalists. You can always deal with a capitalist with money."[112] Similarly, a high-profile *Hollywood Reporter* series on black filmmaking was titled "Black Capitalism Big Factor in PUSH Drive on Hollywood." In it, Jesse Jackson declared that black independent filmmaking was "stronger than a picketline." He promulgated a vision of "civil economics . . . to cash in on civil rights at the cash register."[113] This was, no doubt, a pragmatic response to a situation of declining political racial leverage and the industry's reliance on the black film market in the early 1970s. However, the black audience never, even at its peak, represented 40 percent of the overall market. Although, as I have shown, there were opportunities for black filmmaking at that moment because of the generous tax environment, exhibition patterns, and heightened identity politics, these factors were subject to change, and activists had little control over them. With the collapse of black-oriented film productions after 1976, calls for "civil economics" fell on deaf ears. The industry could even use the heightened "blaxploitation" critiques by advocacy groups as a rationale for its turn away from black-themed texts. As the industry that had first briefly flooded the market with black-oriented films now pronounced the black film trend over, the activists who had prioritized both ethical and pragmatic arguments had few places left to turn.

In 1976, the year of *Rocky* and of the demise of the studio-made black film wave, the California Advisory Committee of the U.S. Civil Rights Commission went to Hollywood to try to assess the progress made on minority employment in motion pictures. It found that the craft unions' seniority roster system, overseen by the unions and the studios, persisted almost entirely unchanged, with many creative openings still advertised through word of mouth and thus reproducing a predominantly white workforce.[114] As a consequence, minorities were still very underrepresented in nearly all areas of film's technical workforce, which actor Raymond St. Jacques described as the "last holdout of blatant racism."[115] The loud calls of reverse discrimination and threat of litigation from the GUE that had helped see off the Justice

Department at the height of the federal challenge in 1969 and 1970 were no longer needed as Hollywood's craft unions could freely return to unobstructed closed-shop labor-market practices that hoarded opportunities for white men. Blacks still represented only a paltry 2.8 percent of the film-industry technical workforce overall in the Los Angeles area (based on figures from twenty-four union locals). With contraction in the size of the total film workforce between 1969 and 1976 and a surge in minority numbers in the Los Angeles–area population, the Civil Rights Commission concluded that any net gains in numbers over this period were "negligible." Minority-inclusion rates were especially bad in some of the prestigious crafts, including camera operating, where black participation was lower than 2 percent.[116] Prospects were therefore bleak for individuals such as Audley Simpson, a young black assistant cameraman on *Claudine* and graduate of the Third World Cinema program, as he tried to forge a career. He had first been hired as a trainee by Otto Preminger, who had met him during a hospital stay and later put him in touch with Third World. But as Simpson stated, "I have a union card now and I'll be on *Claudine*. Seven weeks' work, it's great! But when I ask the unions about other work they look at me as if I'm crazy. Right now it's all glamorous. But what happens to me after *Claudine*?"[117] Once the black film boom was over, the outlook for Simpson and the other forty or so Third World graduates who had achieved union cards looked grim.

If craft unions were free to continue with their nepotistic, word-of-mouth, white-male ways, some of the major studios had ostensibly done a bit better on minority employment. The California Advisory Committee figures suggest that overall there had been at least a doubling of the employment percentage of nonwhites and women at the studios between 1969 and 1976 (though these studio-devised figures were underverified, with the committee finding incomplete and "conflicting data").[118] Some employers had taken a stand on inclusion, whereas others had made no efforts: Walt Disney and Twentieth Century-Fox, both of which had refused even to participate in the Justice Department probe of 1970, were basically free to carry on as usual. By contrast, Warner Bros., for instance, converted promises for more minority representation into some concrete jobs. Of 144 new office employees put on the payroll at the Warners studio during 1973, 35 percent were from minority groups. Accepting a Corporate Image Award for this achievement, Warner chairman Ted Ashley offered an eloquent rejoinder to Valenti's nonredistributive version of job-market equality: "Corporations have a responsibility to make certain that equal opportunity in employment is not merely a slogan, but rather a reality. In doing so, we're not doing anybody here a favor. People of the minority groups are talented, are skilled and dedicated. Bringing more of them into our office and into our studios serves our company as much as it serves broader goals."[119]

However, although representing progress, Warners' inclusiveness was a limited achievement. It had focused much of its minority hiring on administrative and clerical positions—far away from the executives and symbol creators of motion pictures, who are the principal workers in shaping movie outcomes and thus in shaping film's role in the production of social meaning. Figures submitted by the studios to the Justice Department showed that there remained very little evidence of minority representation in decision-making positions: in the wake of the voluntary agreement, still only a handful of minority members served as board members, corporate officers, and subsidiary vice presidents, with not many more in the lower corporate ranks of executives and managers.

Though there was no consensual view on race among the studio bosses in this polarized and transitional period, the encroaching antiquota, laissez-faire discourse won out. Few studios had made real efforts to produce an affirmative-action plan, and some outright refused (without penalty) to offer any information to the commission in 1976, while others offered self-reported figures that were very unreliable. Minority union members protested against major studios for defaulting on hiring pledges and reneging on their legal commitments to put pressure on unions to end their closed-shop practices. But they gained very little traction, and the craft unions had mainly stopped presenting data for audit purposes.[120] In sum, the Civil Rights Commission concluded that "sporadic and weak enforcement efforts by the Federal Government have allowed the industry to shirk its responsibilities."[121] By the mid-1970s, several of the majors, including Warner, were no longer operating their own studio lot, instead leasing facilities and employees from other studios. Thus, in-house staff numbers, which were relatively easy to audit, dropped precipitously in a trend that came to typify the outsourcing and "flexibly specializing" cultural industries more generally.[122]

Studios and unions had learned from the neoconservatives that they could defend the status quo far more effectively by espousing color-blindness à la Valenti than by adopting an old-fashioned defense of privilege. The neoconservatives, including the ideology's powerful Hollywood communicators, mobilized against the politics of redress, which lost much of its mainstream purchase in line with the diminishing national concern for equal employment. The engulfing discourse of color-blind meritocracy (stoked by a thinly veiled politics of white resentment) that had been so powerfully fomented in the film arena won out more and more.

• • •

This production-focused account of black-oriented filmmaking from 1972 to 1976 has explored the film industry's post–civil rights alacrity in projecting exaggerated images of racial difference and racial conflict as entertainment. Alongside the integrationist moralizing of white film-industry executives were many lurid and cheap white-scripted depictions of black life circulated at this moment of black cinematic awakening. Just as the industry was declaring race an irrelevant anachronism, it was producing and profiting from many hyperracialized film products. But I have also emphasized that many other kinds of cinematic portrayals of black life and race relations were on offer, presenting powerful negotiations of black class and gendered identities and critiques. This contradictory complexity in black film culture of the 1970s, which established many of the coordinates of African American filmmaking practice in contemporary Hollywood, is lost when it is dubbed simply "blaxploitation."

Black and progressive filmmakers of the 1970s came up against a rising Right, forged and consolidated in cinema's institutional discourses and practices. This new conservatism was spearheaded by pro-corporate players such as Jack Valenti, Lew Wasserman, and Charlton Heston and aided by neoconservative politicians Richard Nixon and Ronald Reagan. Indeed, the film industry, its long downturn starting much earlier than most industries and leading to new-style corporate maneuvering against taxes, state regulations, and organized labor, was a vital site of right-wing rehabilitation as conservatism crossed into mainstream American politics, deploying discourses of race and reaction to do so. Hollywood continued to influence policy debates through its lobbying and public relations but also on a popular-cultural level through its iconic films, which often vigorously consolidated its messaging of white revival. Cinematic blackness, when it found its way onto cinema screens at all after the mid-1970s, tended to be figured as irredeemably abject, unduly entitled, hyperindividualist, or comfortingly comedic and deferential. In the year of *Rocky*'s dominance, 1976, the Civil Rights Committee's audit uncovered the total defanging of federal activism in an industry that—following the boom of the early to mid-1970s—had failed to make substantial racial change and instead had a refreshed sense of white racial vindicationism.

CONCLUSION

RACE, CREATIVE LABOR, AND REFLEXIVITY IN POST-CIVIL RIGHTS HOLLYWOOD

In 1978, Universal Pictures released *Blue Collar*, a dark portrayal of a Detroit automobile plant. Cowritten and directed by Paul Schrader of *Taxi Driver* fame, the film dramatizes the unraveling interracial friendship of three assembly-line workers, Zeke (Richard Pryor), Jerry (Harvey Keitel), and Smokey (Yaphet Kotto). *Blue Collar* showcased new charismatic onscreen black masculinity. Richard Pryor was the biggest African American screen star of the late 1970s, and as Vincent Canby remarked, in this role he made "use of the wit and fury that distinguish his straight comedy routines." According to the critic J. Hoberman, Pryor's Zeke was "the most cogent . . . and most complicated member of the trio."[1] Kotto's excon bachelor Smokey, as film critic Andrew Sarris proclaimed, was "played with picture-stealing force and charm," recalling Kotto's earlier performance in *Bone*.[2] At the outset, Zeke, Smokey, and white Polish Jerry are shown to have a close camaraderie, consecrated through shared work and leisure practices; together they project a proletarian consciousness that makes them look ready to rise up against their oppressive employer. The factory scenes, which were widely admired, conjured both a vérité and an expressionistic vision of "the grinding sweaty noisy awfulness of assembly-line work."[3] *Blue Collar* captures the capacity in the cinema of the 1970s for memorable African American protagonists as well as for bleak social comment and is a highly regarded film. However, it is also in several important ways antilabor and antiblack. As with earlier Hollywood Renaissance–era films that I have discussed in this book, *Blue Collar* reveals how the renaissance was shaped by important yet unacknowledged black creative input and how a burgeoning politics of racial retreat and resentment about black people in the workplace, including film workplaces, made its way onto the screen.

The antiunion themes of *Blue Collar* were widely acknowledged at the time, and scholars since then have pointed them out.[4] The film begins by showing workers exploited by their employer but very soon finds its real antagonist: their union. Though most liberal commentators celebrated the film on its release, many leftists took issue with the way its anti-institutional tenor targeted organized labor—in this case what is called the Associated Auto Workers—rather than car corporations such as General Motors or Ford. The three friends soon decide to rob their union, and the sense that their decision is a just response is corroborated when they find little money but instead an accounting ledger showing deep union corruption and pay-offs to racketeers. When they use the ledger to bribe the union, its malfeasant response is to have Smokey murdered.

These antiunion dimensions of *Blue Collar* are well known. However, the film's antiblack themes are not. This omission is probably owing to the hip virtuosity of Pryor and Kotto's performances, which distract from the film's racist notes. As with my reading of *In the Heat of the Night*, which showed how Sidney Poitier's beguiling performance of Virgil Tibbs both warranted and undercut the racial retreatism of the text, the performative space opened by Kotto and Pryor in *Blue Collar* cannot be read simply as servicing the white racial frame. Like Tibbs, Smokey and Zeke offered early evidence of the vast cultural salience as well as the marketability of post–civil rights black masculine screen portrayals.

However, the fact remains that the film relies on racist stereotypes. Though all three friends are heavily indebted in the inflation-ridden 1970s, it is only the white protagonist Jerry's penury that isn't self-inflicted. Failed by the American dream, he is the white ethnic hero who is striving to be the responsible breadwinner. After a day at the plant, he moonlights at a gas station in order to buy braces for his daughter's teeth. By contrast, Zeke, who also has a wife and kids, is a self-confessed "slave" to consumer goods, so his indebtedness derives mainly from his chaotic finances. He is fiddling his taxes, claiming to have six children when he actually has three—thus, he is a welfare cheat in the year that Ronald Reagan would popularize his "welfare queen" rhetoric.[5] Street-smart Smokey is even more hedonistic than

Zeke, using his money to gamble, buy a Cadillac, and get high. In what Sarris describes as "an apparently gratuitous orgy scene" at Smokey's pad, he is the full-on black stud. In sum, white ethnic Jerry, even though he participates in the orgy, is basically forbearing and decent—not unlike Rocky Balboa—while the blacks are spendthrift, tax-cheating, government-dependent pleasure seekers. Such a racial logic is furthered by the denouement, when Smokey is killed—presumably in part as punishment for his black pride and sexual activity. His murder is an extended, garish suffocation scene in which he is locked inside the plant's paint room. Though the ending is extremely bleak for all the characters, with Zeke and Jerry coming to blows, only Jerry, backed into a corner, does the right thing: he avenges Smokey's murder by going to the authorities. By contrast, Zeke, presented at the outset as someone who wants to bring about progressive racial reform to the union, emerges as the race traitor. He is bought off by the union officials who have killed his friend, accepting their offer of promotion to shop steward to stay quiet. Like politician Howard Brunswick in *Coffy*, it is the outspoken black reformer and radical who ultimately emerges as devious, weak, and self-serving—an early blueprint of what became an anti-black-nationalist refrain in mainstream-film representational politics thereafter.[6]

Blue Collar's story idea did not originate with Paul Schrader and his cowriter, brother Leonard. It instead came from a young African American writer named Sydney Glass. The son of a Detroit assembly-line worker, Glass had worked in various plants to pay his way through school. He first approached Paul Schrader following a Screen Writers Guild seminar run by the *Taxi Driver* scripter and in follow-up meetings shared his idea. It centered on the grim experiences of his own black auto-worker father. But as Schrader recounted to the *Village Voice*, he soon thought: "Why should he write that? I should write that."[7] Some Hollywood Renaissance white writers (as well of course as many black ones) had mentored minority writers to counter pervasive racial cronyism and exclusion. But although Schrader was already a highly esteemed writer, his first thought was simply to steal the ideas of the younger black creative, and he had no qualms about telling journalists so. When Glass later learned that his story had been taken, he mounted a challenge to get his writing credit, backed by the black caucus of the Writers Guild of America. The Schraders were forced to relent, not because it was the right thing to do but instead because, as Paul put it, "the guy had a gun to my head."[8] Reflecting his leading role in the story's inception,

FIGURE 6.1 Auto-plant coworkers Jerry (Harvey Keitel), Zeke (Richard Pryor), and Smokey (Yaphet Kotto) in *Blue Collar* (Paul Schrader, 1978).
Source: Courtesy of the Academy of Motion Picture Arts and Sciences.

Glass ended up with one-third of the fee and one-third of the percentage points, and the credit read, "Suggested by source material by Sydney A. Glass."[9] As with other black creative interventions examined in this book, this case stands as an important, successful challenge, mounted against the attempted erasure of a black symbol creator on a race-themed film, which forced the white filmmakers to pay off and recognize the black artist whose work they had stolen.

The Schraders were also dependent on another African American creative to bring their film into production. The involvement of Richard Pryor, who was by then a major star, helped them to obtain project financing. Then, once the Schraders had funding, they couldn't find an auto-plant location in Detroit to shoot the film because they were "locked out" due to their film project's antiunion content.[10] But they ultimately secured a Checker Cabs plant in nearby Kalamazoo, Michigan, because the owner's wife thought Pryor was funny.[11] When it came time to market the film, Pryor's pivotal importance is further evident: the front page of the *Blue Collar* pressbook features two photos of the black comedian but none of the other two actors (including second-billed Harvey Keitel).[12]

Such white reliance on high-value black creative labor renders very troubling the resultant coding of African Americans in terms of gratuitous sex and violence (Smokey) and cheating co-optation (Zeke), in contrast with the coding of the white ethnic Jerry in terms of beset but ultimately honorable family values. We have no way of knowing what Sydney Glass's original story was (beyond that it was bleak in that his father, who inspired it, killed himself). But the auto-plant story that the Schraders produced must have departed significantly from the one Glass envisaged, informed by his own and his father's direct intersectional experiences of being black and blue collar. The color-blind comity between the workers at the outset of *Blue Collar* likely bears little resemblance to Glass's (never mind his father's) experiences of the shop floor. The reflexive model of reading films developed in this book suggests that the comfortably middle-class-raised Schraders, with no personal experience of auto plants and their unions, for their antiunion (and antiblack) ire drew in part on their immediate experience of dealing with organized labor in the cultural industries. Their dispute with Glass, arbitrated by the new black caucus of the Writers Guild, had meant losing money and credit. The Schraders' animus toward organized labor was likely fueled by their intersectional contempt toward both the black writer and labor guild. Paul Schrader remarked at the time: "I hate unions. I've always been in trouble with unions. They hate the individualists, the nonconformists."[13] As Sarris posits, the film is representative of Paul Schrader's "radical individualism in line with his own romantic impulses."[14] This episode bundles what would become the principal ingredients of the white, individualist backlash against affirmative action: supposedly overintrusive institutions supporting affirmative action on behalf of overentitled minorities.

Well-regarded interdisciplinary studies of class, politics, and culture in the 1970s by the historian Jefferson Cowie and the film scholar Derek Nystrom have identified and explored *Blue Collar* as a significant film in illuming detail.[15] However, both fail to see the significance of its black creative input or of the dispute about that input. Peter Biskind's rollicking book about the Hollywood Renaissance, *Easy Riders, Raging Bulls,* may well have set the terms of later scholarly debate. *Blue Collar,* which features on Biskind's canon-forming "Selected Filmography" of renaissance classics (all of them white- and male-directed films), is discussed in some detail. But in this book Biskind ignores Glass, instead asserting that "it was . . . Leonard who came up with the story." Notably, this claim ran counter to Biskind's own shorter review of the film in 1978 in which he asserted that the film was "ripped off from a black screenwriter named Sydney A. Glass, who foolishly came to Schrader with his idea."[16] Following Biskind's later whitening of the film's inception, Cowie, in *Stayin' Alive: The 1970s and the Last Days of the Working Class*, asserts in his account of the film's making that the famous strike at "Lordstown gave [Paul Schrader] his topic"—again, no mention of Glass.[17] In *Hard Hats, Rednecks, and Macho Men: Class in 1970s American Cinema*, Nystrom briefly mentions Glass's involvement but only to establish that Schrader, whom Nystrom seems to cast as an enlightened figure, developed his interest in "the auto industry's racial conflicts" in part "during conversations with Glass."[18] Film projects have no single point of origin, and to be sure the Schraders had a significant role in the story's inception. However, the erasure of black creative input and of the disagreement over writing credits in the film historiography is significant because it is indicative of a wider scholarly tendency to underplay racialized creative labor dynamics that I have traced across this book.

Film historians have often discounted both black creative labor and the battle for the recognition of that labor. Cowie's eloquent reading of the film emphasizes the experience of white, male, working-class identity—which is "at [his book's] fulcrum," as other historians have noted—in ways that chime with the Schraders' investment in the elegiac crisis of the white anti-hero Jerry.[19] Nystrom, more than Cowie, presents a broadly racially recuperative reading of the film: rather than being part of the "broader investment in hard hats, rednecks, and macho men" of the 1970s, which is the central focus of his book, *Blue Collar* is one of his counter case studies that apparently make visible "liberatory . . . possibilities of working-class solidarity" and "the connections between class struggles and those of race and gender identity movements."[20] But Paul Schrader's flagrant white theft of Glass's idea ("Why should he write that? I should write that") is far removed from a liberatory vision of racial solidarity. Schrader's theft is especially galling because it occurred in the creatively important sector of film writing, which was and remains today one of the most shockingly exclusionary areas of all in the film industry.[21]

Cinema and Racial Containment

Released at a moment of fundamental change in U.S. politics and society, *Blue Collar* is a fitting, if pessimistic film with which to close my story. With the triumph of Ronald Reagan in 1980, color-blind anti-interventionism became dominant, and cinema's strategic need to incorporate movement demands dissipated. Although the 1980s saw the rise of a few crossover black megastars in the entertainment fields of sport, television, and popular music, shockingly few black and minority ethnic film directors and producers—or even stars—were required during this decade to legitimate the industry's thin professions of racial meritocracy. The closing off of funding for black filmmaking was determined in part, as we have seen, by shifts in the tax environment, by demographic changes with the rise of the suburban multiplex, and by the slashing of the overall number of film releases from an increasingly blockbuster-driven industry. But the abrupt end of black-directed films by 1980, recounted in chapter 5, remains startling. The industry's backlash was so formidable that, like Paul Schrader, it generally didn't even feel the need to pay lip service to cultural justice in production contexts. As with the World War II–era demise of black-directed race films that was powered by Hollywood incorporation, some integration of film casts in the 1980s replaced the brief black film wave of the 1970s. As Sidney Poitier, his vision of black production units scuppered, lamented angrily in the early 1980s, "The scriptwriters, the producers, and the casting directors simply don't have the courage to say to the studios: 'it would only be honest and fair and humane and decent and proper to reflect that we are in fact a multiracial society.' "[22]

Many historiographies of the transitional period in the 1970s fall into what the historian Matthew Lassiter calls the "all-roads-lead-to-Reagan" seamless descent into neoconservatism and deregulated capitalism, spurred by white race reaction.[23] Although Hollywood's contribution to this path is a central intervention of this book, I have also detailed cinema's multilayered racial-justice movement and black film culture, propelled by heightened social activism, burgeoning black-nationalist politics, and the instability of the film industry during these years. Black filmmakers and their allies, backed by black advocacy groups and the federal government, mounted strong campaigns against Hollywood exclusion. By looking at different spheres of cinema—creative workers, technicians, executives, activists, entrepreneurs, and institutions—I have tried to show the complex ways in which constructive change can happen in the cultural industries on both a microlevel and a mesolevel. This book has told a complex story of political flight by many, but not all, white people in and through film. Although there were strong currents of anti-affirmative-action and anti-black-power backlash in the cultural industries, a considerable number of white creatives were committed to racial change at this heightened political moment. As John Downing and Charles Husband remind us in their account of race in the cultural industries, white workers who self-consciously interrupt the white opportunity hoarding of behind-the-camera employment are very important and need to be better understood. [24] Throughout this book, I have tried to show what this constituency looked like, from film directors to studio executives and from union local leaders to writers.

At the heart of this story of the Hollywood Renaissance moment marked by politicoaesthetic ferment were highly politicized African Americans who turned to popular film, a medium about which many of them were deeply skeptical. Sidney Poitier, Harry Belafonte, Ruby Dee, Bill Gunn, Gordon Parks Sr., Ossie Davis, Diana Sands, Cliff Frazier, Melvin Van Peebles, Pam Grier, Ivan Dixon, Jim Brown, Diahann Carroll, Yaphet Kotto, Richard Pryor, and many others made both individual and collective inroads into the exclusionary motion-picture industry. The symbolic salience of individual blacks' stories led to important commercial and creative leverage that generated some jobs and representational clout for African Americans. Though there were unavoidable compromises all along the way, these African American symbol creators nonetheless ably attempted to open up different political perspectives, social identities, representational values, and distributive streams. Their experiences of forging political and cultural alternatives—to racism, to material exclusion, and to the legacy of McCarthyist persecution—equipped them with deep stores of black-diasporic cultural capital with which they sought to interrupt and enrich film's commercial, generic, and typological imperatives. One of the most surprising discoveries I made while doing the research for this book was the sheer breadth and richness of black-oriented popular film in the so-called "blaxploitation era" of the early 1970s—a richness and range that I have tried to capture in this book.

The African American filmmakers and actors who emerged into the cinematic limelight in this period were aware that their newfound visibility and success unavoidably gave credence to the self-serving white view that America (and its film industry) had moved beyond racial hierarchies. Many of these black symbol creators—committed as they often were to popular film as a medium for shaping public consciousness—were at the same time deeply concerned about the antiblack dimensions of the cult of individualism that was inherent in mainstream cinema. To avoid the danger of simply being "black faces in visible places," mascots on screen, many black actors became filmmakers and developed producing units to strengthen their efforts to change Hollywood's business and organizational models. The sheer number of new black directors for a few short years in the 1970s guarded against discourses of individual ascension, allowing these filmmakers to expand race-representational priorities, to distribute some wealth back to minority creative workers, to train and employ more people of color, and to organize for change in the cultural industries. This precarious black elite pushed into Hollywood's exclusionary domains often by working first as performers and then by converting this performative clout to production behind the scenes. These biographies highlight the need for approaches to cinema history that think about the vital linkages between production and text. The film stories that such black filmmakers produced, germinated in a deeply unequal and profit-driven industry run by whites, were often animated by the reflexive foregrounding of negotiations over jobs, wealth, and power in which they were engaged. In line with the cultural-industries framework developed in this book and emphasized by Anamik Saha in his study of race and media,[25] my story has continually emphasized and exposed the inherent unpredictability (rather than predetermination) of racial politics in commercial cultural production.

In response to the heightened black activism in cinema, the industry was forced to acquiesce to some of the movement's demands. At the critical moment of challenge by the racial-justice movement, whites had to give up or find new strategies and narratives for retaining their racial privilege. From major and smaller studios to independent companies, the film business made some concessions: hiring minority symbol creators, setting some targets for traineeships and jobs, and green-lighting more black-oriented stories. If the federal government and minority activists and workers *pushed* the industry into concessions, the freedom struggle and its cultural repertoires also generated striking new stories from previously representationally marginalized and maligned peoples that also *pulled* the industry toward change. The industry responded to activists' demands for commercial as well as political reasons, and it turned out that there was a great and previously vastly underestimated fetishistic appetite for "getting a bit of the other" (to paraphrase Stuart Hall) on cinema screens.[26] The marketability of post–civil rights cinematic blackness (and of black masculinity in particular) at home and abroad was first fully revealed in the late 1960s and early 1970s: iconically in the extraordinary cross-racial success of Sidney Poitier and Richard Pryor and in the charismatic appeal of black street heroes and heroines, starting with the pro-black entrepreneurial creative Melvin Van Peebles and consolidated by the linkages between the making of *Sweetback*, *Super Fly*, *The Mack*, and *Coffy* and "making it" as portrayed in these films.

Although the mounting calls for systemic change led to some short-term industry concessions, they also set off virulent counteroffensives at an individual, institutional, and textual level. To install meaningful diversification in the film industry and its texts as a new norm would have taken two things: top-down, binding implementation of laws to enforce and sustain change and many well-disposed whites to mobilize for the reform of on-the-ground communities of practice in cinema. Instead, as we have seen, the realigning state backed off, and most white workers and executives would not voluntarily desist from hoarding opportunities. The new civil rights laws were faced down not just on the ground by retreatist filmmakers and hostile technicians but also by big management and big labor. The industry, as I have argued, played a forceful role in suppressing the freedom struggle and allied movements when it defeated the federal government and black advocacy groups in battles that, in discursive and policy terms, reached well beyond the world of motion pictures. In the era after Jim Crow–style, state-sanctioned white supremacy, the industry's most formidable move to contain antiracist demands—along with helping to bring about the barefaced sacking of Clifford Alexander from the EEOC at a moment of crisis—came in the form of the soft ideological apparatuses: the post–civil rights *rearticulation* of racial-justice politics. As Michael Omi and Howard Winant explain in their account of shifting racial formations, "Identities of emancipation, speaking broadly, could be rearticulated as identities of incorporation. Ideals of redistribution and justice, again speaking broadly, could be rearticulated as ideals of formal, but not substantive, equality."[27]

Cinema was formidably placed to contribute to this rearticulation. Along with powerful corporate communicators and lobbyists such as Jack Valenti and Charlton Heston who fomented neoconservative "color-blind" language and incipient new-right "reverse-discrimination" discourses and legal actions by labor organizations such as the Group for Union Equality, cinema could mobilize striking racialized "screen speaks for itself" filmic stories. As this book has suggested, although films such as *The Godfather* and *Dirty Harry* are customarily understood as the signal texts of white backlash in the late 1960s and 1970s, an equally far-reaching and usually ignored story may be the soft white revival represented in film projects by Norman Jewison, Paul Schrader, and others. Hollywood was thus a potent player in the national shift toward a rearticulated politics of civil rights incorporation, and through this embrace it detoxified and rehabilitated the racial image of its predominantly white workforce and owners. From the racial embarrassment, defensiveness, and ignorance displayed at the public hearing in 1969, Hollywood transformed its image into one of expansive neoliberal multiculturalism—in which white men "naturally" rose to the top—with little reform of its institutions and hiring practices.

The corporate resurgence in the U.S. film industry in the 1970s led to financial growth and profits that were not enjoyed by most of its workers. Indeed, the new Hollywood consensus was marked by a growing divergence between film's core, shrinking prestige workforce and a mushrooming peripheral labor pool.[28] Core workers, made up overwhelmingly of white men, managed mainly to maintain their pay, conditions, and seniority structures, assiduously policing the labor supply through cruel and tokenistic workplace practices at moments when minority hiring and training initiatives showed up. By contrast, the peripheral pool of workers, starting in the mid-1970s, were typically un-unionized, precariously positioned, and much more racially diverse.[29] Within cinema's seemingly liberal yet overwhelmingly white hierarchies of creative labor, affirmative-action measures were largely avoided and rejected as antithetical to the ideals of individualism, market-based opportunity, and what has come to be called "color-blind meritocracy"— "color-blindness in theory, but race discrimination in practice," as the communications scholar Christopher Boulton explains in his insightful account of racial politics in the comparable U.S. advertising industry.[30]

This book has suggested that scholars need to be vigilant not to reproduce color-blind assumptions that can lead to the neglect of racial power relations in film-production studies. I believe color-blind assumptions help explain the "alarming" lack of research in the subfield of race and cultural production, identified by David Hesmondhalgh and Anamik Saha.[31] This book insists that the examination of race in the film industry must include a much closer look at white identity politics to uncover the complexity of how morphing white supremacy has been reinforced and contested in cinema. It has always been in the interests of the film industry's liberal retreatists and new conservatives to focus attention on "divisive" black-power radicals (the Nat Turner agitators), on "exceptional" black creative workers, on "unfair" affirmative-action policies, and on "ignorant" hard-hat white film technicians. All of these defenses have deflected from the Hollywood elite's own quiet but momentous move to retain and grow its race/class interests. My account, drawing on the work of many others, has tried to deconstruct some of these reasonable-sounding, white-normalizing Hollywood narratives.

Race, Work, and Reflexivity After the Transition

This book has suggested that approaching race and film from the purview of production and industry unlocks new insights about these important, neglected cinematic fields at the same time as it casts new light on filmic content. Production relations, an arena of extremely unequal racial power relations, inform textual outputs in complex ways. Racial dramas very often reflect the professional, entrepreneurial, and political dimensions of cinema's production contexts in ways that invigorate and credentialize the texts, evident in both the color-blind liberal-retreatist narratives and the color-conscious antiracist narratives in my story. In turn, racial dramas perform important communication work, projecting stories about race and the cinematic field to wider publics as well as back to the industry's own workers. Because film narratives and spectacles are so central to the industry's significance, they can come to generate behind-the-scenes leverage for both racist and antiracist social actors. Close scrutiny of the circuitry between production and text, I have argued, thus offers a way of understanding and

evaluating cinema's social power. In this final section, I make some suggestive rather than definitive points about how the model of production/text
reflexivity developed in this book holds explanatory power for understanding more recent racial developments in American cinema.

At the time of writing, an overwhelming proportion of those who make
films and decide what films get made are white men. Cinema's executive
branch, which was exclusively white in the transitional years, remains a
shocking 98 percent white, according to a study done in 2016 (when whites
constituted around 61 percent of the U.S. population).[32] As the film scholar
Monica Ndounou has explored, the color-coded economic principles of
white executives continue to shape investment decisions and distribution
deals in ways that repeatedly curtail the commercial potential of minority-
oriented films—something that the black producers in my story understood only too well.[33] People of color remain heavily underrepresented
among talent agents, the powerful industry gatekeepers who put film packages together. In turn, a large percentage of those on the rosters of the top
agencies are white, including film directors (87 percent white), who heavily
shape individual projects. On screen, whites (in particular white men)
remain overrepresented in both lead and overall cast roles in mainstream
film.[34] With color-blind race discrimination having won the day, textual
outputs remain heavily circumscribed by white commercial and social attitudes, producing race-themed texts that foreground economic and employment relations that tend to both legitimate and conceal their own racial
identity politics. Many prestige and middlebrow "problem pictures" that
deal with race and have multiracial casts continue to shore up the possessive
investment in whiteness. They foreground employment themes in ways that
posture as "racially liberal" but that are archly against affirmative action,
such as Best Picture Oscar winner *Crash* (Paul Haggis, 2004), or they
instead consign the glorious fight for racial employment justice safely to the
past. In the latter, racial workplace amelioration, usually of exceptional
individual blacks, tends to be overseen not by black-movement activists,
worker struggles, or the federal government but by individual white saviors
(as stand-ins for sincere-fiction Hollywood benevolence).[35] This is evident
in the recent flurry of race-themed dramas such as *The Help* (Tate Taylor,
2011) and *Hidden Figures* (Theodore Melfi, 2016). As commentators have
pointed out, these films, almost all directed and scripted by whites, offer
nostalgic retrospections on the freedom struggle. An important film that

nonetheless negotiates such postracial assumptions is *12 Years a Slave* (Steve McQueen, 2014), in which the film's coproducer Brad Pitt writes himself reflexively into the narrative to make a cameo appearance as one of the white liberating heroes.

The cumulative danger of such narratives is that they propose that individual blacks and whites have slowly come together to settle injustices in employment without the need for structural intervention and in ways that deny continuing structural racism—shoring up an alarmingly taken-for-granted attitude among many whites about present-day continuing workplace exclusions. Resentment about race-based affirmative action has remained "vivid and salient in [whites'] minds," explain Robert Entman and Andrew Rojecki, "despite its being mainly beyond the realm of personal experience."[36] The persisting sense of antipathy toward affirmative action among white people, including those in the film industry, seems to derive largely from the realms of rhetoric and representation, including powerful film dramas. As we have seen, the pervasive informal hiring of friends, acquaintances, and family in the production of motion pictures—which amounts on a structural level to a system of white affirmative action—is not deemed to be antimeritocratic and discriminatory. The hoarding of jobs by many industry whites is thus built on a basic racist double standard. As texts and production discourses privilege white stories and white workers, employment activism by minority workers, advocacy groups, and federal government has consequently had very little traction in general.

Within this intractably hostile, supposedly color-blind environment following the transitional decade, black talent in Hollywood has tended to focus on building star-fronted companies, as I have explored elsewhere.[37] After all, short of a new top-down comprehensive implementation of civil rights laws and a change in discrimination-denying white attitudes, negotiating individual agency by black talent has presented one of the only real possibilities for ad hoc diversification. This negotiation amounts to what sociologists Marcus Hunter and Zandria Robinson call an "assets-based" approach to black cultural production, predicated on the hard-won knowledge that there is no point in waiting for the (neo)liberal racial state to bring about constructive change.[38] Where, at best, industry whites made sporadic efforts to redress the industry's overwhelming whiteness in moments of acute pressure and embarrassment, black performer-producers have mobilized whatever individual creative and commercial leverage they had, starting in the post-transition moment with Eddie Murphy, who

worked under the major-studio umbrella of Paramount. The rise of individual African American talents after that—Spike Lee, Will Smith, Oprah
Winfrey, Whoopi Goldberg, Forest Whitaker, Denzel Washington, Tyler
Perry, Ava DuVernay, Lee Daniels, Steve McQueen, Jordan Peele, Ryan
Coogler, Barry Jenkins, Dwayne Johnson, Boots Riley, and many others—
marks progress in some creative areas of cinema. Like many of the black
filmmakers in my story, they usually are both performers and producers,
and/or they emerged through less-exclusionary artistic spheres such as
stand-up comedy, television, fine art, music, sport, and theater, where they
were first able to establish themselves before moving into film production.
Time and again in contemporary Hollywood (as in the transitional years),
it has been members of the black creative elite rather than white filmmakers
and executives who have brought minority workers onto projects in meaningful ways, building in their own informal *inclusion riders.*

The two reflexive mainstream black screen typologies of the transitional
years have endured in this contemporary cinematic field. Poitier's progeny
are the postracial black patriarchal uberprofessionals (often, as Jared Sexton has incisively shown, like Virgil Tibbs in the guise of police or former
military heroes[39]), typified in the by turns comedic and tough star images
of Eddie Murphy, Danny Glover, Will Smith, Denzel Washington, and
Dwayne Johnson. In iconic, diverse roles, these stars have showcased black
professionals in predominantly white spaces in ways that have generally
been ingratiating to whites but also attractive to minorities. As we have seen,
Poitier's influential early postracial portrayals drew their strength from
being genuinely rooted in the possibilities and perils of working as black top
talent within the white-dominated film industry. Such performances tried
to reproduce dominant color-blind norms because they speak to the star's
own charismatic exceptionalism, thus disavowing structural racism.

But such ostensibly postracial performances can be inserted into more
discomforting texts, as in the recent hit *Get Out* (2017), a horror film made
by African American comedian writer-director Jordan Peele. The isolated
black hero, meeting his white girlfriend's family for the first time (in a nod
to the Poitier vehicle *Guess Who's Coming to Dinner*), is a photographer and
thus, armed with a camera, serves as a stand-in for Peele. The film lampoons white "tolerance," which is revealed to mask monstrous practices of
racially embodied exploitation. Through his black protagonist, Peele is commenting in part on his own experiences in the cultural industries, stating
that the film "reflects real fears of mine and issues I've dealt with before."[40]

He insists on the reflexive nature of his film's black reverse gaze as he tries to process his own unsettling lone-professional experiences in the supposedly racially meritocratic but actually racist U.S. cultural industries. The film's lead actor, Daniel Kaluuya, concurs: "I just knew the dynamic of being the only black guy in the room—I work in the creative arts."[41] Peele's greater creative authority in his position as writer and director marks progress from Poitier's experience of marginalization in the late 1960s, when costar Rod Steiger's baiting racial slurs offscreen were sanctioned on the all-white production set as good method-acting practice.

The second main archetype mapped in this book, the black-nationalist-informed hustler creative, launched above all by Melvin Van Peebles in *Sweetback*, has been most powerfully developed, along with the mighty rise of hip-hop culture, by film auteur Spike Lee. Lee's salience, like Van Peebles's, has often come from producing post–civil rights racial dramas that are much less ingratiating to liberal-retreatist whites. In his most iconic film, *Do the Right Thing* (1989), the main protagonist, Mookie (played self-referentially by Lee), repeatedly insists that he needs to "get paid," and at the end of the film, with his friend murdered by police, he cuts through the sanctimonious speech of his white pizzeria-owner boss, Sal (Danny Aiello), by emphatically picking up his money. Onscreen and reflexively as the self-determined new black filmmaker, Lee ultimately does get paid on his own terms though not in conditions of his own choosing. In *Jungle Fever* (1991), the white partners of the architectural firm spout "best person for the job" sincere-fiction rhetoric as they deny black lead protagonist Flipper Purify (Wesley Snipes) his rightful promotion to partner. Spike Lee, in these texts and in his stark cultural-industries racial satire *Bamboozled* (2000), dramatizes unequal material and job relations that have clear correlatives in his experiences in the film industry.[42]

The cultural-industries reflexivity that energizes certain kinds of black screen stories has, to be sure, led to the neglect of other stories. Notably, reflexivity has tended to erase narratives about black women in a deeply patriarchal film business, nonblack minorities in a complexly discriminatory environment, and black poverty in the age of inequality—it is to these three neglected areas that I finally turn.

First, the two main post–civil rights reflexive archetypes, first formulated by Poitier's uberprofessional and Van Peebles's hustler creative, mobilize versions of the black-masculinist cool pose. Black men have continued to be the main beneficiaries of onscreen diversification in cinema, coming to enjoy near parity of roles (though not of leading roles) in mainstream films vis-à-vis their numbers in the U.S. population. The story has been very different for women of all colors.[43] Behind the scenes, as the #MeToo campaign has flagrantly exposed, women remain desperately underrepresented in creative and executive roles, and this is especially true for black and minority women. Although there were a surprising number of nondemeaning screen roles for black women in the early 1970s, once the door on black filmmaking slammed shut in the late 1970s, these roles all but disappeared. Mainstream screen space for black women in the post–civil rights period has too often circulated the grim Moynihan-laced typologies of bad mothers, drug addicts, and sex workers.[44] This negative portrayal is indexed by the Oscar-winning roles of two failing black mothers played by Halle Berry in *Monster's Ball* (Marc Forster, 2001), who is ultimately saved by a white racist patriarch, and the monstrous welfare-cheating matriarch played by Mo'Nique in *Precious* (Lee Daniels, 2009). Both the roles and the industry accolades they received can be read within the context of what Ange-Marie Hancock calls "the politics of disgust"[45]—a far stretch from the black mothers who feature in *Claudine, Sounder, Five on the Black Hand Side*, and *Cornbread, Earl, and Me* and indeed from the recent Oscar-winning mother role played by Viola Davis in *Fences* (Denzel Washington, 2016). Other recent black actress Oscar winners continue to index the importance of employment and economic themes to racial dramas, demonstrating partial progress since the early 2000s: Lupita Nyong'o won for her role in *12 Years a Slave* and Octavia Butler for her maid role in *The Help*. But these parts still consign black women's labor struggles to the past. Much more could be said, but the point I want to stress is that the dearth of good screen roles for black women is spurred not only by their severe underrepresentation behind the camera but also by their scant reflexive leverage.[46] Where select black men have been able to operationalize their dynamic screen images to gain a foothold in archpatriarchal production contexts, women—notwithstanding striking exceptions, such as Oprah Winfrey—have been less able to draw resources from such production/text reflexivity.

Second, the capacity for African Americans to mobilize reflexive energies to feed into and market their films has been much greater than for other racial minority groups. As observed in the introduction, because of black Americans' distinct history of labor persecution and their central role in economic-justice movements, which has made them prime targets of white backlash, they have particular race–labor salience. This salience has been repeatedly fed into both progressive and reactionary cinematic narratives, as I have shown. With discursive and performative acuity, black people have folded these material struggles into their cultural outputs in ways that lend discursive energy, ambivalence, and value to black popular culture.[47] African Americans' particular experience of state-sanctioned social exclusion across centuries fed into the development of vital black-diasporic cultural repertoires in the areas of music, stylization, and the body. These rich politicoaesthetic repertoires have turned out to be highly commoditizable and have been channeled in particular through action and comedy genres and developed through cross-platform synergies that enable stars to consolidate and grow their brand image. Native Americans, Asian Americans, and Latinxs, with different distinct indigenous, indigent, and immigrant histories, have not been able to engage equivalent cultural-industries politicoperformative reflexivity, which may help explain their much lower inclusion rates onscreen.[48]

The greater underrepresentation of black women (relative to black men) and of nonblack people of color in front of and behind the camera in mainstream film renders the careful auditing of intersectional racial and gender trends in Hollywood very important. Longitudinal studies such as the Hollywood Diversity Report project that looks at both race and gender, headed by the media sociologists Darnell Hunt and Ana-Cristina Ramon, are thus crucial for moving analysis beyond black/white and male/female binaries. In the period after civil rights implementation laws first required the film industry to start producing its own employment audits, in which the self-reporting by the industry has been either nonexistent (many of the craft unions) or so unreliable as to be all but useless (the studios), the Hollywood Diversity Report project is a vital guide. It allows us to scrutinize quantitatively the trends in the industry and onscreen to explore macropatterns in contemporary Hollywood with precision and complexity.[49]

The final way in which black cultural-industries reflexivity leads to erasure pertains to redistributive questions of persisting and expanding economic inequality and extreme poverty in the post–civil rights years of neoliberal consolidation. Rather than income, the racial wealth gap remains the most acute indicator of black–white inequality, as economists such as

Darrick Hamilton explore, and has expanded catastrophically since the Great Recession starting in 2008.[50] The median net worth of white households as of 2013 was $144,200, approximately thirteen times greater than the net worth of black households, $11,200. The wealth gap between white and Latinx households was also massive, with white households holding ten times as much wealth. Racial wealth chasms between whites and the rest are widening, with trend lines (calculated in 2017) pointing in the alarming direction of median wealth for blacks falling to zero by midcentury.[51] One contributory factor is the mass incarceration of African Americans, another trend with its roots in the 1970s, which amounts to a new system of segregation, as scholars such as Ruth Gilmore and Michelle Alexander have shown.[52] How can we reconcile and understand the relationship between the new black elite, such as those showcased in the entertainment industries, including film, and those facing what Lisa Cacho calls "social death"?[53] There is a worrying symbolic interdependency between black "winners" and black "losers" within neoliberalism, as many scholars have explored, so that black stars' achievements, whatever their political intentions, play a part in normalizing staggering disparities in life and work chances in the post-1970s period.[54] As the philosopher Falguni Sheth describes the situation starkly, "More and more men and women of color have been invited into the office of white supremacy to share in the destruction of other men and women of color who are vulnerable, disenfranchised, and rapidly being eviscerated through the policies of a multi-racial white supremacy."[55] My book has revealed how such postracial, stripped-down diversity discourses in which a few "lucky" individuals of color are invited into the Hollywood fold first took hold and were powerfully contested in industry politics after the racial break in the late 1960s.

Structural immiseration for many black people has propelled the influential arrival of Afro-pessimist interpretations that stress the impossibility of meaningful black agency (an ideological "ruse") within pervasive, systemic conditions of white domination. Indeed, Afro-pessimist approaches to film, such as those by Frank Wilderson and Jared Sexton, would likely reject the premise adopted in a book like this one, which takes seriously the struggles to try to reform and transform the film industry. Provocatively interpreting contemporary power dynamics as those between "slaves" and "masters," these thinkers might understand the possibility of changing an industry such as film as an ideologically distracting scholarly fiction.[56]

However, black radical thought is of course not monolithic. Although some of the most exciting recent black films animate Afro-pessimist perspectives, others have taken a different path, acknowledging the bleak landscape that has given rise to such perspectives but also imagining contemporary racial capitalism as contingent and destructible rather than fixed and inevitable.

Ava DuVernay's masterful documentary *13th* (2016, distributed by Netflix) is very important in that in full Afro-pessimist mode it foregrounds historic and continuing state-sponsored black-labor persecution. It is an exploration of the invisible workforce of the mass incarcerated—the diametric opposite of exhilarating bootstrap cultural-industries mobility—and the film powerfully engages Hollywood imagery as a regime of symbolic violence that has helped normalize the new Jim Crow landscape. However, the absurdist dark comedy *Sorry to Bother You* (2018) offers a much more contingent picture of racial capitalism, which Robin Kelley describes as being about "the gravediggers of capitalism."[57] Its writer and director, Boots Riley, like Harry Belafonte before him, first developed his career in the more open space of music, combining it with radical race and labor activism before turning to film. Like Sydney Glass, who had worked in an automobile plant before planning his blue-collar drama, Riley had worked as a telemarketer before setting *Sorry to Bother You* in such a workplace environment. Riley was able to resist the incorporative pull that many creatives feel when they are vertiginously swept into Hollywood's ambit and so was able to produce a film that lampoons extreme individual upward mobility and the costly racial identity transactions of black workers (in telesales as in acting). In different ways, this film and *13th* expose and critique the force of status-quo-affirming black celebrity and individual mobility in an era that, as Cornel West remarks, has seen a troubling rise in indifference among the elite to poverty.[58]

Indeed, the grim trends about race, work, and wealth mapped in these films tend to be nonreflexive stories for Hollywood's black elite, thus remaining, until recently, very undertold. Through their film content, anti-racist advocacy, employment practices, and profit distribution, filmmakers such as DuVernay and Riley do important work to interrupt the discursive embrace of them by a persistently racist industry. Through these various means, they can continue to mount critique and make microlevel and perhaps mesolevel changes. And it is worth reemphasizing that filmmakers of color have continued to be the main engine for diversification of the industry workforce as well as for the production of films that foreground material inequality and racial complexity. Indeed, at the time of writing this conclusion, a black filmmaking cultural formation has tentatively begun to reestablish itself, its networked creatives starting to move beyond self-reflectively liberal-individualist stories to bring a wider and more collective and complex vision of racial identities, repertoires, and economics into view (as it briefly did in the 1970s).

A film such as *Black Panther* (Ryan Coogler, 2018), which has made more than a billion dollars, is representative of both the new possibilities in and the continuing constraints on mainstream black-focused and black-directed cinema.[59] It marks progress in terms of onscreen visibility and behind-the-scenes black creative authority, particularly in light of the previous hyperwhiteness of the Marvel film franchise. Its huge commercial success and tent-pole status have enabled the green-lighting of other black-oriented productions. However, with the racial political economy of cinema having changed hardly at all, *Black Panther* also typifies constraints. White people reaped the biggest financial reward from the film, which performed particularly well with nonwhite audiences: it filled the coffers of exhibitors and delivered for its almost exclusively white funders and executives at Disney and Marvel Studios.[60] Moreover, the narrative logic of *Black Panther*, as scholar Christopher Lebron persuasively argues, repudiates "toxic" black nationalism (revealed, as in many Hollywood films encountered in this book, as boiling down to black thuggery).[61] Moving confidently beyond tokenism in its visuals and soundtrack, *Black Panther* employed many black creative workers and technicians, while nonetheless doing excellent postracial public-relations work for liberal-capitalist America and its film industry at home and abroad. Within a broader context of a gaping wealth divide, the disjuncture between a blackness empowered by a virtuosic cultural elite versus the film's mainly white profit structures remains troubling. As Herman Gray asserts in his magisterial book *Cultural Moves: African Americans and the Politics of Representation*, "Representations of black achievement do recognize and effectively make visible black presence and accomplishment in the national culture. But they are no guarantors of progressive projects for racial justice. Indeed, these representations of black people can just as easily be used to support political projects that deny any specific claim or warrant on the part of black folk to experiencing disproportionately the effects of social injustice, economic inequality, racism, and so on."[62]

The dominant way in which production/text reflexivity has worked in my story remains, of course, to reproduce pro-capitalist white advantage. The racial circuits of cinema have generally served to resolve and conceal contradictions between the industry's rhetoric of tolerance and practices of separation. Producing films that feature mainly white characters—with the added showcasing of marketable minorities (mainly black male) and demeaned and exoticized others—the white-run film industry has communicated its sincere fictions to wider publics and back to itself. Indeed, this reflexive ideological masking has generally worked so well at reproducing white identity politics that it has led to its own instabilities. Textual obfuscations can help maintain white workplaces to such a degree that, paradoxically, they inevitably give rise to crises—especially given the increasingly multiracial nature of America (with minorities constituting nearly 40 percent of the population in 2019). Take, for instance, the "Oscars so White" storm in 2016 following the announcement that for the second year running the Academy of Motion Picture Arts and Sciences had nominated only whites among the twenty available spots in the four acting categories. In the Venn diagram of production and text, actors inhabit the point of overlap between the circles. Thus, these workers do the racial signaling on screen that helps the industry protect its informal segregation behind the camera, as this book has shown. When even strategically vital acting professionals are not visible in the industry's awards categories, then "color-blind meritocracy" is baldly revealed as white supremacy. The crisis turned a spotlight on the demographic makeup of academy members, who vote to nominate individuals for these accolades: fully 91 percent white. This crisis gave rise to some institutional change, and the demographics of the academy as of 2018 were shifting: 87 percent white, with trend lines pointing perhaps to less-white (and less-male) cultural formations ahead.[63]

This book has shown that Hollywood, as industry and representational medium, was a powerful national arena in which the race-conscious approaches to employment and economic justice, following the racial break, were negotiated and generally repudiated in the 1960s and 1970s. Film catalyzed battles over resources and discourses during the inception of the complementary projects of racial neoconservatism and the broader neoliberal turn against poor and working people by elites. The approach developed in this book offers a starting point for thinking about Hollywood's complex yet pivotal role in the ongoing battle for jobs and economic justice in the age of job insecurity and wealth inequality, which are strongly determined by race. In the activist transitional years that I have mapped in this book, the intertwined identity politics of productions and films were exposed and operationalized to fight for constructive change. But in times of white and corporate backlash, racial discrepancies between production and screen actually became a means of further obfuscating racial disparities in order to maintain white privilege. We have seen that cinema is a contradictory as well as an oppressive field of racial structure and signification. Perhaps once again in the period of white nationalism and Black Lives Matter, of workplace precarity and raging inequality, and of Time's Up and Trump, material and discursive fault lines can be revealed and reactivated for deeper change. Returning to the late 1960s and early 1970s, when things seemed far from predetermined, allows us to see that racial power relations in the contemporary film industry are not fixed—however entrenched the racial exclusion and racist meritocracy frame can seem.

NOTES

INTRODUCTION

1. "Charlton Heston Joins Integration Marchers," *Los Angeles Times*, May 28, 1961, Charlton Heston Papers, Special Collections, Margaret Herrick Library (MHL), Academy of Motion Picture Arts and Sciences, Los Angeles, Calif.
2. "Hollywood March Committee," press release, July 31, 1963, Heston Papers, MHL; "Hollywood March Committee," press release, August 4, 1963, Heston Papers, MHL.
3. Eartha Kitt, quoted in "Top Film Group Plans to Join Rights March," *Los Angeles Times*, August 8, 1963.
4. Josephine Baker, quoted in James Donald, *Some of These Days: Black Stars, Jazz Aesthetics, and Modernist Culture* (New York: Oxford University Press, 2015), 213.
5. There was pressure from the state and the media on individuals not to attend the march, which was disapproved of by a majority of Americans according to a Gallup Organization poll, cited in Roper Center for Public Opinion Research, *Public Opinion on Civil Rights: Reflections on the Civil Rights Act of 1964* (Ithaca, N.Y.: Cornell University, 2015), http://ropercenter.cornell.edu/public-opinion-on-civil-rights-reflections-on-the-civil-rights-act-of-1964/. On the pressure faced by black stars, including some who decided not to participate, see Peter Ling, "A Question of Expectations: African American Celebrities and Civil Rights Protest in 1963," unpublished paper, copy in author's files. For negative reporting in the media, including the film-trade press, see, for instance, Mike Mosettig, "March Tramples on D.C. Boxoffice; Showfolk Figure in Demonstration," *Variety*, August 29, 1963.
6. Harry Belafonte, with Michael Schnayerson, *My Song: A Memoir of Art, Race, and Defiance* (Edinburgh: Canongate, 2011), 279.
7. On NAACP advocacy in the mid-1960s, see A. D. Murphy, "Pix Gains 'Disappoint' NAACP: Taking Hard Look at New Federal Law," *Daily Variety*, July 23, 1965.
8. On Hollywood executive support for the moderate wing of the civil rights movement in the 1960s, see Connie Bruck, *When Hollywood Had a King: The Reign of Lew Wasserman, Who Leveraged Talent Into Power and Influence* (New York: Random House, 2003), chap. 3.

9.   Daniel Steiner, "General Counsel's Statement," in U.S. Equal Employment Opportunity Commission, *Hearings Before the U.S. Equal Employment Opportunity Commission on Utilization of Minority and Women Workers in Certain Major Industries*, Los Angeles, March 12–14, 1969 (Washington, D.C.: U.S. Government Printing Office, 1969), 228. On the film industry being worse than other Los Angeles industries, including television, see Clifford Alexander, Interview III by Joe Frantz, June 4, 1973, transcript, 3, Lyndon Baines Johnson Oral History Collection, Lyndon Baines Johnson Presidential Library, Austin, Tex.

10. For an influential account of the distinction between professions and practices of racial tolerance by whites in the post–civil rights period, see Howard Schuman, Charlotte Steeh, Lawrence Bobo, and Maria Krysan, *Racial Attitudes in America: Trends and Interpretations*, rev. ed. (Cambridge, Mass.: Harvard University Press, 1997), 108–20. On color-blindness, developed in chapter 5 of this book, see, for instance, Eduardo Bonilla-Silva, *Racism Without Racists: Color-Blind Racism and the Persistence of Racial Inequality in the United States* (New York: Rowman and Littlefield, 2006).

11. Lawrence Bobo and Ryan Smith, "From Jim Crow Racism to Laissez-Faire Racism: The Transformation of Racial Attitudes," in *Beyond Pluralism: The Conception of Groups and Identities in America*, ed. Wendy Katkin, Ned Landsman, and Andrea Tyree (Urbana: University of Illinois Press, 1998), 182–220.

12. This meeting in 1976 was later published as a report: California Advisory Committee to the U.S. Commission on Civil Rights, *Behind the Scenes: Equal Employment Opportunity in the Motion Picture Industry* (Washington, D.C.: U.S. Government Printing Office, September 1978).

13. See Susan Christopherson, "Labor: The Effects of Media Concentration on the Film and Television Workforce," in *Contemporary Hollywood Film Industry*, ed. Paul McDonald and Janet Wasko (Malden, Mass.: Wiley-Blackwell, 2008), 155–66.

14. Matthew Frye Jacobson, *Roots Too: White Ethnic Revival in Post–Civil Rights America* (Cambridge, Mass.: Harvard University Press, 2006).

15. Ed Guerrero, *Framing Blackness: The African American Image on Film* (Philadelphia: Temple University Press, 1993), 110. The number of black-focused features declined sharply after 1976, per figures in Keith Corson, *Trying to Get Over: African American Directors After Blaxploitation, 1977–1986* (Austin: University of Texas Press, 2016), 14.

16. David Hesmondhalgh and Anamik Saha, "Race, Ethnicity, and Cultural Production," *Popular Communication* 11 (2013): 179–95; David Hesmondhalgh, *The Cultural Industries*, 3rd ed. (London: Sage, 2013), introduction and chap. 1, esp. 4–6.

17. The social scientists Desmond King and Rogers Smith use "transitional decade" in *Still a House Divided: Race and Politics in Obama's America* (Princeton, N.J.: Princeton University Press, 2011), 98–101, 116.

18. On the U.S. "racial break" that gave rise to the transition, see Howard Winant, *The World Is a Ghetto: Race and Democracy Since World War II* (New York: Basic Books, 2001), 147–77.

19. On neoconservatism and race reaction around the turn of the 1970s, see Michael Omi and Howard Winant, *Racial Formation in the United States*, 3rd ed. (New York: Routledge, 2015), chaps. 1, 7, and 8. I consider the racial neoconservatism of film industry management in chapters 3 and 5 of this book.

20. Nancy MacLean, *Freedom Is Not Enough: The Opening of the American Workplace* (Cambridge, Mass.: Harvard University Press, 2006), introduction and chaps. 1–3.

21. National Advisory Commission on Civil Disorders, *Report of the National Advisory Commission on Civil Disorders* (New York: Bantam Books, 1968), 11.

22. For critical race studies of labor that inform this book, see Robin Kelley, *Race Rebels: Culture, Politics, and the Black Working Class* (New York: Free Press, 1994); Michael Brown, Martin Carnoy, Elliott Currie, Troy Duster, David Oppenheimer, Marjorie Schultz, and David Wellman, *Whitewashing Race: The Myth of a Color-Blind Society* (Berkeley: University of California Press, 2003), chap. 5; Bonilla-Silva, *Racism Without Racists*; Devon Carbado and Mitu Gulati, *Acting White? Rethinking Race in "Post-racial" America* (New York: Oxford University Press, 2013), chaps. 1 and 2; Christopher Boulton, "Under the Cloak of Whiteness: A Circuit of Culture Analysis of Opportunity Hoarding and Colour-Blind Racism Inside US Advertising Internship Programs," *TripleC: Communication, Capitalism, & Critique* 13, no. 2 (2015): 390–403.

23. Joe Feagin, Hernan Vera, and Pinar Batur, *White Racism: The Basics* (New York: Routledge, 2001), 186.

24. The labor sociologist John Skrentny makes a comparable distinction between what he terms the "classical liberal strategy" and "affirmative-action liberalism," though he risks underplaying the political gulf between these two projects—one laissez-faireist, the other interventionist—in his study *After Civil Rights: Racial Realism in the New American Workplace* (Princeton, N.J.: Princeton University Press, 2014), chap. 1.

25. Stephen Steinberg, "The Liberal Retreat from Race During the Post–Civil Rights Era," in *The House That Race Built*, ed. Wahneema Lubiano (New York: Vintage, 1998), 13–47.

26. Thomas Sugrue, *Sweet Land of Liberty: The Forgotten Struggle* (New York: Random House, 2008), xxvi.

27. Robin Kelley, *Yo' Mama's Disfunktional! Fighting the Culture Wars in Urban America* (Boston: Beacon, 1997), 119.

28. Richard Dyer, *White: Essays on Race and Culture* (London: Routledge, 1997).

29. S. Craig Watkins, *Representing: Hip Hop Culture and the Production of Black Cinema* (Chicago: University of Chicago Press, 1998), esp. 155; Monica Ndounou, *Shaping the Future of African American Film: Color-Coded Economics and the Story Behind the Numbers* (New Brunswick, N.J.: Rutgers University Press, 2014); Kara Keeling, *Witch's Flight: The Cinematic, the Black Femme, and the Image of Common Sense* (Durham, N.C.: Duke University Press, 2007), esp. 27–28; Judith Smith, *Becoming Belafonte: Black Artist, Public Radical* (Austin: University of Texas Press, 2014), chap. 4; Maryann Erigha, *The Hollywood Jim Crow: The Racial Politics of the Movie Industry* (New York: New York University Press, 2019).

30. Lindsay Patterson, ed., *Black Films and Filmmakers: A Comprehensive Anthology from Stereotype to Superhero* (New York: Dodd, Mead, 1975); Thomas Cripps, *Making Movies Black: The Hollywood Message Movie from World War II to the Civil Rights Era* (New York: Oxford University Press, 1993), 250–94; Mark Reid, *Redefining Black Film* (Berkeley: University of California Press, 1993); Guerrero, *Framing Blackness*, 69–111; Scot French, "Mau-mauing the Filmmakers: Should Black Power Take the Rap for Killing *Nat Turner*, the Movie?" in *Media, Culture, and the Modern American Freedom Struggle*, ed. Brian Ward (Gainesville: University Press of Florida, 2001), 233–54; Mark Anthony Neal, *Soul Babies: Black Popular Culture and the Post-Soul Aesthetic* (New York: Routledge, 2002); Melvin Donalson, *Black Directors in Hollywood* (Austin: University of Texas Press, 2003); Paula Massood, *Black City Cinema: African American Urban Experiences in Film* (Philadelphia: Temple University Press, 2003), 79–116; William Grant, *Post-soul Black*

Cinema: Discontinuities, Innovations, and Breakpoints, 1970–1995 (New York: Routledge, 2004); Yvonne Sims, *Women of Blaxploitation: How the Black Action Film Heroine Changed American Popular Culture* (Jefferson, N.C.: McFarland, 2006); Mia Mask, "1971: Movies and the Exploitation of Excess," in *American Cinema of the 1970s: Themes and Variations*, ed. Lester Friedman (New Brunswick, N.J.: Rutgers University Press, 2007), 48–70; Novotny Lawrence, *Blaxploitation Films of the 1970s: Blackness and Genre* (New York: Routledge, 2008); Stephane Dunn, *Baad Bitches and Sassy Supermamas: Black Power Action Films* (Urbana: University of Illinois Press, 2008); Steven Ross, *Hollywood Left and Right: How Movie Stars Shaped American Politics* (New York: Oxford University Press, 2011), chap. 5; Christopher Sieving, *Soul Searching: Black-Themed Cinema from the March on Washington to the Rise of Blaxploitation* (Middletown, Conn.: Wesleyan University Press, 2011); Ian Strachan and Mia Mask, eds., *Poitier Revisited: Reconsidering a Black Icon in the Age of Obama* (New York: Bloomsbury, 2014); Allyson Field, Jan-Christopher Horak, and Jacqueline Stewart, eds., *LA Rebellion: Creating a New Black Cinema* (Oakland: University of California Press, 2015); Corson, *Trying to Get Over*, chap. 1; Charlene Regester, "A Matter of Race and Gender: *Lady Sings the Blues* (1972) and the Hollywood Renaissance Canon," in *The Hollywood Renaissance: Revisiting American Cinema's Most Celebrated Era*, ed. Peter Krämer and Yannis Tzioumakis (London: Bloomsbury Academic, 2018), 185–202; Michael Martin, David Wall, and Marilyn Yaquinto, eds., *Race and the Revolutionary Impulse in "The Spook Who Sat by the Door"* (Bloomington: Indiana University Press, 2018).

31. Renee Ward, "Black Films, White Profits," *The Black Scholar* 7, no. 8 (May 1976): 13–24; Gladstone Yearwood, "The Hero in Black Film: An Analysis of the Film Industry and the Problems in Black Cinema," *Wide Angle* 5 (Spring 1982): 67–81; Jesse Rhines, *Black Film/White Money* (New Brunswick, N.J.: Rutgers University Press, 1996), 36–50; Robert Weems, *Desegregating the Dollar: African American Consumerism in the Twentieth Century* (New York: New York University Press, 1998), 80–99.

32. Ossie Davis, quoted in Nat Hentoff, "Never Sell More of Yourself Than You Can Buy Back," *New York Times*, May 5, 1968.

33. Harry Belafonte, in Ralph Blumenfeld, "A Talk with Harry Belafonte," *New York Post*, August 1, 1970.

34. Jacqueline Najuma Stewart, *Migrating to the Movies: Cinema and Black Urban Modernity* (Berkeley: University of California Press, 2005), 5.

35. Linda Williams, *Playing the Race Card: Melodramas of Black and White from Uncle Tom to O. J. Simpson* (Princeton, N.J.: Princeton University Press, 2001), chaps. 3 and 5.

36. Cedric Robinson, *Forgeries of Memory and Meaning: Blacks and the Regimes of Race in American Theater and Film Before World War II* (Chapel Hill: University of North Carolina Press, 2007), 82–126, esp. 87.

37. Williams, *Playing the Race Card*, 188. See also Thomas Cripps, "The Winds of Change," in *Recasting "Gone with the Wind" in American Culture*, ed. Darden Pyron (Miami: University Press of Florida, 1983), 143–59.

38. "*Gone with the Wind*," Box Office Mojo, n.d., https://www.boxofficemojo.com/movies/?id=gonewiththewind.htm.

39. For figures and discussion, see Peter Krämer, *The New Hollywood: From "Bonnie and Clyde" to "Star Wars"* (London: Wallflower Press, 2005), 46. Film scholars often also call the Hollywood Renaissance the "New Hollywood."

40. Massood, *Black City Cinema*, 11–44.

41. On race and the musical, see Desiree Garcia, *The Migration of Musical Film: From Ethnic Margins to American Mainstream* (New Brunswick, N.J.: Rutgers University Press, 2014); on black-cast filmmaking in the 1930s, see Ryan Friedman, *Hollywood's African American Films: The Transition to Sound* (New Brunswick, N.J.: Rutgers University Press, 2011); on postwar liberal reformist filmmaking, see Ellen Scott, *Cinema Civil Rights: Regulation, Repression, and Race in the Classical Hollywood Era* (New Brunswick, N.J.: Rutgers University Press, 2014).

42. See Richard Brody, "What Hollywood Lost When the Communists Were Purged," *New Yorker*, August 14, 2014.

43. David James, "Chained to Devilpictures: Cinema and Black Liberation in the Sixties," in *The Year Left 2: An American Socialist Yearbook*, ed. Mike Davis, Manning Marable, Fred Pfeil, and Michael Sprinker (London: Verso, 1987), 127.

44. Anamik Saha, *Race and Cultural Industries* (Cambridge: Polity, 2018), 18.

45. Herman Gray, *Watching Race: Television and the Struggle for "Blackness"* (Minneapolis: University of Minnesota Press, 1995), 6.

46. Robert Stam, *Reflexivity in Film and Literature: From Don Quixote to Jean-Luc Goddard* (New York: Columbia University Press, 1992), 122.

47. John Caldwell, *Production Culture: Industrial Reflexivity and Critical Practice in Film and Television* (Durham, N.C.: Duke University Press, 2008), 1.

48. Hesmondhalgh, *Cultural Industries*, 411–12. See also David Hesmondhalgh, "Normativity and Social Justice in the Analysis of Creative Labour," *Journal of Cultural Research* 14, no. 3 (2010): 231–49.

49. On postracialism, a topic developed in the next chapter, see David Goldberg, *Are We All Postracial Yet?* (Cambridge: Polity, 2015).

50. I adopt Hesmondhalgh's term *symbol creator* (*Cultural Industries*, 420) rather than the narrower term *filmmaker* because many of the creatives in my story worked across platforms and in different creative sectors and roles (as writers, actors, musicians, producers, photographers, etc.).

51. I appropriate the phrase *ghetto action production trend* from Watkins's study of black action films of the 1990s (*Representing*, chaps. 6 and 7).

52. Sharon Willis, though invoking a rich range of sources, describes Poitier as an enduring "effigy" in *The Poitier Effect: Racial Melodrama and Fantasies of Reconciliation* (Minneapolis: University of Minnesota Press, 2015), 39, 49.

53. *Stir Crazy* (1980), which Poitier directed, held the number-one spot in *Variety*: "Top Films by Black Directors," *Variety*, March 18, 1991.

1. "THE SCREEN SPEAKS FOR ITSELF": INSTITUTIONAL DISCRIMINATION AND THE DAWNING OF HOLLYWOOD POSTRACIALISM

1. Bosley Crowther, "The Significance of Sidney," *New York Times*, August 6, 1967.

2. Charles Champlin, "Sidney Poitier Becomes No. 1 Box-Office Draw," *Los Angeles Times*, February 2, 1969.

3. George Lipsitz, *The Possessive Investment in Whiteness: How White People Profit from Identity Politics* (Philadelphia: Temple University Press, 2006). See also Thomas Shapiro, *The Hidden Cost of Being African American: How Wealth Perpetuates Inequality* (New York: Oxford University Press, 2005).

4. Figure from Gary Sandefur, "Blacks, Hispanics, American Indians, and Poverty—and What Worked," in *Quiet Riots: Race and Poverty in the United States*, ed. Fred Harris and Roger Wilkins (New York: Pantheon, 1988), 48.

5. Figures from Fred Harris, "The 1967 Riots and the Kerner Commission," in *Quiet Riots*, ed. Harris and Wilkins, 6, and from the Social Security Administration, 1964, cited in Sandefur, "Blacks, Hispanics, American Indians, and Poverty," 47.

6. Melvin Oliver and Thomas Shapiro, *Black Wealth/White Wealth: A New Perspective on Racial Equality* (New York: Routledge, 1995), 4.

7. On early black cinema, see Jacqueline Najuma Stewart, *Migrating to the Movies: Cinema and Black Urban Modernity* (Berkeley: University of California Press, 2005), 189–244; Pearl Bowser, Jane Gaines, and Charles Musser, eds., *Oscar Micheaux and His Circle: African-American Filmmaking and the Race Cinema of the Silent Era* (Bloomington: Indiana University Press, 2001); Allyson Field, *Uplift Cinema: The Emergence of African American Film and the Possibility of Black Modernity* (Durham, N.C.: Duke University Press, 2015).

8. See Clayton Koppes and Gregory Black, "Blacks, Loyalty, and Motion Picture Propaganda in World War II," *Journal of American History* 73 (September 1986): 383–406; Thomas Cripps and David Culbert, "*The Negro Soldier* (1944): Film Propaganda in Black and White," *American Quarterly* 31, no. 5 (1979): 616–40.

9. See Charles Musser, "Paul Robeson and the End of His 'Movie' Career," in *Contemporary Black American Cinema: Race, Gender and Sexuality at the Movies*, ed. Mia Mask (New York: Routledge, 2012), 30–31.

10. Anna Everett, *Returning the Gaze: A Genealogy of Black Film Criticism, 1909–1949* (Durham, N.C.: Duke University Press, 2000), 302–3. See also Thomas Cripps, *Black Film as Genre* (Bloomington: Indiana University Press, 1978).

11. William Grant, *Post-soul Black Cinema: Discontinuities, Innovations, and Breakpoints, 1970–1995* (New York: Routledge, 2004), 8.

12. Figure from Robert Weems, *Desegregating the Dollar: African American Consumerism in the Twentieth Century* (New York: New York University Press, 1998), 88.

13. Dan Knapp, "An Assessment of the Status of Hollywood Blacks," *Los Angeles Times*, September 28, 1969, calendar 1. On the federal government finding less exclusion in television than in motion pictures, see Collette Wood, "EEOC Says Too Little 'Color' TV," *Hollywood Reporter*, March 17, 1969. On the integration of other cultural industries, see, for instance, Christine Acham, *Revolution Televised: Prime Time and the Struggle for Black Power* (Minneapolis: University of Minnesota Press, 2004), and Brian Ward, *Radio and the Struggle for Civil Rights in the South* (Gainesville: University of Florida Press, 2004).

14. Figures from U.S. Equal Employment Opportunity Commission (EEOC), *Hearings Before the U.S. Equal Employment Opportunity Commission on Utilization of Minority and Women Workers in Certain Major Industries*, Los Angeles, March 12–14, 1969 (Washington, D.C.: U.S. Government Printing Office, 1969), 537–49.

15. Figures from U.S. EEOC, "EEOC Reveals Statistics on Minority Membership in Unions," press release, September 28, 1969, EEOC folder, box 84, Leonard Garment files, Staff Member and Office Files, White House Central Files, Richard Nixon Presidential Library, Yorba Linda, Calif.

16. Figures from U.S. EEOC, *Hearings*, 152–53.

17. Figures quoted in Vincent Canby, "Cheers for 'Claudine,'" *New York Times*, May 5, 1974.

18. Vincent Burke, "US Plans to Prod Film Industry on Job Discrimination Charges," *Los Angeles Times*, October 19, 1969.

19. Robert Grant, quoted in "Sidney Poitier: The Acceptable Negro," *Los Angeles FM Fine Arts*, June 1968, core collection, Sidney Poitier Papers, Margaret Herrick Library (MHL), Academy of Motion Picture Arts and Sciences, Los Angeles.

20. James Bacon, "Hollywood 1968—in the Black," *Los Angeles Herald-Examiner*, October 20, 1968.

21. Figure from A. D. Murphy, "Pix Gains 'Disappoint' NAACP: Taking Hard Look at New Federal Law," *Daily Variety*, July 23, 1965.

22. See "Off-Camera Minorities Employment," chart in Vance King, "Behind-the-Camera Minorities Employment Takes a Big Leap," *Daily Variety*, October 16, 1972.

23. Davis Roberts, quoted in Murphy, "Pix Gains 'Disappoint' NAACP."

24. Knapp, "Assessment," calendar 18.

25. "Unless Negroes Get More Film Jobs, Peterson Group Threatens to Picket," *Daily Variety*, August 27, 1968.

26. Leonard Feather, "Hollywood: Inglorious Black and White," *Entertainment World*, December 19, 1969.

27. John Downing and Charles Husband, *Representing "Race": Racisms, Ethnicities, and Media* (London: Sage, 2006), 163; Vance King, "Hiring Check Worries H'Wood," *Film and Television Daily*, July 7, 1969.

28. On the complex labor conditions and perceptions of creative workers, see David Hesmondhalgh and Sarah Baker, *Creative Labour: Media Work in Three Cultural Industries* (Abingdon, U.K.: Routledge, 2011), chap. 1.

29. Cliff Frazier, quoted in Ronald Gold, "Community Film Exec Says Majors Must Face Down Unions on Crew Bias," *Variety*, November 10, 1971. See also Downing and Husband, *Representing "Race,"* 164–66.

30. The situation for women trying to forge careers in the film industry was also dire, and many of the dynamics that I map also pertain to their exclusion (see the brief discussion of this issue in chapter 5). Though the Civil Rights Act banned gender bias, too, the state reform efforts directed at the film industry at the time were far more concerned with race.

31. Howard Schuman, Charlotte Steeh, Lawrence Bobo, and Maria Krysan, *Racial Attitudes in America: Trends and Interpretations*, rev. ed. (Cambridge, Mass.: Harvard University Press, 1997), 3, 108–20, 4.

32. Figure from Raymond Wolfinger and Fred Greenstein, "The Repeal of Fair Housing in California: An Analysis of Referendum Voting," *American Political Science Review* 62, no. 3 (September 1968): 753–69.

33. Joe Feagin, Hernan Vera, and Pinar Batur, *White Racism: The Basics* (New York: Routledge, 2001), 186.

34. Feagin, Vera, and Batur, *White Racism*, 196.

35. White executive quoted in Bob Hull, "Dramatic Upsurge in Hiring Negroes in Features and TV," *Hollywood Reporter*, April 29, 1968.

36. Charles Boren, quoted in "Boren Reminds Gov't AMPTP Has Tried to Hire Minorities," *Daily Variety*, March 18, 1969.

37. Arthur Schaefer, quoted in Collette Wood, "Blast H'Wood 'All-White' Hiring," *Hollywood Reporter*, March 14, 1969.

38. Schuman et al., *Racial Attitudes in America*, 153.

39. Boren, quoted in Knapp, "Assessment," calendar 18.

40. Feagin, Vera, and Batur, *White Racism*, 192; Joe Feagin, *Systemic Racism: A Theory of Oppression*, rev. ed. (New York: Routledge, 2006), 247; Mark Reid, "The Black Action Film: The End of the Patiently Enduring Black Hero," *Film History* 2, no. 1 (Winter 1988): 24.

41. Christine Gledhill, "Pleasurable Negotiations" (1988), reprinted in *Cultural Theory and Popular Culture: A Reader*, 3rd ed., ed. John Storey (Harlow, U.K.: Pearson Longman, 2006), 250–51.

42. Bosley Crowther, "Screen: Poitier Meets the Cockneys," *New York Times*, June 15, 1967, http://www.nytimes.com/movie/review?res=9E06E3DF103AE63ABC4D52DFB066838C 679EDE.

43. Bosley Crowther, "'In the Heat of the Night,' a Racial Drama," *New York Times*, August 3, 1967; Richard Schickel, "Two Pros in a Super Sleeper," *Life*, July 28, 1967, Stirling Silliphant Collection, Film and Television Archive (FTA), University of California, Los Angeles; Joseph Bell, "'Heat of the Night' Has the Taste, Feel, and Smell of Authenticity," *National Observer*, August 7, 1967.

44. Hernan Vera and Andrew Gordon, *Screen Saviors: Hollywood's Fictions of Whiteness* (Lanham, Md.: Rowman and Littlefield, 2003), 159.

45. Emma Hamilton and Troy Saxby, "'Draggin' the Chain': Linking Civil Rights and African American Representation in *The Defiant Ones* and *In the Heat of the Night*," in *Poitier Revisited: Reconsidering a Black Icon in the Obama Age*, ed. Ian Strachan and Mia Mask (New York: Bloomsbury, 2015), 75, 91.

46. Howard Winant, *The World Is a Ghetto: Race and Democracy Since World War II* (New York: Basic Books, 2001), 166.

47. John Ball, *In the Heat of the Night* (London: Michael Joseph, 1966).

48. Crowther, "'In the Heat of the Night,'" 26.

49. Rolf Stromberg, "Degradation Is No Fiction," *Seattle Post-Intelligencer*, May 14, 1968.

50. Malcolm X, "The Ballot or the Bullet" (1964), speech reprinted in *Say It Loud: Great Speeches on Civil Rights and African American Identity*, ed. Catherine Ellis and Stephen Smith (New York: New Press, 2010), 12.

51. Andrea Levine, "Sidney Poitier's Civil Rights: Rewriting the Mystique of White Womanhood in *Guess Who's Coming To Dinner* and *In the Heat of the Night*," *American Literature* 73, no. 2 (June 2001): 365–66; Hamilton and Saxby, "'Draggin' the Chain,'" 88, 89.

52. Bell, "Heat of the Night"; Mark Harris, "Telling It Like We'd Like It to Be," *National Catholic Reporter*, July 1967, Silliphant Collection, FTA; Ann Faber, "Hollywood Epic at Its Very Best," *Seattle Post-Intelligencer*, August 30, 1967.

53. Crowther, "Significance of Sidney"; "'In the Heat of the Night,'" *Daily Variety*, June 21, 1967.

54. Norman Jewison, *This Terrible Business Has Been Good to Me: An Autobiography* (New York: St. Martin's Press, 2005), 143.

55. James Baldwin, *The Devil Finds Work* (London: Michael Joseph, 1976), 51.

56. Schickel, "Two Pros in a Super Sleeper."

57. Advertisement for *In the Heat of the Night*, *New York Times*, n.d., Silliphant Collection, FTA.

58. Hamilton and Saxby, "'Draggin' the Chain,'" 87.

59. Hamilton Carroll, *Affirmative Reaction: New Formations of White Masculinity* (Durham, N.C.: Duke University Press, 2011).

60. Allison Graham, *Framing the South: Hollywood, Television, and Race During the Civil Rights Struggle* (Baltimore: Johns Hopkins University Press, 2001), 180.

61. Myra Johnson to Stirling Silliphant, February 27, 1968, Silliphant Collection, FTA.

62. Charles Champlin, no title, *Los Angeles Times*, March 19, 1968, Silliphant Collection, FTA. On healthy returns in the South, see "Selected Shorts," *Memphis Commercial Appeal*, June 22, 1967, Silliphant Collection, FTA.

63. Michael Omi and Howard Winant, *Racial Formation in the United States*, 3rd ed. (New York: Routledge, 2015), chaps. 4, 7, and 8.

64. Baldwin, *Devil Finds Work*, 55.

65. Tino Balio, "New Producers for Old: United Artists and the Shift to Independent Production," in *Hollywood in the Age of Television*, ed. Tino Balio (Cambridge, Mass.: Unwin Hyman, 1990), 168–73.

66. Walter Mirisch, quoted in Daniel Nemet-Nejat, "MoMA Toasts Hollywood Independent," *The Reeler*, November 27, 2006, http://www.thereeler.com/features/moma_toasts_holly wood_independ.php.

67. Tino Balio, *United Artists*, vol. 2: *1951–1978: The Company That Changed the Film Industry* (Madison: University of Wisconsin Press, 2009), 185.

68. Harry Belafonte, with Michael Schnayerson, *My Song: A Memoir of Art, Race, and Defiance* (Edinburgh: Canongate, 2012), 348.

69. Compare the annotated script drafts of Stirling Silliphant, *In the Heat of the Night*, dated March 14, 1966 ("first script") and July 5, 1966 ("revised first script"), Silliphant Collection, FTA.

70. Stirling Silliphant, "'In the Heat of the Night' Character File Notes," December 15, 1965, Silliphant Collection, FTA.

71. See Mark Harris, *Scenes from a Revolution: The Birth of the New Hollywood* (Edinburgh: Canongate, 2008), 288, which provides rich detail on these creative negotiations but largely refrains from commenting on their political implications.

72. Nelson George, "Sidney and Me," in *Blackface: Reflections on African Americans and the Movies* (New York: Harper Collins, 1994), 19–20.

73. Jewison, *This Terrible Business*, 146.

74. Ball, *In the Heat of the Night*, 14.

75. Compare *In the Heat of the Night* "first draft" screenplay by Silliphant, dated January–February 1966, with the later scripts from March 14, 1966, and July 5, 1966, Silliphant Collection, FTA. See the detailed comparative account of these changes in Darcy Meeker, "Novel to Script to Film: The Case of *In the Heat of the Night*," MA thesis, University of Florida, 1981, 12, 58–59, Silliphant Collection, FTA.

76. Ball, *In the Heat of the Night*, 28.

77. Figure from Balio, *United Artists*, 2:168.

78. David Bordwell, Janet Staiger, and Kristen Thompson, *The Classical Hollywood Cinema: Film Style and Mode of Production to 1960* (New York: Routledge, 1985), 12–17, esp. 16.

79. Diahann Carroll, quoted in Rex Reed, "Like They Could Cut Your Heart Out," *New York Times*, August 21, 1966.

80. Sidney Poitier, *This Life* (New York: Ballantine, 1981), 289; Stirling Silliphant, quoted in Dave Kaufman, "Token Use of Negroes in Pix and TV Could Be Dangerous, Says Silliphant," *Daily Variety*, January 23, 1969.

81. Figure from March on Washington memo, August 8, 1963, Charlton Heston Papers, Special Collections, MHL.

82. Jewison, *This Terrible Business*, 141.

83. Haskell Wexler, in Trevor Hogg, "Daring Ideas: Haskell Wexler Talks About *In the Heat of the Night* and *Medium Cool*," September 12, 2012, http://www.flickeringmyth.com/2012 /09/daring-ideas-haskell-wexler-talks-about.html.

84. See Larry Ceplair and Steven Englund, *The Inquisition of Hollywood: Politics in the Film Community, 1930–1960* (Berkeley: University of California Press, 1979), xi.

85. Haskell Wexler interview, Criterion Collection, video, posted September 7, 2014, http://www.youtube.com/watch?v=v7qMNXu2dXQ.

86. Richard Dyer, *White: Essays on Race and Culture* (London: Routledge, 1997), 98, 99.

87. George, "Sidney and Me," 19.

88. Dyer, *White*, 13.

89. David Roediger, "White Workers, New Democrats, and Affirmative Action," in *The House That Race Built*, ed. Wahneema Lubiano (New York: Vintage, 1998), 58.

90. Angus Campbell and Howard Schuman, *Racial Attitudes in Fifteen American Cities* (Ann Arbor: Institute for Social Research, University of Michigan, 1969), https://babel.hathitrust.org/cgi/pt?id=mdp.39015054478352;view=1up;seq=2.

91. Howard Winant, *The New Politics of Race: Globalism, Difference, Justice* (Minneapolis: University of Minnesota Press, 2004), 23.

92. Ossie Davis and Ruby Dee, *With Ossie and Ruby: In This Life Together* (New York: HarperCollins, 1998), 195.

93. Norman Jewison, quoted in Scot French, "Mau-mauing the Filmmakers: Should Black Power Take the Rap for Killing *Nat Turner*, the Movie?" in *Media, Culture, and the Modern American Freedom Struggle*, ed. Brian Ward (Gainesville: University Press of Florida, 2001), 240.

94. Gregory Peck, quoted in "Tribute Paid Dr King," *Los Angeles Times*, n.d., *In the Heat of the Night* clipping file, Silliphant Collection, FTA.

95. Jewison, *This Terrible Business*, 153.

96. See, for instance, Thomas Jackson, *From Civil Rights to Human Rights: Martin Luther King Jr. and the Struggle for Economic Justice* (Philadelphia: University of Pennsylvania Press, 2006).

97. Downing and Husband, *Representing "Race,"* 203.

98. Martin Luther King Jr., quoted in Adam Fairclough, "Was Martin Luther King a Marxist?" *History Workshop Journal* 15, no. 1 (1983): 120; Belafonte, *My Song*, 328.

99. David Chappell, *Waking from the Dream: The Struggle for Civil Rights in the Shadow of Martin Luther King, Jr.* (New York: Random House, 2014); Lewis Baldwin and Rufus Burrow, eds., *The Domestication of Martin Luther King Jr.: Clarence B. Jones, Right-Wing Conservatism, and the Manipulation of the King Legacy* (Eugene, Ore.: Cascade Books, 2013).

100. Winant, *New Politics of Race*, xxiii.

101. Ed Guerrero, *Framing Blackness: The African American Image in Film* (Philadelphia: Temple University Press, 1993), 70–75.

102. Clifford Mason, "Why Does White America Love Sidney Poitier So?" *New York Times*, September 10, 1967; Larry Neal, "Beware the Tar Baby," *New York Times*, August 3, 1969.

103. James Baldwin, "Sidney Poitier," *Look*, July 23, 1968; Ruby Dee, "A Talk About Film with Sidney Poitier," 1969, transcript, 1, Ossie Davis and Ruby Dee files, Schomburg Center for Research in Black Culture, New York Public Library.

104. Figures from Peter Krämer, *The New Hollywood: From "Bonnie and Clyde" to "Star Wars"* (London: Wallflower Press, 2005), 106.

105. Stuart Hall, "New Ethnicities" (1989), reprinted in *Stuart Hall: Critical Dialogues in Cultural Studies*, ed. David Morley and Kuan-Hsing Chen (London: Routledge, 1996), 441–49.

106. Crowther, "The Significance of Sidney." On *A Raisin in the Sun*, see Judith Smith, *Visions of Belonging: Family Stories, Popular Culture, and Postwar Democracy, 1940–1960* (New York: Columbia University Press, 2004), chap. 9.

107. See Jeff Smith, "Whisper Campaign on Catfish Row: Sidney Poitier and *Porgy and Bess*," in *Poitier Revisited*, ed. Strachan and Mask, 97–128.

108. George, "Sidney and Me," 19.

109. On Beah Richards, see the excellent documentary *Beah: A Black Woman Speaks* (LisaGay Hamilton, 2003).

110. Harry Haun, "Tolerance and Detection: *In the Heat of the Night* in Review," *Nashville Tennessean*, September 28, 1967; Hollis Alpert, "The Admirable Sidney," *Saturday Review*, July 8, 1967; Baldwin, "Sidney Poitier"; George, "Sidney and Me," 19.

111. Stuart Hall, "What Is This 'Black' in Black Popular Culture?" in *Black Popular Culture*, ed. Gina Dent (Seattle: Bay, 1992), 26.

112. Devon Carbado and Mitu Gulati, "The Law and Economics of Critical Race Theory," *Yale Law Journal* 112 (2003): 1757–828.

113. Champlin, "Sidney Poitier Becomes No. 1."

114. Figures from salary sheets and cast contact information, Norman Jewison Collection, Wisconsin Center for Film and Theater Research, Madison, cited in Harris, *Scenes from a Revolution*, 177.

115. Robert Landry, "Poitier: Negro Image-Maker," *Variety*, July 26, 1967.

116. Harris, *Scenes from a Revolution*, 139.

117. Sidney Poitier, quoted in Jack Slater, "Poitier Lashes Hollywood's 'Racist' Ways," *Los Angeles Herald-Examiner*, February 20, 1981.

118. Poitier, *This Life*, 289; Terry Morse and Norman Jewison, quoted in Harris, *Scenes from a Revolution*, 224, 222.

119. William Schallert, quoted in Harris, *Scenes from a Revolution*, 224; Remi Joseph-Salisbury, "Institutionalized Whiteness, Racial Microaggressions, and Black Bodies Out of Place in Higher Education," *Whiteness and Education*, 2019, DOI:10.1080/23793406.2019.1620629. Jewison's account of the positive influence of Steiger's immersive approach on Poitier and of his reassurances to "Sidney that Rod knew exactly what he was doing" are in his autobiography, *This Terrible Business*, 142–46, esp. 144–45.

120. Poitier, *This Life*, 289; Poitier, in Dee, "Talk About Film with Sidney Poitier," 6.

121. Devon Carbado and Mitu Gulati, *Acting White? Rethinking Race in "Post-racial" America* (New York: Oxford University Press, 2013), 15.

122. Sidney Poitier, in Claudia Dreifus, "Conversation with Sidney Poitier," *Los Angeles Herald-Examiner*, September 9, 1980.

123. Poitier, in Dreifus, "Conversation with Sidney Poitier," 10.

124. Baldwin, "Sidney Poitier."

125. Jack Valenti to Stirling Silliphant, February 23, 1968, Silliphant Collection, FTA.

2. RACIALIZING THE HOLLYWOOD RENAISSANCE: BLACK AND WHITE SYMBOL CREATORS IN A TIME OF CRISIS

1. National Advisory Commission on Civil Disorders, *Report of the National Advisory Commission on Civil Disorders* (New York: Bantam Books, 1968), 366.

2. On new black-oriented television trends, see Devorah Heitner, *Black Power TV* (Durham, N.C.: Duke University Press, 2013); Christine Acham, *Revolution Televised: Prime Time and the Struggle for Black Power* (Minneapolis: University of Minnesota Press, 2004); Gayle Wald, *It's Been Beautiful: Soul! and Black Power Television* (Durham, N.C.: Duke University Press, 2015).

3. Cliff Frazier, interview by the author, New York, April 17, 2007.

4. Lee Beaupre, "One-Third Film Public: Negro; Columbia, and UA Pitch for Biz," *Variety*, November 29, 1967.

5. Ed Guerrero, *Framing Blackness: The African American Image on Film* (Philadelphia: Temple University Press, 1993), 9–111; Jesse Rhines, *Black Film/White Money* (New Brunswick, N.J.: Rutgers University Press, 1996), 36–50; Joseph Morgenstern, "How to Stop Telling It Like It Isn't," *Newsweek*, August 5, 1968.

6. Stefan Kanfer, "The Shock of Freedom in Films" (1967), reprinted in *The Movies: An American Idiom*, ed. Arthur McClure (Rutherford, N.J.: Farleigh Dickinson University Press, 1971), 322–33. On the Hollywood Renaissance, which David Cook dates from 1967 to 1975, see his *Lost Illusions: American Cinema in the Shadow of Watergate and Vietnam, 1970–1979* (New York: Scribner's, 2000), 6–7, 67–158.

7. Peter Krämer and Yannis Tzioumakis, eds., *The Hollywood Renaissance: Revisiting American Cinema's Most Celebrated Era* (London: Bloomsbury, 2018). In the introduction to this volume, the editors, in an unusual turn, draw self-reflective attention to the white (male) identities of both Hollywood Renaissance filmmakers and most scholars who examine such films, identifying an "extreme white male bias" in Hollywood Renaissance canon formation (xix).

8. Harry Belafonte, quoted in William Wolf, "A Melting Pot Cast for NY's 'Angel Levine,'" *Los Angeles Times*, April 15, 1969.

9. Ossie Davis and Ruby Dee, *With Ossie and Ruby: In This Life Together* (New York: HarperCollins, 1998), 112.

10. Charles Hobson, "The Film-Makers: Focusing In," *Newark Sunday News*, February 1970.

11. Ossie Davis, quoted in Nat Hentoff, "Never Sell More of Yourself Than You Can Buy Back," *New York Times*, May 5, 1968.

12. William Styron, *The Confessions of Nat Turner* (New York: Random House, 1967).

13. Eliot Fremont-Smith, "Books of the Times; Nat Turner I: The Controversy," *New York Times*, August 1, 1968.

14. John Henrik Clarke, ed., *William Styron's "Nat Turner": Ten Black Writers Respond* (Boston: Beacon Press, 1968).

15. Fremont-Smith, "Books of the Times."

16. William Styron, quoted in Douglas Barzelay and Robert Sussman, "William Styron on *The Confessions of Nat Turner*: A Yale Lit Interview" (1968), reprinted in *Conversations with William Styron*, ed. James West (Jackson: University of Mississippi Press, 1985), 100. Styron makes very disparaging remarks about black nationalism in this interview.

17. Michael Brown, Martin Carnoy, Elliott Currie, Troy Duster, David Oppenheimer, Marjorie Schultz, and David Wellman, *Whitewashing Race: The Myth of a Color-Blind Society* (Berkeley: University of California Press, 2003), 2.

18. Norman Jewison, quoted in Wayne Warga, "Civil Rights and a Producer's Dilemma," *Los Angeles Times*, April 14, 1968, calendar 19.

19. Herbert Aptheker, "A Note on the History," *Nation*, October 16, 1967, 375–76.

20. Norman Jewison, *This Terrible Business Has Been Good to Me: An Autobiography* (New York: St. Martin's Press, 2005), 154.

21. Association to End Defamation of Black People to David Wolper and Norman Jewison, March 26, 1968, Ossie Davis and Ruby Dee Collection, Schomburg Center for Research in Black Culture, New York Public Library.

22. Association to End Defamation of Black People, "End Defamation of Black People," press release, n.d., Davis and Dee Collection, Schomburg Center.

23. BADA (Ossie Davis), advertisement, *Hollywood Reporter*, April 18, 1968.

24. Norman Jewison, quoted in "Wolper and Jewison Brush 'Turner' Beef," *Daily Variety*, March 29, 1968, and in Warga, "Civil Rights."

25. William Styron, quoted in Gerald Peary, "Nat Turner's Second Coming," *Village Voice*, September 4, 2001.

26. Jewison, *This Terrible Business*, 154.

27. John Downing and Charles Husband, *Representing "Race": Racisms, Ethnicities, and Media* (London: Sage, 2006), 200.

28. Styron, quoted in Peary, "Nat Turner's Second Coming."

29. For a detailed account of developments in the *Nat Turner* project, see Scot French, "Mau-mauing the Filmmakers: Should Black Power Take the Rap for Killing *Nat Turner*, the Movie?" in *Media, Culture, and the Modern American Freedom Struggle*, ed. Brian Ward (Gainesville: University Press of Florida, 2001), 242.

30. Joe Feagin, Hernan Vera, and Pinar Batur, *White Racism: The Basics* (New York: Routledge, 2001), 191.

31. French, "Mau-mauing the Filmmakers," 242–46.

32. Jewison, *This Terrible Business*, 155; William Styron, quoted in James Campbell, "Tidewater Traumas," *Guardian*, March 22, 2003, https://www.theguardian.com/books/2003/mar/22/featuresreviews.guardianreview34.

33. David Wolper, quoted in "Wolper Makes Change in 'Turner' Film Name," *Los Angeles Times*, February 15, 1969.

34. See Christopher Boulton, "Under the Cloak of Whiteness: A Circuit of Culture Analysis of Opportunity Hoarding and Color-Blind Racism Inside US Advertising Internship Programs," *Triple C* 13, no. 2 (2015): 390–403; Downing and Husband, *Representing "Race,"* 175–93.

35. French, "Mau-mauing the Filmmakers," 233–54.

36. Christopher Sieving, "The Concessions of *Nat Turner*," *Velvet Light Trap* 61 (Spring 2008): 46.

37. Christopher Sieving, *Soul Searching: Black-Themed Cinema from the March on Washington to the Rise of Blaxploitation* (Middletown, Conn.: Wesleyan University Press, 2011), 116.

38. Davis and Dee, *With Ossie and Ruby*, 338.

39. Judith Smith, *Visions of Belonging: Family Stories, Popular Culture, and Postwar Democracy, 1940–1960* (New York: Columbia University Press, 2004), 304.

40. Figure from Peter Biskind, *Easy Riders, Raging Bulls: How the Sex-Drugs-and-Rock'n'Roll Generation Saved Hollywood* (New York: Simon and Schuster, 1998), 35.

41. Bruce Kerner, "An Interview with Kenneth Hyman," *Cinema* 4, no. 2 (Summer 1968): 9; Kenneth Hyman, quoted in Robert Koehler, "Times They Were A-Changin'," *Daily Variety*, April 3, 1998.

42. Bosley Crowther, "The Dirty Dozen," *New York Times*, June 16, 1967, http://www.nytimes.com/movie/review?res=EE05E7DF173DE267BC4E52DFB066838C679EDE; Jim Brown, in Alex Haley, "*Playboy* Interview: Jim Brown," *Playboy*, February 1968.

43. Gordon Parks, *The Learning Tree* (New York: Harper and Row, 1963).

44. Bill Ornstein, "Progress Reported in Industry Efforts Up Negro Employment," *Hollywood Reporter*, September 6, 1968. For Parks's own account of his signing, see the interview in George Alexander, *Why We Make Movies: Black Filmmakers Talk About the Magic of Cinema* (New York: Broadway Books, 2003), 3–15.

45. Film-industry worker, quoted in Bob Hull, "Use of Negroes in Industry Just Tokenism," *Hollywood Reporter*, May 2, 1968.

46. Gordon Parks Sr., quoted in "Gordon Parks Tells of Union Aid on 'Learning,' " *Hollywood Reporter*, August 14, 1969.

47. " 'The Learning Tree' Ranks with the Very Best Films," *Hollywood Reporter*, June 20, 1969.

48. Gordon Parks Sr., quoted in Bob Hull, "Dramatic Upsurge in Hiring Negroes in Features and TV," *Hollywood Reporter*, April 29, 1968.

49. Gordon Parks Sr., quoted in Dan Knapp, "An Assessment of the Status of Hollywood Blacks," *Los Angeles Times*, September 28, 1969, calendar 17.

50. Figures from Keith Corson, *Trying to Get Over: African American Directors After Blaxploitation, 1977–1986* (Austin: University of Texas Press, 2016), 222 n. 12.

51. Bill Edwards, "MGM's Solow Okays Ralph Nelson Training an Assistant from Minority," *Daily Variety*, April 11, 1969. On Nelson's earlier career, see Smith, *Visions of Belonging*, 355, 357.

52. Downing and Husband, *Representing "Race,"* 164.

53. See Peter Krämer, *The New Hollywood: From "Bonnie and Clyde" to "Star Wars"* (London: Wallflower Press, 2005), 1–5, 6–37.

54. William Turner, "Pulping the Black Atlantic: Race, Genre, and Commodification in the Detective Fiction of Chester Himes," Ph.D. thesis, University of Manchester, 2011, http://ethos.bl.uk/OrderDetails.do?uin=uk.bl.ethos.532251#sthash.Bnes2ZTR.dpuf.

55. *"Cotton Comes to Harlem,"* *Variety*, June 10, 1970.

56. Figures from Taylor Clyde (G. P. Putnam's Sons) to Chester Himes, October 14, 1968, Chester Himes Papers, Amistad Research Center (ARC), Tulane University; Rosalyn Targ (Targ Literary Agents) to Chester Himes, March 3, 1968, Himes Papers, ARC.

57. Sam Goldwyn Jr., interview by the author, Los Angeles, April 13, 2008.

58. Goldwyn, interview by the author; Ossie Davis, quoted in "Ossie Davises (Ruby Dee) Thriving," *New York Morning Telegraph*, August 18, 1970, Davis and Dee Collection, Schomburg Center.

59. Davis and Dee, *With Ossie and Ruby*, 240.

60. See Michael Denning, *The Cultural Front: The Laboring of American Culture in the Twentieth Century* (New York: Verso, 1998); George Lipsitz, *Rainbow at Midnight: Labor and Culture in the 1940s* (Urbana: University of Illinois Press, 1994).

61. Davis and Dee, *With Ossie and Ruby*, 225, 226.

62. Cynthia Young, *Soul Power: Culture, Radicalism, and the Making of a US Third World Left* (Durham, N.C.: Duke University Press, 2006), 54–99; Sidney Poitier, interview by Ruby Dee, "A Talk About Film with Sidney Poitier," unedited version, 1969, 5, Davis and Dee Collection, Schomburg Center.

63. Frazier, interview by the author; figure from Ossie Davis, *Life Lit by Some Large Vision: Selected Speeches and Writings* (New York: Atria, 2006), 33.

64. Melvin Van Peebles, interview in *Reflections on Blaxploitation: Actors and Directors Speak*, ed. David Walker, Andrew Rausch, and Chris Watson (Lanham, Md.: Scarecrow, 2009), 170.

65. For a detailed account of Belafonte's earlier film career, see Judith Smith, *Becoming Belafonte: Black Artist, Public Radical* (Austin: University of Texas Press, 2014), 176–201.

66. Harry Belafonte, quoted in and figure from Wolf, "A Melting Pot Cast."

67. Kristin Hunter, *The Landlord* (New York: Scribner's, 1966).

68. Erich Segal to Norman Jewison, January 1, 1967, Norman Jewison Collection, Wisconsin Center for Film and Theater Research, Madison, quoted in Sieving, *Soul Searching*, 171–72.

69. Sieving, *Soul Searching*, 187.

70. Haskell Wexler, quoted in Biskind, *Easy Riders*, 171.

71. Hal Ashby to Norman Jewison, June 20, 1970, Hal Ashby Collection, Margaret Herrick Library (MHL), Academy of Motion Picture Arts and Sciences, Los Angeles.

72. Ashby to Jewison, July 8, 1970, Ashby Collection, MHL.

73. Jewison to Ashby, November 11, 1970, Ashby Collection, MHL.

74. Krämer, *New Hollywood*, 81–87.

75. Stirling Silliphant, quoted in Dave Kaufman, "Token Use of Negroes in Pix and TV Could Be Dangerous, Says Silliphant," *Daily Variety*, January 23, 1969.

76. Sieving, *Soul Searching*, 161–99.

77. Figures from Nelson George, *Blackface: Reflections on African Americans and the Movies* (New York: Harper Collins, 1994), 52.

78. See Sieving's illuminating reading of the film's production in *Soul Searching*, chap. 4.

79. Thomas Cripps, "*Sweet Sweetback's Baadasssss Song* and the Changing Politics of Genre," in *Close Viewings: An Anthology of New Film Criticism*, ed. Peter Lehman (Tallahassee: Florida State University Press, 1990), 245.

80. See the Van Peebles interview in *Reflections on Blaxploitation*, 170.

81. Harry Belafonte, with Michael Schnayerson, *My Song: A Memoir of Art, Race, and Defiance* (Edinburgh: Canongate, 2011), 318, emphasis in original.

82. Ishmael Reed to Chester Himes, June 24, 1974, Himes Papers, ARC.

83. On the black and white press reception of *A Time for Laughter*, see Smith, *Becoming Belafonte*, 229–31.

84. Vincent Canby, "Milestones Can Be Millstones," *New York Times*, July 19, 1970.

85. Davis and Dee, *With Ossie and Ruby*, 335.

86. The CBS series *Of Black America* (1968) and the WNET black-produced series *Black Journal* (launching in 1968) were among the high-profile television offerings about African Americans. On the air time devoted to race-relations-themed shows, see Richard Doan, "How Television Is Waging a Summer Campaign for Racial Understanding," *TV Guide*, August 17, 1968.

87. Bill Gunn, *The Landlord* treatment, February 12, 1968, 13, Ashby Collection, MHL.

88. A handful of earlier features were shot on location in urban settings, including Leo Penn's *A Man Called Adam* (1965) and Jules Dassin's *Up Tight* (1968).

89. Denis Jamill, "Hollywood Comes to Harlem," *Daily News*, January 27, 2002, http://www .nydailynews.com/hollywood-harlem-hood-stands-explored-ammi-film-series-article -1.483789; Davis, quoted in "Ossie Davises."

90. Davis and Dee, *With Ossie and Ruby*, 105.

91. See Paula Massood, *Black City Cinema: African American Urban Experiences in Film* (Philadelphia: Temple University Press, 2003), 85.

92. Belafonte, *My Song*, 348.

93. Harry Belafonte, in Ralph Blumenfeld, "A Talk with Harry Belafonte," *New York Post*, August 1, 1970.

94. Smith, *Becoming Belafonte*, chap. 4.

95. "Unless Negroes Get More Film Jobs, Peterson Group Threatens to Picket," *Daily Variety*, August 27, 1968.

96. Melvin Van Peebles, quoted in Jack Slater, "The Death of Diana Sands," *Ebony*, January 1974.

97. Robert Weems, *Desegregating the Dollar: African American Consumerism in the Twentieth Century* (New York: New York University Press, 1998), 80–99.

98.   "Columbia Aims at Negro Community," *Hollywood Reporter*, January 18, 1965; "Col, 'Several Other Studios' Trying to Make Pix Biz Less 'Notoriously White,'" *Variety*, August 18, 1966.

99.   See D. Parke Gibson's influential volume on marketing to blacks, *$70 Billion in the Black: America's Black Consumers* (New York: Macmillan, 1969).

100. On policies and discourses of social disorder in New York around this time, see Themis Chronopoulos, *Spatial Regulation in New York City: From Urban Renewal to Zero Tolerance* (New York: Routledge, 2013).

101. John Patterson, "Hal Ashby's *The Landlord*," *Guardian*, October 4, 2012, https://www.theguardian.com/film/filmblog/2012/oct/04/hal-ashby-the-landlord-classic.

102. Belafonte, *My Song*, 192. On white flight, see, for instance, the early influential article by William Frey, "Central City White Flight: Racial and Nonracial Causes," *American Sociological Review*, June 1979, 425–48.

103. Brown, in Haley, "*Playboy* Interview," 58.

3. CHALLENGING JIM CROW CREWS: FEDERAL ACTIVISM AND INDUSTRY REACTION

1.   Sidney Poitier, quoted in Louie Robinson, "The Expanding World of Sidney Poitier," *Ebony*, November 1971.

2.   U.S. Equal Employment Opportunity Commission, Title VII of the Civil Rights Act of 1964, Record Group 11, pub. L. no. 88-352, SEC. 2000e-2 (Section 703), 2000e-4 (Section 705), General Records of the U.S. Government, National Archives and Records Administration, Washington, D.C., https://www.eeoc.gov/laws/statutes/titlevii.cfm.

3.   Herbert Hill to Branch Presidents, July 27, 1965, quoted in Nancy MacLean, *Freedom Is Not Enough: The Opening of the American Workplace* (Cambridge, Mass.: Harvard University Press, 2006), 76.

4.   MacLean, *Freedom Is Not Enough*, 76.

5.   Vance King, "Behind-the-Camera Minorities Employment Takes a Big Leap," *Daily Variety*, October 16, 1972; A. D. Murphy, "Pix Gains 'Disappoint' NAACP: Taking Hard Look at New Federal Law," *Daily Variety*, July 23, 1965. The first union figures were published in U.S. Equal Employment Opportunity Commission (EEOC), "EEOC Reveals Statistics on Minority Membership in Unions," press release, September 28, 1969, EEOC folder 4 of 4, box 84, Leonard Garment files, Staff Member and Office Files, White House Central Files, Richard Nixon Presidential Library (NPL), Yorba Linda, Calif.

6.   "Unless Negroes Get More Film Jobs, Peterson Group Threatens to Picket," *Daily Variety*, August 27, 1968.

7.   Clifford Alexander, Interview III by Joe Frantz, June 4, 1973, transcript, 3, Lyndon Baines Johnson Oral History Collection, Lyndon Baines Johnson Library, Austin, Tex.

8.   Daniel Steiner, "General Counsel's Statement," in U.S. EEOC, *Hearings Before the U.S. Equal Employment Opportunity Commission on Utilization of Minority and Women Workers in Certain Major Industries*, Los Angeles, March 12–14, 1969 (Washington, D.C.: U.S. Government Printing Office, 1969), 227, 228.

9.   A. D. Murphy, "Gov't Charges: Pix Discriminate in Jobs," *Daily Variety*, March 14, 1969; Vincent Burke, "US Plans to Prod Film Industry on Job Discrimination Charges," *Los Angeles Times*, October 19, 1969; "Gov't Crackdown on H'Wood," *Daily Variety*, October 20, 1969; Dan Knapp, "An Assessment of the Status of Hollywood Blacks," *Los Angeles Times*, September 28, 1969, calendar 1, calendars 17–18.

10. Arthur Schaefer, quoted in U.S. EEOC, *Hearings*, 179, 185.

11. Clifford Alexander and Kenneth Sieling, quoted in U.S. EEOC, *Hearings*, 211–12.

12. On Universal, see Burke, "US Plans to Prod Film Industry"; Knapp, "Assessment," calendar 17.

13. Collette Wood, "Blast H'Wood 'All-White' Hiring," *Hollywood Reporter*, March 14, 1969.

14. Dave Kaufman, "EEOC Brushed Off One IA Union," *Daily Variety*, March 20, 1969. Whatever the skill level, all costumers had their conditions and wages protected under the collective-bargaining agreement for their local, so the 20 percent minority membership represents a small pocket of meaningful integration in motion pictures. On Costumers Local 705 in the postwar period, see Hugh Lovell and Tasile Carter, *Collective Bargaining in the Motion Picture Industry* (Berkeley: University of California Press, 1955), 30–32.

15. Vance King, "Hiring Check Worries H'Wood," *Film and Television Daily*, July 7, 1969.

16. "Questions Union Asks on Registration Form," in U.S. EEOC, *Hearings*, 158–65, esp. 58.

17. Josef Bernay, quoted in U.S. EEOC, *Hearings*, 159.

18. John Downing and Charles Husband, *Representing "Race": Racisms, Ethnicities, and Media* (London: Sage, 2006), chap. 8.

19. Alexander, Interview III, 13.

20. See Murphy, "Pix Gains 'Disappoint' NAACP." On the more recent lack of minority film writers, see Denise Bielby and William Bielby, "Hollywood Dreams, Harsh Realities: Writing for Film and Television," *Contexts* 4, no. 1 (2002): 21–27.

21. On the new Directors Guild of America requirements, see Bill Edwards, "MGM's Solow Okays Ralph Nelson Training an Assistant from Minority," *Daily Variety*, April 11, 1969.

22. On the "racial signaling" work done by minority actors, see John Skrentny, *After Civil Rights: Racial Realism in the New American Workplace* (Princeton, N.J.: Princeton University Press, 2014), 153–55.

23. A. D. Murphy, "Students: Stay Out of Hollywood," *New York Times*, August 18, 1968.

24. Charles Allen, "Boris Karloff . . . Too Dark?" *New York Times*, February 28, 1971.

25. Steiner, "General Counsel's Statement," 227–28.

26. On the lack of awareness of affirmative-action procedures, see testimony in U.S. EEOC, *Hearings*, 184, 200, 228.

27. Murphy, "Gov't Charges," 23.

28. Leonard Feather, "Hollywood: Inglorious Black and White," *Entertainment World*, December 19, 1969.

29. Clifford Frazier, quoted in Ronald Gold, "Community Film Exec Says Majors Must Face Down Unions on Crew Bias," *Variety*, November 10, 1971.

30. On consent decrees, see Robert Zieger, *For Jobs and Freedom: Race and Labor in America Since 1865* (Lexington: University Press of Kentucky, 2007), 175–207.

31. King, "Hiring Check Worries H'Wood." See also Collette Wood, "Justice Dept. Here on Probe," *Hollywood Reporter*, May 15, 1969.

32. Burke, "US Plans to Prod Film Industry."

33. On Title VII and the built-in restraints, see, for instance, Charles Whalen and Barbara Whalen, *The Longest Debate: A Legislative History of the 1964 Civil Rights Act* (Washington, D.C.: Seven Locks, 1985), 200–201, 149–93.

34. MacLean, *Freedom Is Not Enough*, 71.

35. Alexander, Interview III, 8.

36. Senator Everett Dirksen, quoted in David Broder, "Dirksen Threatens to Get Job Equality Chief Fired," *Los Angeles Times*, March 28, 1969; "Response of Clifford Alexander," U.S.

Congress, Senate Committee on Interior and Insular Affairs, *Committee Prints*, vol. 3 (Washington, D.C.: U.S. Government Printing Office, 1971), 801–2.

37. Senator Edward Kennedy, quoted in Broder, "Dirksen Threatens to Get Job Equality Chief Fired."

38. William Brown, quoted in James Batten, "Equal Employment Boss: Slaying a Dragon with a Pea-Shooter," *Miami Herald*, October 23, 1969.

39. Everett Dirksen to Irene Leander, May 26, 1969, Clifford Alexander file, Alphabetical File 1969, Everett Dirksen Papers, Everett Dirksen Collection, Pekin, Ill.; Everett Dirksen to Bryce Harlow, April 7, 1969, Alexander file, Dirksen Papers.

40. Hugh Davis Graham, *The Civil Rights Era: Origins and Development of National Policy 1960–1972* (New York: Oxford University Press, 1990), 238.

41. Figure from "Civil Rights Preview: Progress, 1954–71," n.d., 3, Civil Rights Preview folder, box 84, Bradley Patterson files, Staff Member and Office Files, White House Central Files, NPL.

42. See Dean Kotlowski, *Nixon's Civil Rights* (Cambridge, Mass.: Harvard University Press, 2001), 118–21.

43. William Brown, press conference, August 29, 1969, EEOC 1969 folder, box 84, Garment files, NPL.

44. Clifford Alexander, quoted in Batten, "Equal Employment Boss."

45. Burke, "US Plans to Prod Film Industry."

46. Kevin Sandler, "The Future of U.S. Film Censorship Studies," *Velvet Light Trap* 63 (Spring 2009): 69.

47. "Valenti Feels Easier in Approaching Republicans on Film Trade's Behalf," *Variety*, February 16, 1969.

48. Jack Valenti, Interview V by Joe Frantz, July 12, 1972, transcript, 11, Lyndon Baines Johnson Oral History Collection. On Valenti's relationship with Dirksen, see also Jack Valenti, *My Life: In War, the White House, and Hollywood* (New York: Harmony, 2007), 46–47.

49. Wilkins and Andrews photo in "Negro Film Roles Show Sharp Increase," *Hollywood Citizen News*, April 22, 1969, Blacks and Film (–1969) File, Margaret Herrick Library (MHL), Academy of Motion Picture Arts and Sciences, Los Angeles.

50. Jack Valenti, quoted in Bill Ornstein, "Black Employment Pics, TV Up," *Hollywood Reporter*, April 22, 1969.

51. Schaefer, testimony in U.S. EEOC, *Hearings*, 177.

52. Jack Valenti and Roy Wilkins, quoted in Jim Mullen, "Roy Wilkins Praises Pic Biz: NAACP Leader Asserts Film-TV Industry 'Has Done a Very Satisfactory Job,'" *Daily Variety*, April 22, 1969.

53. Ornstein, "Black Employment Pics, TV Up."

54. Roy Wilkins, statement in "Alexander's Resignation Forced by Bias," *Crisis*, May 1969, 217.

55. On Wilkins's criticism of Nixon and Dirksen, see Roy Wilkins, with Tom Mathews, *Standing Fast: The Autobiography of Roy Wilkins* (New York: Da Capo, 1994), 333–34. On his public rejection of black power, see 315–21.

56. Roy Wilkins, quoted in Ornstein, "Black Employment Pics, TV Up."

57. Stephen Vaughn, *Freedom and Entertainment: Rating the Movies in an Age of New Media* (New York: Cambridge University Press, 2006), 24.

58. Clifford Alexander, quoted in A. D. Murphy, "TV and Pix Hiring Practices to Get Public Hearings on Coast This Week," *Variety*, March 12, 1969.

59. Wilkins, quoted in Mullen, "Roy Wilkins Praises Pic Biz."

60. Valenti, quoted in Ornstein, "Black Employment Pics, TV Up," and in "Negro Film Roles Show Sharp Increase."

61. Irving Kristol, *Reflections of a Neoconservative: Looking Back, Looking Ahead* (New York: Basic Books, 1983), xii; Peter Steinfels, *The Neoconservatives: The Men Who Are Changing America's Politics* (New York: Simon and Schuster, 1979), 3. On the genesis of neoconservatism around the turn of the 1970s, see Howard Winant, *The World Is a Ghetto: Race and Democracy Since World War II* (New York: Basic Books, 2001), 150–51, 171–72; Angela Dillard, *Guess Who's Coming to Dinner Now? Multicultural Conservatism in America* (New York: New York University Press, 2001), 56–98; MacLean, *Freedom Is Not Enough*, 196–99. For seminal texts that fed into the neoconservative racial project, see the writing in *Commentary* magazine in the 1960s, starting with Norman Podhoretz, "My Negro Problem—and Ours" (1963), reprinted in *The "Commentary" Reader: Two Decades of Articles and Stories*, ed. Norman Podhoretz (New York: Atheneum, 1967), 376–87, and Nathan Glazer, "Negroes and Jews: The New Challenge to Pluralism" (1964), reprinted in *Ethnic Dilemmas: 1964–1982* (Cambridge, Mass.: Harvard University Press, 1983), 70–93.

62. Daniel Moynihan to Richard Nixon, memorandum, January 16, 1970, Civil Rights Preview folder, box 84, Patterson files, NPL.

63. Michael Omi and Howard Winant, *Racial Formation in the United States: From the 1960s to the 1990s*, 2nd ed. (New York: Routledge, 1994), 56, 128–32.

64. Steinfels, *Neoconservatives*, 228.

65. "Urge Reagan Pressure Nixon in H'Wood's Unemployment," *Daily Variety*, January 15, 1971.

66. Peter Flanigan to the President, April 5, 1971, box 84, President's Office Files, White House Special Files, NPL. See also Connie Bruck, *When Hollywood Had a King: The Reign of Lew Wasserman, Who Leveraged Talent Into Power and Influence* (New York: Random House, 2003), 270–76; A. D. Murphy, "Tax Break to Ease Pix Crisis: 'Schreiber Plan' to Cut Charges," *Variety*, September 15, 1971; and A. D. Murphy, "U.S. Grant Pushed for Pic Jobs," *Daily Variety*, September 24, 1971.

67. David Cook, *Lost Illusions: American Cinema in the Shadow of Watergate and Vietnam, 1970–1979* (New York: Scribner's, 2000), 9–14, esp. 11–12.

68. Estimate cited in Cook, *Lost Illusions*, 12.

69. "Heston Cites Casting Growth for Minorities," *Hollywood Reporter*, August 27, 1968.

70. On the rise of "runaway productions," see U.S. House of Representatives, *Hearings Before the General Subcommittee on Labor, Committee on Labor and Education, House of Representatives: Unemployment Problems in American Film Industry*, October 29 and 30, 1971 (Los Angeles: U.S. Government Printing Office), 37, 44.

71. "Nixon Gets Backing of Charlton Heston," *Los Angeles Herald-Examiner*, August 4, 1972, Charlton Heston Papers, MHL.

72. Charlton Heston, *In the Arena: An Autobiography* (New York: Harper Collins, 1996), 354, emphasis in original.

73. "Nixon Gets Backing of Charlton Heston"; "Heston Asks Aid to Films: Up to Reagan," *Hollywood Citizen News*, November 21, 1966, Heston Papers, MHL.

74. Charlton Heston, quoted in Charles Champlin, "Heston's Rx for Ailing Hollywood," *Los Angeles Times*, July 20, 1969.

75. "Charlton Heston's Speech Introducing Mrs. Coretta Scott King at the Dinner in Her Honor, Cocoanut Grove, Ambassador Hotel, Los Angeles, December 2, 1969," transcript, Heston Papers, MHL.

76. Charlton Heston, *This Actor's Life: Charlton Heston Journals, 1956–1976* (New York: Viking, 1979), 326.

77. Irving Kristol, quoted in Barry Gwen, "Irving Kristol, Godfather of Modern Conservatism, Dies at 89," *New York Times*, September 19, 2009. Emilie Raymond uncritically reproduces Heston's neoconservative logic as simply "standing in place," contending that "Heston remained devoted to his core values . . . throughout his political career" (*From My Cold Dead Hands: Charlton Heston and American Politics* [Lexington: University Press of Kentucky, 2006], 4–5). Steven Ross offers a more nuanced reading, yet his interpretation of these new conservatives also tends to normalize them (and by extension Heston) as centrists: "Disturbed by what they saw as the party's distinctly left agenda, a small group of liberal intellectuals, led by *Commentary* editors Irving Kristol and Norman Podhoretz, criticized Democrats for no longer championing the values they used to stand for, *values that appealed to a broad spectrum of middle- and working-class Americans*" (*Hollywood Left and Right: How Movie Stars Shaped American Politics* [New York: Oxford University Press, 2011], 291–92, emphasis added).

78. Nancy MacLean, *Democracy in Chains: The Deep History of the Radical Right's Stealth Plan for America* (New York: Penguin, 2017).

79. At this time, Heston was reorienting his screen image somewhat, most successfully with the socially redolent hit *Planet of the Apes* (Franklin Schaffner, 1968), which drew on topical themes of racial discrimination and oppression but ends with the hero (Heston) saving a white woman from the marauding apes. See Eric Greene, *"Planet of the Apes" as American Myth: Race, Politics, and Popular Culture* (Middletown, Conn.: Wesleyan University Press, 1996).

80. Richard Walsh, quoted in King, "Hiring Check Worries H'Wood," and in Bill Ornstein, "Walsh Rips Race Bias Charge," *Hollywood Reporter*, April 10, 1969. See also Dave Kaufman, "Unions Prep Seniority Defense," *Daily Variety*, July 11, 1969.

81. Frazier, quoted in Gold, "Community Film Exec."

82. Howard Fabrick, quoted in Robert Kistler, "Film Executive Blames Hiring Bias on Unions," *Los Angeles Times*, October 19, 1969.

83. Heston, *This Actor's Life*, 178.

84. Alexander, Interview III, 14.

85. See Thomas Frank, *Listen, Liberal, or Whatever Happened to the Party of the People?* (London: Scribe, 2016); Jefferson Cowie, *Stayin' Alive: The 1970s and the Last Days of the Working Class* (New York: New Press, 2010), 21–209.

86. Robert Brenner, "The Economics of Global Turbulence: 1950–1998," special issue of *New Left Review* 229 (May–June 1998): 6, 93.

87. On overall U.S. unemployment rates in the 1960s, see Brenner, "Economics of Global Turbulence," 96–97.

88. See Susan Christopherson and Michael Storper, "The Effects of Flexible Specialization on Industrial Politics and the Labor Market: The Motion Picture Industry," *Industrial and Labor Relations Review* 42, no. 3 (April 1992): 331–47.

89. Judith Stein, *Running Steel, Running America: Race, Economic Policy, and the Decline of Liberalism* (Chapel Hill: University of North Carolina Press, 1998), 318.

90. Dave Kaufman, "Industry on Gov't Griddle," *Daily Variety*, October 27, 1969.

91. See Cook, *Lost Illusions*, 3–6, 64; Janet Wasko, *Movies and Money: Financing the American Film Industry* (Norwood, N.J.: Ablex, 1982), 176–89; Jon Lewis, *Hollywood v. Hard Core: How the Struggle Over Censorship Saved the Modern Film Industry* (New York: New York University Press, 2000), 151–56.

92. Dave Kaufman, "More Pic-TV Jobs for Minorities," *Daily Variety*, April 1, 1970.

93. Dave Kaufman, "Racial Minority Pact's Future?" *Variety*, April 26, 1972. For a summary of the terms of the agreement, see California Advisory Committee to the U.S. Commission on Civil Rights, *Behind the Scenes: Equal Employment Opportunity in the Motion Picture Industry* (Washington, D.C.: U.S. Government Printing Office, September 1978), 13–14; "Justice Backed Down on 'Race,'" *Variety*, April 8, 1970.

94. MacLean, *Freedom Is Not Enough*, 225–61.

95. Downing and Husband, *Representing "Race,"* 50.

96. Dave Kaufman, "Unions Race Time Re Minorities," *Daily Variety*, April 21, 1972.

97. Figures from Tino Balio, "The Recession of 1969," in *Hollywood in the Age of Television*, ed. Tino Balio (Boston: Unwin Hyman, 1990), 259.

98. Dave Kaufman, "Hollywood Unemployment at 42.8%," *Variety*, March 4, 1970. By 1967, fully 70 percent of American films were made abroad, as reported in U.S. House of Representative, *Hearings on Unemployment Problems in American Film Industry*, Los Angeles, October 29 and 30, 1971, cited in Daniel Peltzman, "The Impact of Runaway Productions on Hollywood Labor Organizations," *InMedia* 1 (2012): 3.

99. Stein, *Running Steel, Running America*, 315.

100. Kaufman, "Hollywood Unemployment at 42.8%."

101. Unnamed union executive, quoted in Kaufman, "Unions Prep Seniority Defense."

102. "Locals in Minority Job Pinch to Decide on Filing Law Suit," *Daily Variety*, July 10, 1970.

103. Doyle Nave, quoted in Dave Kaufman, "IA Hits Race Pledge Un-Doers," *Variety*, December 30, 1970.

104. Kaufman, "EEOC Brushed Off One IA Union."

105. Peter Levy, *The New Left and Labor in the 1960s* (Urbana: University of Illinois Press, 1994), 188, 194.

106. "Tokenism to Minorities Resented by White Studio Local with Idle Men," *Variety*, July 9, 1969.

107. Cliff Frazier, interview by the author, New York, April 17, 2007.

108. Harry Belafonte, quoted in William Wolf, "A Melting Pot Cast for NY's 'Angel Levine,'" *Los Angeles Times*, April 15, 1969.

109. Belafonte, quoted in Wolf, "Melting Pot Cast."

110. Ralph Blumenfeld, "A Talk with Harry Belafonte," *New York Post*, August 1, 1970.

111. Kaufman, "Racial Minority Pact's Future?" See also Dave Kaufman, "Dissident Film Workers Seek Coin to Challenge Minority Hiring Pact," *Daily Variety*, October 30, 1970.

112. Kaufman, "Unions Race Time."

113. Allen Hill, quoted in Dave Kaufman, "Minority Program Opponent Denounces Other Union Reps Who Support Project," *Daily Variety*, December 30, 1970.

114. Hill, quoted in Kaufman, "Minority Program Opponent."

115. Donald Zimmerman, quoted in "Locals in Minority Job Pinch."

116. David Daar, paraphrased in Howard Lucraft, "Court Weighs Minority Job Issue," *Daily Variety*, May 2, 1972.

117. Downing and Husband, *Representing "Race,"* 163.

118. Deirdre Royster, *Race and the Invisible Hand: How White Networks Exclude Black Men from Blue-Collar Jobs* (Berkeley: University of California Press, 2003).

119. Trevor Griffey, "'The Blacks Should Not Be Administering the Philadelphia Plan': Nixon, the Hard Hats, and 'Voluntary' Affirmative Action," in *Black Power at Work: Community Control, Affirmative Action, and the Construction Industry*, ed. David Goldberg and Trevor Griffey (Ithaca, N.Y.: Cornell University Press, 2010), 134.

120. See Dave Kaufman, "Laborers Exec Says Minority Hiring Distressing His IA Local," *Daily Variety*, May 21, 1970; "H'wood IATSE Local Raps Minority Hiring Under Department of Justice Deal," *Variety*, June 10, 1970.

121. Jefferson Cowie, "Nixon's Class Struggle: Romancing the New Right Worker, 1969–1973," *Labor History* 43, no. 3 (2002): 257–83; figure from Randolph Hohle, *Race and the Origins of American Neoliberalism* (New York: Routledge, 2015), 200. See also Thomas Sugrue and John Skrentny, "The White Ethnic Strategy," in *Rightward Bound: Making America Conservative in the 1970s*, ed. Bruce Schulman and Julian Zelizer (Cambridge, Mass.: Harvard University Press, 2008) 171–92.

122. Frazier, quoted in Gold, "Community Film Exec," 54.

123. George Lipsitz, *The Possessive Investment in Whiteness: How White People Profit from Identity Politics*, rev ed. (Philadelphia: Temple University Press, 2006), 25.

124. Eduardo Bonilla-Silva, *Racism Without Racists: Color-Blind Racism and the Persistence of Racial Inequality in the United States* (New York: Rowman and Littlefield, 2006), 83–87.

125. Kaufman, "Unions Race Time"; Kaufman, "Racial Minority Pact's Future?"

126. Basil Patterson, quoted in Ronald Gold, "Harlem Film Training Program for Blacks Face Funding, Labor Pains," *Daily Variety*, May 24, 1972.

127. Wendell Franklin, quoted in Knapp, "Assessment," calendar 17.

4. "GETTING THE MAN'S FOOT OUT OF OUR COLLECTIVE ASSES": BLACK LEFT FILM PRODUCERS AND THE RISE OF THE HUSTLER CREATIVE

1. Ossie Davis, "It's Not the Man, It's the Plan," speech to the Congressional Black Caucus (1971), reprinted in Ossie Davis, *Life Lit by Some Large Vision: Selected Speeches and Writings* (New York: Atria, 2006), 33.

2. See Judith Smith, *Becoming Belafonte: Black Artist, Public Radical* (Austin: University of Texas Press, 2014), 176–250; Steven Ross, *Hollywood Left and Right: How Movie Stars Shaped American Politics* (New York: Oxford University Press, 2011), 187, 202–4.

3. Harry Belafonte, with Michael Schnayerson, *My Song: A Memoir of Art, Race, and Defiance* (Edinburgh: Canongate, 2011), 157.

4. Smith, *Becoming Belafonte*, 176–250.

5. Ross, *Hollywood Left and Right*, 210.

6. Figures from Gill Noble, "Entertainment, Politics, and the Movie Business: An Interview with Sidney Poitier," *Cineaste* 8, no. 3 (1978): 18.

7. Charles Champlin, "Sidney Poitier Becomes No. 1 Box-Office Draw," *Los Angeles Times*, February 2, 1969.

8. Sidney Poitier, *This Life* (New York: Ballantine, 1981), 283.

9. See, for instance, the fund-raising and organizing efforts detailed in Sidney Poitier to Stanley Kramer, October 24, 1968, Stanley Kramer Collection, UCLA Film and Television Archive, Los Angeles.

10. Poitier, *This Life*, 323.

11. Poitier, *This Life*, 178–79. See also Adam Goudsouzian, *Sidney Poitier: Man, Actor, Icon* (Chapel Hill: University of North Carolina Press, 2004), chap. 5.

12. Keith Corson, *Trying to Get Over: African American Directors After Blaxploitation, 1977–1986* (Austin: University of Texas Press, 2016), 65.

13. Figures from Barbara Campbell, "Third World Pins Movie Hopes on 'Claudine' Run," *New York Times*, June 5, 1975.

14. Edmund Newton, "Picture Brightens for Blacks in Movies," *New York Post*, October 1, 1973.

15. Davis, "It's Not the Man," 33.

16. Champlin, "Sidney Poitier."

17. Ossie Davis, quoted in Maurice Peterson, "Movies: Being About Ossie Davis," *Essence*, February 1972.

18. Ossie Davis and Ruby Dee, *With Ossie and Ruby: In This Life Together* (New York: HarperCollins, 1998), 420.

19. Davis and Dee, *With Ossie and Ruby*, 369.

20. Davis and Dee, *With Ossie and Ruby*, 371–72.

21. Davis, quoted in Peterson, "Movies."

22. Figure from "*Lady Sings the Blues*," The Numbers, n.d., http://www.the-numbers.com/movie/Lady-Sings-the-Blues#tab=summary.

23. Allyson Field, Jan-Christopher Horak, and Jacqueline Stewart, introduction to *LA Rebellion: Creating a New Black Cinema*, ed. Allyson Field, Jan-Christopher Horak, and Jacqueline Stewart (Oakland: University of California Press, 2015), 4.

24. Melvin Van Peebles, *The Making of "Sweet Sweetback's Baadasssss Song"* (1971; reprint, Edinburgh: Canongate, 1996), 11.

25. Van Peebles, *Making of "Sweet Sweetback's Baadasssss Song,"* 44.

26. Van Peebles, *Making of "Sweet Sweetback's Baadasssss Song,"* 13.

27. Van Peebles, *Making of "Sweet Sweetback's Baadasssss Song,"* 16, 53.

28. Van Peebles, *Making of "Sweet Sweetback's Baadasssss Song,"* 16.

29. Huey Newton, "He Won't Bleed Me: A Revolutionary Analysis of *Sweet Sweetback's Baadasssss Song*," *Black Panther*, June 19, 1971.

30. James Murray, "Now, a Boom in Black Directors," *New York Times*, June 8, 1972.

31. Figures from "*Sweet Sweetback's Baadasssss Song*," The Numbers, n.d., http://www.the-numbers.com/movie/Sweet-Sweetbacks-Baad-Asssss-Song#tab=summary. On the film's impressive box-office and release pattern in Chicago, see Gerald Butters, *From "Sweetback" to "Super Fly": Race and Film Audiences in Chicago's Loop* (Columbia: University of Missouri Press, 2016).

32. Van Peebles, *Making of "Sweet Sweetback's Baadasssss Song,"* 12.

33. Stuart Hall, "What Is This 'Black' in Black Popular Culture?" in *Black Popular Culture*, ed. Gina Dent (Seattle: Bay, 1992), 27, 28.

34. Hall, "What Is This 'Black'?" 27, emphasis in the original.

35. Van Peebles, *Making of "Sweet Sweetback's Baadasssss Song,"* 14.

36. Hall, "What Is This 'Black'?" 27.

37. Van Peebles, *Making of "Sweet Sweetback's Baadasssss Song,"* 45, 13. See also Mike Gross, "Black Tracks Cue New Sales Mart," *Billboard*, July 24, 1971.

38. Hall, "What Is This 'Black'?" 27.

39. Van Peebles, film script, in *Making of "Sweet Sweetback's Baadasssss Song,"* 18.

40. Jon Lewis, *Hollywood v. Hard Core: How the Struggle Over Censorship Saved the Modern Film Industry* (New York: New York University Press, 2000), 150.

41. See Eithne Quinn, *Nuthin' but a "G" Thang: The Culture and Commerce of Gangsta Rap* (New York: Columbia University Press, 2005), chaps. 1 and 2.

42. David Cook, *Lost Illusions: American Cinema in the Shadow of Watergate and Vietnam, 1970–1979* (New York: Scribner's, 2000), 260.

43. Jeff Menne, *Post-Fordist Cinema: Hollywood Auteurs and the Corporate Counterculture* (New York: Columbia University Press, 2019).

44. John Caldwell, "Cultures of Production: Studying Industry's Deep Texts, Reflexive Rituals, and Managed Self-Disclosures," in *Media Industries: History, Theory, and Method*, ed. Jennifer Holt and Alisa Perren (Malden, Mass.: Wiley-Blackwell, 2009), 207.

45. Van Peebles, *Making of "Sweet Sweetback's Baadasssss Song,"* 14.

46. Van Peebles, *Making of "Sweet Sweetback's Baadasssss Song,"* 7, 8.

47. Van Peebles, *Making of "Sweet Sweetback's Baadasssss Song,"* 8, 50.

48. See Adam Coombs, "Queer Oedipal Drag in *Sweet Sweetback's Baadasssss Song* and *Baadasssss!*" *African American Review* 50, no. 1 (2017): 41–58.

49. Mark Anthony Neal, *Soul Babies: Black Popular Culture and the Post-soul Aesthetic* (New York: Routledge, 2002), 24–26.

50. Van Peebles, *Making of "Sweet Sweetback's Baadasssss Song,"* 3.

51. S. Craig Watkins, *Representing: Hip Hop Culture and the Production of Black Cinema* (Chicago: University of Chicago Press, 1998), 95.

52. Van Peebles, *Making of "Sweet Sweetback's Baadasssss Song,"* 21.

53. Mia Mask, "1971: Movies and the Exploitation of Excess," in *American Cinema of the 1970s: Themes and Variations*, ed. Lester Friedman (New Brunswick, N.J.: Rutgers University Press, 2007), 57.

54. Darius James, *That's Blaxploitation! Roots of the Baadasssss 'Tude* (New York: St. Martin's Griffin, 1995), 81.

55. Figures from Bob Johnson, "Black Films Popular in Chicago's Loop," *Boxoffice*, April 14, 1975; Addison Verrill, "'Super Fly' a Blackbuster Phenom.," *Variety*, October 4, 1972; Ron Pennington, "*Mack*'s Boxoffice Strength Activates Planning for Sequel," *Hollywood Reporter*, April 27, 1973; Lawrence Cohn, "All-Time Film Rental Champs," *Variety*, May 10, 1993.

56. Dick Anthony Williams, interview by the author, Los Angeles, March 2006.

57. Mark Reid, "The Black Action Film: The End of the Patiently Enduring Black Hero," *Film History* 2, no. 1 (1988): 35 n. 36. Reid notes the employment opportunities created by black action films, though he does not elaborate (23, 34, 30).

58. Thomas Frank, *The Conquest of Cool: Business Culture, Counterculture, and the Rise of Hip Consumerism* (Chicago: University of Chicago Press, 1997), 13.

59. Philip Fenty, interview in "One Last Deal: A Retrospective," *Super Fly*, DVD (Warner Home Video, 2004).

60. Lois Baumoel, "Producer and Star of 'Super Fly' Are Interviewed in Cleveland," *Boxoffice*, October 9, 1972.

61. Sigissmund Shore, quoted in David Mills, "Blaxploitation 101," *Washington Post*, November 4, 1990, https://www.washingtonpost.com/archive/lifestyle/style/1990/11/04/blaxploitation-101/4f5d248e-d98b-4777-bf9d-0fbb3ecb4bc3/; Hall, "What Is This 'Black'?"

62. "White Negro" is Norman Mailer's famous term for a white male who has an exoticized attraction to black cool in *Advertisements for Myself* (New York: Putnam, 1959).

63. Addison Verrill, "'Super Fly's' Happy Harlem Stay; Crew Black and Hispanic; Financing, Script, Director, PR All Black," *Variety*, April 12, 1972.

64. Figure from Archer Winsten, "Rages and Outrages," *New York Post*, August 28, 1972.

65. Ronald Gold, "Harlem Film Fund: Bumpy," *Variety*, May 24, 1972; Verrill, "'Super Fly's' Happy Harlem Stay."

66. An important exception was first-time white cinematographer James Signorelli.

67. Verrill, "'Super Fly's' Happy Harlem Stay."

68. Donald Bogle, *Toms, Coons, Mulattoes, Mammies, and Bucks: An Interpretive History of Blacks in American Films*, 3rd ed. (New York: Continuum, 1997), 239–40.

69. Michael Campus, quoted in Joseph McBride, "Campus, Director with Hit 'Carson,' Wants Pix 'That Make My Blood Boil,'" *Daily Variety*, August 20, 1974; Michael Campus, interview by the author, Los Angeles, March 10, 2006.

70. Ron Pennington, "Producer of 'Mack' Gains Confidence of Oakland Gang Lords to Shoot Film," *Hollywood Reporter*, September 14, 1972; Andrew Bausch, "Reflections on Blaxploitation," interview of Michael Campus, *Reality Check TV*, n.d., http://www.realitychecktv.com/birchgrove/Reflections%20_Blaxploitation.htm.

71. Pennington, "*Mack*'s Boxoffice Strength."

72. Campus, interview by the author.

73. Curtis Mayfield, *Super Fly*, soundtrack album (Curtom, 1972).

74. Campus, interview by the author.

75. On Uniworld's promotional work for the related case of *Shaft*, see Jason Chambers's illuminating study *Madison Avenue and the Color Line: African Americans in the Advertising Industry* (Philadelphia: University of Pennsylvania Press, 2009), 237.

76. James Booker Associates executive, quoted in Verrill, "'Super Fly' a Blackbuster Phenom," 3.

77. Michael Campus, quoted in Pennington, "*Mack*'s Boxoffice Strength."

78. James Murray, *To Find an Image: Black Films from "Uncle Tom" to "Super Fly"* (Indianapolis, Ind.: Bobbs-Merrill, 1973), 168, 170; figures from Verrill, "'Super Fly' a Blackbuster Phenom," 3.

79. Hank Werba, "'Super Fly' B.O. Bonanza Cues Fast Sequel as Producer, Others Cash In," *Daily Variety*, January 19, 1973.

80. Baumoel, "Producer and Star of 'Super Fly.'"

81. Figures from Pennington, "*Mack*'s Boxoffice Strength."

82. Verrill, "'Super Fly' a Blackbuster Phenom," 3; Werba, "'Super Fly' B.O. Bonanza."

83. See Robert Pruter, *Chicago Soul* (Urbana: University of Illinois Press, 1991), chap. 13.

84. Figures from Chuck Philips, "Cruel Twist to a Comeback Dream," *Los Angeles Times*, August 26, 1990, http://articles.latimes.com/1990-08-26/entertainment/ca-196_1_curtis -mayfield; Werba, "'Super Fly' B.O. Bonanza"; and Isaac Hayes, *Shaft*, soundtrack album (MGM, 1971).

85. Willie Hutch, *The Mack*, soundtrack album (Motown, 1973).

86. Ralph Cooper's "race film" *Dark Manhattan* (1937) is an important progenitor to ghetto action film's subcultural enterprise of the early 1970s. See Mark Reid, "The Black Gangster Film," in *The Film Genre Reader II*, ed. Barry Grant (Austin: University of Texas Press, 1995), 456–73.

87. Melvin Oliver and Thomas Shapiro, *Black Wealth/White Wealth: A New Perspective on Racial Inequality* (New York: Routledge, 1997).

88. James Parish and George Hill, *Black Action Films* (Jefferson, N.C.: McFarland, 1989), 290.

89. Nelson George, *Blackface: Reflections on African Americans and the Movies* (New York: HarperCollins, 1994), 30.

90. Oliver and Shapiro, *Black Wealth/White Wealth*, 6, 7.

91. Vincent Canby, "All but 'Super Fly' Fall Down," *New York Times*, November 12, 1972; "*Super Fly*," *Motion Picture Herald*, September 1972.

92. Robin Kelley, *Yo' Mama's Disfunktional! Fighting the Culture Wars in Urban America* (Boston: Beacon Press, 1997), 20.

93.   George, *Blackface*, 54, 34; Eithne Quinn, "'Tryin' to Get Over': *Super Fly*, Black Politics, and Post–Civil Rights Film Enterprise," *Cinema Journal* 49, no. 2 (Winter 2010): 86–105.

94.   William Van Deburg, *Black Camelot: African American Culture Heroes in Their Times, 1960–1980* (Chicago: University of Chicago Press, 1997), 127–96.

95.   Iceberg Slim (Robert Beck), *Pimp: The Story of My Life* (Los Angeles: Holloway House, 1967). For stand-up comedy routines that feature pimps, see the videos and sound recordings of Redd Foxx, early Richard Pryor, and Rudy Ray Moore (eighteen albums). For pimp pulp fiction, see Donald Goines, *Whoreson: The Story of a Ghetto Pimp* (Los Angeles: Holloway House, 1973).

96.   Bruce Jackson, *Get Your Ass in the Water and Swim Like Me: African American Narrative Poetry from the Oral Tradition* (Cambridge, Mass.: Harvard University Press, 1974), 106.

97.   Kelley, *Yo' Mama's Disfunktional!* 57.

98.   Kevin Thomas, "Dope Dealer Who's in a Fix," *Los Angeles Times*, September 20, 1972.

99.   Lindsay Patterson, introduction to *Black Films and Film-makers: A Comprehensive Anthology from Stereotype to Superhero*, ed. Lindsay Patterson (New York: Dodd, Mead, 1975), x.

100. Nancy MacLean, *Freedom Is Not Enough: The Opening of the American Workplace* (Cambridge, Mass.: Harvard University Press, 2006), 6.

101. William Lyne, "No Accident: From Black Power to Black Box Office," *African American Review* 34, no. 1 (2000): 43.

102. Roy Innis, statement in "Black Movie Boom—Good or Bad?" *New York Times*, December 17, 1972.

103. Huey Newton, quoted in Charles Michener, "Black Movies," *Newsweek*, October 23, 1972.

104. Huey P. Newton, *Revolutionary Suicide* (New York: Ballantine, 1973), 141.

105. Davis and Dee, *With Ossie and Ruby*, 296.

106. Howard Winant, *The World Is a Ghetto: Race and Democracy Since World War II* (New York: Basic Books, 2001), 302.

107. Verrill, "'Super Fly's' Happy Harlem Stay."

108. Harris, interview in "One Last Deal," *Superfly*, DVD.

109. Gold, "Harlem Film Fund."

110. See McBride, "Campus, Director with Hit 'Carson.'"

111. Bausch, "Reflections on Blaxploitation."

112. Newton, *Revolutionary Suicide*, 141.

113. Robin Kelley, *Race Rebels: Culture, Politics, and the Black Working Class* (New York: Free Press, 1994), 163.

114. Campus, quoted in Pennington, "*Mack*'s Boxoffice Strength."

115. Kevin Thomas, "Ring of Truth in 'The Mack,'" *Los Angeles Times*, April 13, 1973.

116. The classic Birmingham School treatments of youth subcultures were published just a few years after these film texts: Stuart Hall and Tony Jefferson, eds., *Resistance Through Rituals: Youth Subcultures in Post-war Britain* (London: Hutchinson, 1976), and Dick Hebdige, *Subculture: The Meaning of Style* (London: Methuen, 1979), in which Hebdige describes style as "signs of forbidden identity, sources . . . of subversive value" (3).

117. William Berry, "How 'Super Fly' Film Is Changing Behavior of Blacks," *Jet*, December 28, 1972. On *Super Fly* and drug consumption, see Alvin Poussaint, "Cheap Thrills That Degrade Blacks," *Psychology Today* 7 (February 1974): 22–26; Will Tusher, "Current Black Films Scored for Free Dope Advertising," *Hollywood Reporter*, September 20, 1972. On *Super Fly* promoting fashion consumerism, see Stella Bruzzi, *Undressing Cinema: Clothing and Identity in the Movies* (London: Routledge, 1997), 98–102.

118. Nathan McCall, *Makes Me Wanna Holler: A Young Black Man in America* (New York: Vintage, 1995), 102.

119. Mary Pattillo-McCoy, *Black Picket Fences: Privilege and Peril Among the Black Middle Class* (Chicago: University of Chicago Press, 1999), 126.

120. Kelley, *Yo' Mama's Disfunktional!* 20. See, for one such ethnography, Ulf Hannerz, *Soulside: Inquiries Into Ghetto Culture and Community* (New York: Columbia University Press, 1969).

121. Christina Milner and Richard Milner, *Black Players: The Secret World of Black Pimps* (1972; reprint, London: Michael Joseph, 1973).

122. William Julius Wilson, *When Work Disappears: The World of the New Urban Poor* (New York: Knopf, 1996).

123. Ossie Davis, in Lindsay Patterson, "An Interview with Ossie Davis: How Can Blacks Make the Money To Be Made on Black Films?" *Black Enterprise*, September 1973, 45.

124. Ron O'Neal offers an eloquent account of how he was subsequently offered few roles, remarking on how difficult it is "to watch your career going down, down, down. . . . I haven't been on an audition in three, four years" (in David Walker, Andrew Rausch, and Chris Watson, *Reflections on Blaxploitation: Actors and Directors Speak* [Lanham, Md.: Scarecrow, 2009], 142–45, esp. 143).

125. Van Peebles, *Making of "Sweet Sweetback's Baadasssss Song,"* vii.

5. COLOR-BLIND CORPORATISM: THE BLACK FILM WAVE AND WHITE REVIVAL

1. Figure from Peter Krämer, *The New Hollywood: From "Bonnie and Clyde" to "Star Wars"* (London: Wallflower Press, 2005), 8.

2. Matthew Frye Jacobson, *Roots Too: White Ethnic Revival in Post-Civil Rights America* (Cambridge, Mass.: Harvard University Press, 2006).

3. Jack Valenti, quoted in Will Tusher, "Valenti Calls Black's [*sic*] Bluff; Rejects 'Special' Treatment," *Hollywood Reporter*, September 29, 1972.

4. James Murray, "Now, a Boom in Black Directors," *New York Times*, June 8, 1972.

5. Figures from Keith Corson, *Trying to Get Over: African American Directors After Blaxploitation, 1977–1986* (Austin: University of Texas Press, 2016), 14.

6. Figures from George Gent, "Black Films Are in, so Are Profits," *New York Times*, July 18, 1972.

7. Figures from A. D. Murphy, "'Crossover' Pix Elude H'Wood," *Daily Variety*, July 17, 1974, and Corson, *Trying to Get Over*, 14.

8. Jack Valenti, "Demographics Cue Upped BO," *Variety*, January 3, 1973.

9. B. J. Mason, "The New Films: Culture or Con Game?" *Ebony*, December 1972.

10. David Cook, *Lost Illusions: American Cinema in the Shadow of Watergate and Vietnam, 1970–1979* (New York: Scribner's, 2000), 11–14, esp. 12.

11. For a discussion of these new black directors, see Corson, *Trying to Get Over*, chap. 1.

12. See Christine Acham and Cliff Ward, dirs., *Infiltrating Hollywood: The Rise and Fall of "The Spook Who Sat by the Door,"* documentary (ChiTrini Productions, 2011).

13. Twentieth Century-Fox Screening Program, *Gordon's War*, 1973, Ossie Davis and Ruby Dee Collection, Schomburg Center for Research in Black Culture, New York Public Library; Kathleen Carroll, "A Black Movie with a Conscience," *New York Daily News*, August 19, 1973.

14. Robert Schaffel (producer) to William Hogan (head of Camera Local 644), January 3, 1973, Davis and Dee Collection, Schomburg Center.

15. "The Education of Sonny Carson," *Ebony*, August 1974. See also Simon Anekwe, "Sonny Carson Expects an Academy Award for His Film Biog!" *New York Amsterdam News*, May 11, 1974.

16. Michael Campus, quoted in Joseph McBride, "Campus, Director with Hit 'Carson,' Wants Pix 'That Make My Blood Boil,'" *Daily Variety*, August 20, 1974. On the impoverished Brooklyn childhood of the Yablanses, see Irwin Yablans, *The Man Who Created Halloween* (North Charlestown, N.C.: CreateSpace, 2012).

17. Paramount Pictures, handbook of production, *The Education of Sonny Carson*, New York (1974), 6, in *Education of Sonny Carson* clipping file, New York Public Library for the Creative and Performing Arts.

18. Marc Mauer, *Race to Incarcerate: The Sentencing Project* (New York: New Press, 1999).

19. Marlene Clark, in Chris Poggiali, "Slinking Through the Seventies: An Interview with Marlene Clark," *Fangoria* 191 (April 2000), http://templeofschlock.blogspot.co.uk/2011/01/slinking-through-seventies-interview.html.

20. James Murray, *Black Creation*, Summer 1973, in *Ganja and Hess* clipping file, New York Public Library for the Creative and Performing Arts.

21. Charles Burnett, quoted in Jan-Christopher Horak, "Tough Enough: Blaxploitation and the L.A. Rebellion," in *LA Rebellion: Creating a New Black Cinema*, ed. Allyson Field, Jan-Christopher Horak, and Jacqueline Stewart (Oakland: University of California Press, 2015), 123.

22. "Brock Peters, Michael Tolan Win Despite Film Biz Proverbs," *Variety*, November 28, 1973; figure from "'Black-Hand Side,' $1.7 Mil in 20," *Variety*, March 13, 1974.

23. Hugh Robertson, quoted in Charles Michener, "Black Movies," *Newsweek*, October 23, 1972.

24. Mason, "New Films."

25. Novotny Lawrence, *Blaxploitation Films of the 1970s: Blackness and Genre* (New York: Routledge, 2008), 49–55.

26. Leerom Medovoi, "Theorizing Historicity, or the Many Meanings of *Blacula*," *Screen* 39, no. 1 (Spring 1998): 1–21.

27. See, for instance, Christopher Sieving, "*Super* Sonics: Song Score as Counter Narration in *Super Fly*," *Journal of Popular Music Studies* 13 (2001): 77–91.

28. Sam Arkoff, with Richard Trubo, *Flying Through Hollywood by the Seat of My Pants* (New York: Birch Lane Press, 1992), 200.

29. Larry Cohen, interview by the author, Los Angeles, April 23, 2008. On the importance of *Black Caesar*, see Thomas Doherty, "The Black Exploitation Picture: *Super Fly* and *Black Caesar*," *Ball State University Forum*, Spring 1983, 30–39.

30. Angela Smith, "Two Fine Actors Inspire Youth in New Film," *New York Amsterdam News*, June 4, 1975.

31. Figure from Lawrence Cohn, "All-Time Film Rental Champs," *Variety*, May 10, 1993.

32. Collins's first film, which didn't get picked up for distribution, was *The Cruz Brothers and Miss Malloy* (1980).

33. Ivan Dixon, quoted in Michener, "Black Movies."

34. Hugh Robertson and Rosalind Cash, quoted in Michener, "Black Movies."

35. Molly Haskell, *From Reverence to Rape: The Treatment of Women in the Movies*, 2nd ed. (Chicago: University of Chicago Press, 1987), 57, 329; Krämer, *New Hollywood*, 34.

36. U.S. Equal Employment Opportunity Commission (EEOC), *Hearings Before the United States EEOC on Utilization of Minority and Women Workers in Certain Major Industries,* Los Angeles, March 12–14, 1969 (Washington, D.C.: U.S. Government Printing Office, 1969), 113–228.

37. Clifford Alexander, Interview III by Joe Frantz, June 7, 1973, transcript, 1, Lyndon Baines Johnson Oral History Collection, Lyndon Baines Johnson Presidential Library, Austin, Tex.

38. Figures from "David Walker," in *What It Is . . . What It Was! The Black Film Explosion of the '70s in Words and Pictures,* ed. Gerald Martinez, Diana Martinez, and Andres Chavez (New York: Hyperion, 1998), 58, and "50 Top-Grossing Films," *Variety,* May 16, 1973.

39. David Oestreicher, "Third World People in Film World Jobs," *New York Daily News,* September 9, 1973.

40. Figures from James Murray, "Third World Cinema Ponders Future," *New York Amsterdam News,* March 15, 1975; Barbara Campbell, "Third World Pins Movie Hopes on 'Claudine' Run," *New York Times,* June 5, 1975.

41. Daniel Patrick Moynihan, *The Negro Family: The Case for National Action* (Washington, D.C.: Office of Policy Planning and Research, U.S. Department of Labor, March 1965), 5; "Tangle of Pathology" is the title of chapter 4, 29–46.

42. William Ryan, quoted in Lee Rainwater and William Yancey, *The Moynihan Report and the Politics of Controversy* (Cambridge, Mass.: MIT Press, 1967), 410 and chaps. 2 and 4.

43. Miriam Thaggert, "Marriage, Moynihan, and *Mahogany*: Success and the Post–Civil Rights Black Female Professional in Film," *American Quarterly* 64, no. 4 (December 2012): 715–40.

44. Donald Bogle, *Brown Sugar: Eighty Years of America's Black Female Superstars* (New York: Da Capo, 1980), 190; Stephane Dunn, *"Baad Bitches" and Sassy Supermamas: Black Power Action Films* (Urbana: University of Illinois Press, 2008), 121, 15.

45. Hannah Weinstein, quoted in the *Claudine* pressbook, Twentieth Century-Fox Film Corp., New York, 1974, copy in author's files.

46. Vincent Canby, "Cheers for 'Claudine,'" *New York Times,* May 5, 1974. See also Penelope Gilliatt, "The Current Cinema," *New Yorker,* April 29, 1974.

47. Clyde Taylor, "Preface: Once Upon a Time in the West . . . LA Rebellion," in *LA Rebellion,* ed. Field, Horak, and Stewart, xxii.

48. "Jack Hill," interview in *What It Is,* ed. Martinez, Martinez, and Chavez, 136.

49. Grier discusses and quotes from the manifesto and talks about her days at UCLA in her memoir *Foxy: My Life in Three Acts* (New York: Springboard, 2010), 137, 125. On UCLA as a training ground for the black film movement, see Allyson Field, Jan-Christopher Horak, and Jacqueline Stewart, "Emancipating the Image: The L.A. Rebellion of Black Filmmakers," in *LA Rebellion,* ed. Field, Horak, and Stewart, 6–15.

50. "Jack Hill," interview in *What It Is,* ed. Martinez, Martinez, and Chavez, 136; Jack Hill, interview by the author, Los Angeles, March 10, 2006; Jack Hill, quoted in Calum Waddell, *Jack Hill: The Exploitation and Blaxploitation Master, Film by Film* (Jefferson, N.C.: McFarland, 2009), 122. Grier had appeared in *Cool Breeze* (Barry Pollack, 1972) and *Hit Man* (George Armitage, 1972).

51. Pam Grier, quoted in "Pam Grier Has a New Role in *Coffy,*" *Chicago Defender,* May 12, 1973; Hill, quoted in Waddell, *Jack Hill,* 122.

52. Diahann Carroll, quoted in Murray, "Third World Cinema Ponders Future."

53. Paul Gardner, "18 Minority Film Trainees Graduate," *New York Times,* August 23, 1973.

54. Murray, "Third World Cinema Ponders Future."

55. Ed Guerrero, *Framing Blackness: The African American Image in Film* (Philadelphia: Temple University Press, 1993), 110.

56. Warrington Hudlin, quoted in David Mills, "Blaxploitation 101," *Washington Post*, November 4, 1990.

57. Cedric Robinson, "Blaxploitation and the Misrepresentation of Liberation," *Race and Class* 40, no. 1 (1998): 1–12; Howard Winant, *The World Is a Ghetto: Race and Democracy Since World War II* (New York: Basic Books, 2001), 312.

58. Hill, interview by the author.

59. Cohen, interview by the author.

60. Hill, quoted in Waddell, *Jack Hill*, 141.

61. Hill, interview by the author.

62. Bob Johnson, "Black Films Popular in Chicago's Loop," *Boxoffice*, April 14, 1975, Blacks and Film Subject Files, Margaret Herrick Library (MHL), Academy of Motion Picture Arts and Sciences, Los Angeles; Ron Wise, "Chicago's Black Pix Dilemma," *Variety*, April 5, 1972.

63. Canby, "All but 'Super Fly.'"

64. See J. Phillip Thompson, *Double Trouble: Black Mayors, Black Communities, and the Call for a Deep Democracy* (New York: Oxford University Press, 2006), introduction.

65. Robin Kelley, "Into the Fire: 1970 to the Present," in *To Make Our World Anew: A History of African Americans*, ed. Robin Kelley and Earl Lewis (New York: Oxford University Press, 2000), 543.

66. Hill, interview by the author.

67. Hill, interview by the author.

68. "United Artists 'Black Hand Side' Draws Big Promotional Budget," *Variety*, February 6, 1974.

69. Sidney Poitier, *This Life* (New York: Ballantine, 1981), 346; figure from Cohn, "All-Time Film Rental Champs."

70. Poitier, *This Life*, 346–47.

71. Acham and Ward, *Infiltrating Hollywood*; Samantha Sheppard, "Persistently Displaced: Situated Knowledges and Interrelated Histories in *The Spook Who Sat by the Door*," *Cinema Journal* 52, no. 2 (Winter 2013): 71–92.

72. Marlene Clark, quoted in Poggiali, "Slinking Through the Seventies."

73. Richard Brody, "Front Row: *Ganja & Hess*," *New Yorker*, August 15, 2016, http://www.newyorker.com/culture/richard-brody/the-front-row-ganja-hess.

74. Cohen, interview by the author.

75. Robin Wood, quoted in "*Bone*," Time Out London, n.d., https://www.timeout.com/london/film/bone.

76. Cohen, interview by the author.

77. Charlayne Hunter, "Sonny Carson's Conflicts Simmer on and off Screen," *New York Times*, July 29, 1974.

78. Cohen, interview by the author.

79. Cohen, interview by the author.

80. Jim Brown, interview by Todd Mason, Flintridge, February 26, 1973, Jim Brown clipping file, Production Files, MHL.

81. Figure from "US Black Audience–Slated Films: 25 New 1974 Titles," *Variety*, January 8, 1975, and Renee Ward, "The 'Crossover' Goes Beyond Blaxploitation," *Los Angeles Times*, December 28, 1975.

82. Murphy, "'Crossover' Pix Elude H'Wood"; Gent, "Black Films Are in, so Are Profits."

83. Cook, *Lost Illusions*, 14.

84. Johnson, "Black Films Popular."

85. Cook, *Lost Illusions*, 11–14, 149, 352.

86. Figures from Corson, *Trying to Get Over*, 14.

87. Following the success of *Greased Lightning* (Michael Schultz, 1977), Pryor had signed a deal with Warner Bros. for four pictures to be made jointly with his company Richard Pryor Enterprises (Warner Bros. press release, July 2, 1977, Richard Pryor clipping file, Production Files, MHL).

88. Sidney Poitier, quoted in Jack Slater, "Poitier Lashes Hollywood's 'Racist' Ways," *Los Angeles Herald-Examiner*, February 20, 1981.

89. Stuart Hall, "New Ethnicities" (1989), reprinted in *Stuart Hall: Critical Dialogues in Cultural Studies*, ed. Kuan-Hsing Chen and David Morley (London: Routledge, 1996), 447.

90. See Steve Toy, "NAACP and CORE Hit Black Capers; Distortion of Race Life-Style," *Variety*, August 23, 1972, and Will Tusher, "Black Capitalism Big Factor in PUSH Drive on Hollywood," *Hollywood Reporter*, September 18, 1972.

91. Junius Griffin, quoted in "Fight 'Black Exploitation' in Pix," *Daily Variety*, August 16, 1972. See also "NAACP Takes Militant Stand on Black Exploitation Films," *Hollywood Reporter*, August 1, 1972.

92. See, for instance, the contributions from Gordon Parks Sr., Jim Brown, Amiri Baraka, and Junius Griffin in "Black Movie Boom—Good or Bad?" *New York Times*, December 17, 1972.

93. Robert Hampton to Heads of Departments and Agencies, memorandum, August 18, 1972, EEO Policy—Remedies (Merit Systems), folder 1 of 4, box 85, Bradley Patterson files, Richard Nixon Presidential Library, Yorba Linda, Calif.

94. Valenti, quoted in Tusher, "Valenti Calls Black's Bluff."

95. Valenti, quoted in Tusher, "Valenti Calls Black's Bluff."

96. Martin Luther King Jr., "I Have a Dream" (1963), reprinted in *Heath Anthology of American Literature*, vol. 2, ed. Paul Lauter (Lexington, Mass.: Heath, 1994), 2483–86; Robin Kelley, *Yo' Mama's Disfunktional! Fighting the Culture Wars in Urban America* (Boston: Beacon, 1997), 89–90.

97. Valenti, quoted in Tusher, "Valenti Calls Black's Bluff."

98. For an example of such ethnicity-based neoconservative writings, see Michael Novak, *The Rise of the Unmeltable Ethnics: Politics and Culture in the Seventies* (New York: MacMillan, 1972).

99. Valenti, quoted in Tusher, "Valenti Calls Black's Bluff."

100. Michael Omi and Howard Winant, *Racial Formation in the United States*, 3rd ed. (New York: Routledge, 2015), chaps. 1–3.

101. Jacobson, *Roots Too*, esp. 177–205.

102. On the intellectuals at the heart of the neoconservative project, see chapter 3 in this volume. On black–Jewish relations in Hollywood, see Thomas Cripps, "African Americans and Jews in Hollywood: Antagonistic Allies," in *Strangers and Neighbors: Relations Between Blacks and Jews in the United States*, ed. Maurianne Adams and John Bracey (Amherst: University of Massachusetts Press, 1999), 457–70.

103. *Stir Crazy* still held the number-one film spot in 2017 according to the chart compiled in Dana Harris and Tom Brueggemann, "The 33 Highest-Grossing Movies Directed by Black Filmmakers," *Indie Wire*, May 12, 2017.

104. Bruce Nelson, *Divided We Stand: American Workers and the Struggle for Black Equality* (Princeton, N.J.: Princeton University Press, 2001), 291.

105. Charlton Heston, quoted in Laura Ingraham, "A Conversation in Hollywood," *Policy Review*, 1987, 23, 21, Charlton Heston Papers, Special Collections, MHL.

106. Charlton Heston, quoted in "Nixon Gets Backing of Charlton Heston," *Los Angeles Herald-Examiner*, August 4, 1972.

107. Steven Ross, *Hollywood Left and Right: How Movie Stars Shaped American Politics* (New York: Oxford University Press, 2011), 292–93.

108. Daniel Patrick Moynihan, address to a National League of Cities conference, Washington, D.C., March 25, 1985, transcribed in "Notable and Quotable," *Wall Street Journal*, April 18, 1985.

109. AMPTP agreement in Steve Toy, "Meeting with Coalition Against Blaxploitation on 12 Demands Deemed 'Very Good,'" *Daily Variety*, October 16, 1972.

110. Clifford Alexander, quoted in "Clifford Alexander Attacks Federal Job Discrimination," *Jet*, October 12, 1972.

111. Jim Brown, statement in "Black Movie Boom."

112. Roy Innis, quoted in Mason, "New Films."

113. Jesse Jackson, quoted in Tusher, "Black Capitalism Big Factor."

114. The open meeting held to collect testimony in Los Angeles in October 1976 was later published as a report: California Advisory Committee to the U.S. Commission on Civil Rights, *Behind the Scenes: Equal Employment Opportunity in the Motion Picture Industry* (Washington, D.C.: U.S. Government Printing Office, September 1978).

115. Ray St. Jacques, quoted in "US Black Money Not Easy for Pix: Ray St. Jacques," *Variety*, August 16, 1972.

116. California Advisory Committee, *Behind the Scenes*, 5–6.

117. Audley Simpson, quoted in Paul Gardner, "18 Minority Film Trainees Graduate," *New York Times*, August 23, 1973. See also Edmund Newton, "Picture Brightens for Blacks in Movies," *New York Post*, October 1, 1973.

118. California Advisory Committee, *Behind the Scenes*, 41–42, esp. 42.

119. Ted Ashley quoted in and figure in Will Tusher, "Industry Tops US on Minority Hiring," *Hollywood Reporter*, January 22, 1974.

120. "Black Stunters' Marvin Walters Scrams MGM: Says 'They Stall,'" *Variety*, December 29, 1976.

121. California Advisory Committee, *Behind the Scenes*, 41–42, esp. 41.

122. See Susan Christopherson, "Labor: The Effects of Media Concentration on the Film and Television Workforce," in *Contemporary Hollywood Film Industry*, ed. Paul McDonald and Janet Wasko (Malden, Mass.: Wiley-Blackwell, 2008), 155–66.

CONCLUSION: RACE, CREATIVE LABOR, AND REFLEXIVITY IN POST-CIVIL RIGHTS HOLLYWOOD

1. Vincent Canby, "On the Auto Front," *New York Times*, February 10, 1978; J. Hoberman, "*Blue Collar,*" *Village Voice*, September 14, 1982.

2. Andrew Sarris, "Off the Assembly Line: One Lemon, One Authentic Model," *Village Voice*, February 27, 1978.

3. "Blue Collar Caper Cop-Out," *Christopher Street*, March 1978.

4. On negative representations of organized labor in *Blue Collar*, see John Watson, "The Far Left Looks at 'Blue Collar,'" *Los Angeles Times*, March 25, 1978; Michael Omi, "Race Relations in *Blue Collar*," *Jump Cut* 26 (December 1981): 7–8; Jefferson Cowie, *Stayin' Alive: The 1970s and the Last Days of the Working Class* (New York: New Press, 2010), 334–37.

5. Reagan first aired his notoriously effective welfare-queen story during his failed presidential election bid of 1976, and by 1978, as he launched his successful bid, he was widely recounting the story. See "'Welfare Queen' Becomes Issue in Reagan Campaign," *New York Times*, February 15, 1976, and Julilly Kohler-Hausmann, "'The Crime of Survival': Fraud Prosecutions, Community Surveillance, and the Original 'Welfare Queen,'" *Journal of Social History* 41, no. 2 (Winter 2007): 329–54.

6. See Robert Entman and Andrew Rojecki, *The Black Image in the White Mind: Media and Race in America* (Chicago: University of Chicago Press, 2000), 186.

7. Paul Schrader, quoted in Terry Fox, "Blue Collar Fever: The Shameless Cinema of Paul Schrader," *Village Voice*, February 27, 1978.

8. Schrader, quoted in Fox, "Blue Collar Fever." See also *"Blue Collar* Production Notes: Motion Picture News," Universal Studios, January 6, 1978, Film Files, Margaret Herrick Library (MHL), Academy of Motion Picture Arts and Sciences, Los Angeles.

9. Figures from Fox, "Blue Collar Fever." Peter Biskind describes the deal as a fee of $15,000 and 1.5 percent of the film in his review of the film in 1978, reprinted in Peter Biskind, "Blue Collar Blues: Proletarian Cinema from Hollywood," in *Gods and Monsters: 30 Years of Writing on Film and Culture* (New York: Thunder's Mouth, 2004), 75.

10. Charles Higham, "When I Do It, It's Not Gore, Says Writer Paul Schrader," *New York Times*, February 5, 1978.

11. Fox, "Blue Collar Fever."

12. *Blue Collar* pressbook, Universal Studios 1978, Film Files, MHL.

13. Paul Schrader, quoted in Paul Tickell, *"Blue Collar*: Workers Without a History," *Socialist Challenge*, February 1, 1979.

14. Sarris, "Off the Assembly Line."

15. Cowie, *Stayin' Alive*; Derek Nystrom, *Hard Hats, Rednecks, and Macho Men: Class in 1970s American Cinema* (New York: Oxford University Press, 2009).

16. Peter Biskind, *Easy Riders, Raging Bulls: How the Sex-Drugs-and-Rock'n'Roll Generation Saved Hollywood* (New York: Simon and Schuster, 1998), 348; Biskind, "Blue Collar Blues," 75.

17. Cowie, *Stayin' Alive*, 334.

18. Nystrom, *Hard Hats*, 161.

19. Cowie, *Stayin' Alive*, 240. See, for instance, the book review by Joseph McCartin, *"Stayin' Alive: The 1970s and the Last Days of the Working Class* by Jefferson Cowie," *Journal of Social History* 47, no. 3 (2014): 795–97, esp. 796.

20. Nystrom, *Hard Hats*,160, xx.

21. In 2017–2018, Hollywood film writers of color remained underrepresented in relation to their overall population numbers by a factor five to one (whites represented a full 92.2 percent of film writers of the top two hundred theatrical releases), as reported in Darnell Hunt, Ana-Christina Ramon, and Michael Tran, *Hollywood Diversity Report 2019: Old Story, New Beginning* (Los Angeles: College of Social Sciences, University of California, 2018), 3.

22. Sidney Poitier, quoted in Jack Slater, "Poitier Lashes Hollywood's 'Racist' Ways," *Los Angeles Herald-Examiner,* February 20, 1981.

23. Matthew Lassiter, "Political History Beyond the Red–Blue Divide," *Journal of American History* 98, no. 3 (December 2011): 761.

24. John Downing and Charles Husband, *Representing "Race": Racisms, Ethnicities, and Media* (London: Sage, 2006), chap. 8.

25. Anamik Saha, *Race and the Cultural Industries* (Cambridge: Polity, 2018), 166.

26. Stuart Hall, "What Is This 'Black' in Black Popular Culture?" in *Black Popular Culture,* ed. Gina Dent (Seattle: Bay, 1992), 467.

27. Michael Omi and Howard Winant, *Racial Formation in the United States,* 3rd ed. (New York: Routledge, 2015), 185–209, esp. 187.

28. Susan Christopherson, "Labor: The Effects of Media Concentration on the Film and Television Workforce," in *The Contemporary Hollywood Film Industry,* ed. Paul McDonald and Janet Wasko (Malden, Mass.: Wiley-Blackwell, 2008), 155–66.

29. Susan Christopherson, "Beyond the Self-Expressive Industry Worker," *Theory, Culture, and Society* 25, nos. 7–8 (2008): 85–88.

30. Christopher Boulton, "Under the Cloak of Whiteness: A Circuit of Culture Analysis of Opportunity Hoarding and Color-Blind Racism Inside US Advertising Internship Programs," *Triple C: Communication, Capitalism, and Critique* 13, no. 2 (2015): 390.

31. David Hesmondhalgh and Anamik Saha, "Race, Ethnicity, and Cultural Production," *Popular Communication* 11, no. 2 (August 2013): 180.

32. Figures from Rebecca Keegan, Sandra Poindexter, and Glenn Whipp, "91% White, 76% Male," *Los Angeles Times,* February 26, 2016, http://graphics.latimes.com/oscars-2016 -voters/.

33. Monica Ndounou, *Shaping the Future of African American Film: Color-Coded Economics and the Story Behind the Numbers* (New Brunswick, N.J.: Rutgers University Press, 2014).

34. Figures from Darnell Hunt, Ana-Christina Ramon, Michael Tran, Amberia Sargent, and Debanjan Roychoudhury, *Hollywood Diversity Report 2018: Five Years of Progress and Missed Opportunities* (Los Angeles: College of Social Sciences, University of California, 2018), 2–3, 14–28.

35. On white saviors in Hollywood film, see Matthew Huey, *The White Savior Film: Content, Critics, and Consumption* (Philadelphia: Temple University Press, 2014).

36. Entman and Rojecki, *Black Image in the White Mind,* 107, 209.

37. Eithne Quinn, "Black Talent and Conglomerate Hollywood: The Case of Will Smith and Tyler Perry," *Popular Communication* 11, no. 2 (August 2013): 196–210.

38. Marcus Hunter and Zandria Robinson, *Chocolate Cities: The Black Map of American Life* (Oakland: University of California Press, 2018), xi–xii.

39. Jared Sexton, "The Ruse of Engagement: Black Masculinity and the Cinema of Policing," *American Quarterly* 61, no. 1 (2009): 39–63.

40. Jordan Peele, in Emanuel Levy, "Get Out: Interview with Writer-Director Jordan Peele," *EL: Cinema 24/7,* February 24, 2017, http://emanuellevy.com/blog/get-out-interview-with -writer-director-jordan-peele/.

41. Daniel Kaluuya, quoted in Kaleem Aftab, "Daniel Kaluuya on His Life-Changing *Get Out* Role," *Screen Daily,* November 18, 2017, https://www.screendaily.com/interviews/daniel -kaluuya-on-his-life-changing-get-out-role-steve-mcqueens-widows-and-black-panther /5124304.article.

42. Spike Lee's recent, industry-lauded hit, the retrospective police drama *BlacKkKlansman* (2018), presents a departure from his racial critique of the American workplace.

43. See Hunt et al., *Hollywood Diversity Report 2018*, 21, 22.

44. On these recurring racist tropes, see the content analysis in Entman and Rojecki, *Black Image in the White Mind*, 194–201.

45. Ange-Marie Hancock, *The Politics of Disgust: The Public Identity of the Welfare Queen* (New York: New York University Press, 2004).

46. Hunt et al., *Hollywood Diversity Report 2018*, 29, 39.

47. See Michael Gillespie, *Film Blackness: American Cinema and the Idea of Black Film* (Durham, N.C.: Duke University Press, 2016).

48. For figures on racial groups in front of and behind the camera in Hollywood, see Hunt et al., *Hollywood Diversity Report 2018*, 20–22.

49. Hunt et al., *Hollywood Diversity Report 2018*.

50. William Darity, Darrick Hamilton, Patrick Mason, Gregory Price, Alberto Davila, and Marie Mora, "Stratification Economics: A General Theory of Intergroup Inequality," in *The Hidden Rules of Race: Barriers to an Inclusive Economy*, ed. Andrea Flynn, Susan Homberg, Dorian Warren, and Felicia Wong (New York: Cambridge University Press, 2017), 35–51; Darrick Hamilton and William Darity, "Race, Wealth, and Intergenerational Poverty," *American Prospect* 20, no. 7 (2009): A10–12.

51. Net wealth figures from Federal Reserve, "Survey of Consumer Finances" (2013), reproduced in Pew Research Center, "On Views of Race and Inequality, Black and Whites Are Worlds Apart," June 27, 2016, http://www.pewsocialtrends.org/2016/06/27/1-demographic-trends-and-economic-well-being/. See also Chuck Collins, Dedrick Asante-Muhammed, Emanuel Nieves, and Josh Hoxie, "The Road to Zero Wealth: How the Racial Wealth Divide Is Hollowing Out America's Middle Class," Institute for Policy Studies, September 11, 2017, https://www.ips-dc.org/report-the-road-to-zero-wealth/.

52. Ruth Gilmore, *Golden Gulag: Prisons, Surplus, Crisis, and Opposition in Globalizing California* (Berkeley: University of California Press, 2007); Michelle Alexander, *The New Jim Crow: Mass Incarceration in the Age of Color-Blindness* (New York: New Press, 2012).

53. Lisa Cacho, *Social Death: Racialized Rightlessness and the Criminalization of the Unprotected* (New York: New York University Press, 2012).

54. See, for instance, Eithne Quinn, "Occupy Wall Street, Racial Neoliberalism, and New York's Hip-Hop Moguls," *American Quarterly* 68, no. 1 (March 2016): 75–101.

55. Fulgani Sheth, "The Irony of MLK Day 2013: A Renewed Invitation Into White Supremacy," *Translation Exercises*, January 21, 2013, https://translationexercises.wordpress.com/2013/01/21/the-irony-of-mlk-day-2013-a-renewed-invitation-into-white-supremacy/.

56. Frank Wilderson, *Red, White, & Black: Cinema and the Structure of U.S. Antagonisms* (Durham, N.C.: Duke University Press, 2010); Sexton, "Ruse of Engagement."

57. Robin Kelley, "Sorry, Not Sorry," *Boston Review*, September 13, 2018, http://bostonreview.net/race-literature-culture/robin-d-g-kelley-sorry-not-sorry.

58. Cornel West, "Ta-Nehisi Coates Is the Neoliberal Face of the Black Freedom Struggle," *Guardian*, December 17, 2017, https://www.theguardian.com/commentisfree/2017/dec/17/ta-nehisi-coates-neoliberal-black-struggle-cornel-west. See also Lester Spence's excellent book *Knocking the Hustle: Against the Neoliberal Turn in Black Politics* (New York: Punctum, 2016).

59. Rebecca Rubin, "'Black Panther' Crosses $1 Billion at Global Box Office," *Variety*, March 10, 2018, http://variety.com/2018/film/news/black-panther-billion-global-box-office-120272 3326/.

60. Pamela McClintock, "Weekend Box Office," *Hollywood Reporter*, February 25, 2018, https://www.hollywoodreporter.com/heat-vision/weekend-box-office-black-panther -scores-massive-1117m-second-outing-1088212.

61. Christopher Lebron, "'Black Panther' Is Not the Movie We Deserve," *Boston Review*, February 17, 2018, http://bostonreview.net/race/christopher-lebron-black-panther.

62. Herman Gray, *Cultural Moves: African Americans and the Politics of Representation* (Berkeley: University of California Press, 2005), 186.

63. Figures from Keegan, Poindexter, and Whipp, "91% White, 76% Male," and Anne Cohen, "How Many Women Are Actually Voting for the Oscar Winners?" *Refinery29*, February 15, 2018, https://www.refinery29.uk/2018/02/190937/academy-members-women-oscar-voters ?bucketed=true&bucketing_referrer=https%3A%2F%2Fwww.google.com%2F.

INDEX

guilds, film, 29–30, 93, 98–99, 109, 143, 174,
209, 211; Publicists' Guild, 29. *See also*
Directors Guild of America; Screen
Actors Guild; Writers Guild of America
Gulati, Mitu, 54, 56
Gunn, Bill, 4, 19, 61, 76, 78–80, 82, 85, 141,
174–75, 178, 192
Gunn, Moses, 177

Haley, Alex, 66
Hall, Stuart, 51, 53–54, 140–41, 147, 195, 216
Hallelujah (film), 15
Hamilton, Darrick, 224–25
Hamilton, Emma, 35, 38–39
Hancock, Ange-Marie, 223
Hansberry, Lorraine, 88
Harlem, 75, 77, 81, 85–86, 118, 130, 136, 146–50,
152, 160–61, 172; 180–81, 191
Harlem Commonwealth Council, 134
Harlem Writers Guild, 174
Harris, Jack, 192
Harris, Julius, 161
Harris, Mark, 55–56
Haskell, Molly, 180
Hayes, Isaac, 151, 176
Hell up in Harlem (film), 189
Help, The (film), 219, 223
Hesmondhalgh, David, 6 17–18, 218
Heston, Charlton, 1–2, 21, 108–14, 200–201,
205, 217
Hidden Figures (film), 219
Hill, George, 153
Hill, Herbert, 95
Hill, Jack, 181, 182–85, 189–91
Hill, The (film), 69
Himes, Chester, 73, 84–85, 87, 132
Hoberman, J., 207
Hobson, Charles, 61–62
Hollywood: as capitalist industry, 15–16, 27,
127–28, 147 166, 218; conservative
rehabilitation in, 4–5, 7, 20, 21, 110, 197–206;
corporate reconfiguration of, 5, 7, 19, 60,
69, 113, 122, 217; economic downturn in,
20, 66, 94, 113–15; generational shift in, 19,
60, 69, 72–73, 80; lobbying power of, 20,
94, 101–4, 107–10, 122; new industry

consensus in, 21, 194, 122, 217; racial
discourses of, 16, 20, 26, 29–34, 58, 93–94,
101–14, 112, 122, 196–99, 205, 217, 227;
runaway productions in, 109, 115–16; as
synecdoche, 15–16. *See also* Association of
Motion Picture and Television Producers
(AMPTP); Motion Picture Association of
America (MPAA); white opportunity
hoarding in Hollywood (cronyism)
Hollywood Diversity Report, 224
Hollywood Renaissance (the New
Hollywood), 14, 60–61, 69, 72, 76–77,
80–82, 86–87, 136, 138–42, 147, 173–74, 193,
209; end of, 194; neglect of black
participation in, 19, 60–61, 80–81, 207–8,
211–12, 214, 242n7; sexism in, 21, 180
Home of the Brave (film), 15, 42
Homesteader, The (film), 15
Hooks, Robert, 30–31
Horak, Jan-Christopher, 137
Horne, Lena, 1, 27, 127, 179
House Un-American Activities Committee
(blacklisting), 15, 36, 74–75, 77, 132, 134,
165, 181, 214
Houston, Clyde, 138
Hudlin, Warrington, 188
Hughes, Langston, 61
Hughes, Rhetta, 145
Hunt, Darnell, 224, 263n21
Hunter, Kristin, 77
Hunter, Marcus, 220
Hurry Sundown (film), 44
Husband, Charles, 31, 48, 64, 72, 98, 115, 119, 214
hustler creatives: depoliticization of, 143–45,
161, 163–66, 222; emergence of, 126–27,
146–48, 216; and masculinity, 144–45,
158–59, 163–64, 222–23; and political
dissidence, 137–44, 153–57, 222; reflexivity
of, 126–27, 144–45, 163–65
Hutch, Willie, 151, 161, 176
Hyman, Elliot, 68
Hyman, Kenneth, 19, 68–72

independent (art-house) film, 15–16, 27, 42, 45,
69, 76, 80, 90, 108, 125–28, 134–43, 148, 166,
174–76. *See also* LA Rebellion filmmaking